PENNSYLVANIA PLACE NAMES

BY

A. HOWRY ESPENSHADE

PROFESSOR IN THE PENNSYLVANIA STATE COLLEGE
MEMBER OF THE HISTORICAL SOCIETY OF PENNSYLVANIA
AUTHOR OF "THE ESSENTIALS OF COMPOSITION AND RHETORIC"

THE PENNSYLVANIA STATE COLLEGE STUDIES
IN HISTORY AND POLITICAL SCIENCE, NO. 1.
COLLEGE SERIES, NO. 1.

CLEARFIELD

Originally Published
The Pennsylvania State College
State College, 1925

Reprinted With Permission
Genealogical Publishing Company
Baltimore, 1970

Reprinted for
Clearfield Company, Inc. by
Genealogical Publishing Co., Inc.
Baltimore, Maryland
1991, 1995, 1998

Library of Congress Catalog Card Number 71-112824
International Standard Book Number 0-8063-0416-2

CONCERNING AMERICAN NAMES

"LOCAL names—whether they belong to provinces, cities, and villages, or are the designations of rivers or mountains—are never mere arbitrary sounds, devoid of meaning. They may always be regarded as records of the past, inviting and rewarding a careful historical interpretation. . . . The colonization of America has been effected during the modern historic period, the process of name-giving is illustrated by numerous authentic documents, and the names are derived from living languages. By means of the names upon the map, we may trace the whole history of the successive stages by which the white men have spread themselves over the Western world. We may discover the dates at which the several settlements were founded; we may assign to each of the nations of Europe its proper share in the work of colonization; and, lastly, we may recover the names of the adventurous captains who led their little bands of daring followers to conquer the wilderness from nature or from savage tribes."—ISAAC TAYLOR: *Words and Places.*

"None can care for literature in itself who do not take a special pleasure in the sound of names; and there is no part of the world where nomenclature is so rich, poetical, humorous, and picturesque, as the United States of America. All times, races, and languages have brought their contribution. Pekin is in the same State with Euclid, with Bellefontaine, and with Sandusky. The names of the States and Territories themselves form a chorus of sweet and most romantic vocables: Delaware, Ohio, Indiana, Florida, Dakota, Iowa, Wyoming, Minnesota, and the Carolinas; there are few poems with a nobler music for the ear; a songful, tuneful land; and if the new Homer shall arise from the Western continent, his verse will be enriched, his pages sing spontaneously, with the names of states and cities that would strike the fancy in a business circular."—ROBERT LOUIS STEVENSON: *Across the Plains.*

PREFACE

PENNSYLVANIA PLACE NAMES is an historical commentary on the names of all the Pennsylvania counties, county seats, and towns with a population of five thousand or more, and on the most noteworthy village and township names. The author has endeavored to make his account of the naming of places more interesting by furnishing important geographical and historical facts about the places named, and brief biographical data about many of the distinguished men whose names are inseparably connected with the counties, cities, and boroughs of Pennsylvania.

The book is a modest effort in a comparatively new field of research. In attempting it the author has been actuated by an intense love for his native State, an absorbing interest in its history, and a fondness for etymological studies, particularly in the field of personal and local nomenclature. So far as he knows, the only other work in any way resembling this is Dr. Charles M. Long's *Virginia County Names,* which presents a somewhat similar but briefer historical commentary on the names of the one hundred counties of Virginia.

Perhaps the writer should add that fourteen years ago, when he first began to collect material bearing upon the origin, historical setting, and meaning of Pennsylvania place names, he had no thought of writing a book, but was simply riding a hobby for his own gratification. An extensive correspondence as Registrar of The Pennsylvania State College gave him some acquaintance with nearly all the places of consequence in Pennsylvania, and aroused his interest in their names, and greatly stimulated his curiosity to learn something about their origin. The large number of letters received from others who seem to be interested in the same subject has led him to believe that the general reader as well as the scholar may possibly find some instruction, entertainment, and profit in learning easily what the writer has found out only after long and patient research.

5

Pennsylvania place names are now pretty firmly fixed. Some new names will be added from time to time, but very few names of any importance are likely to be changed. The time has therefore come when some inquiry can and should be made into their origin and history. The author has tried to show that an interesting and important part of the history of Pennsylvania has been indelibly written in the names of its counties, cities, towns, and townships; and he ventures to hope that his work may stimulate others to prepare similar historical commentaries on the place names of other states. Here is a promising and useful field for the local historian.

To be convinced of some of the difficulties to be met in such an investigation, the reader need only set himself some such task as that of discovering the origin and the meaning of the current English names of the nations of Europe, or of the forty-eight states of our Union and their capitals. Such an effort will convince any one that the amateur historian and etymologist must exercise patience, restraint, judgment, and common sense in seeking the origin and signification of place names.

The author has resisted the temptation to write a much bigger and more pretentious work,—a great hulking ark of a book with its keel deeply barnacled with lengthy and labored footnotes. He has found it pleasanter—and perhaps wiser—to ride his hobby decorously and to set down mainly what may presumably appeal to the normal interest of the general reader. He has searched through hundreds of books and has written countless letters in his quest. He has made every effort to learn all the essential facts about a particular name, and to secure information from the most reliable and authentic sources. His chief printed authorities are mentioned in Appendix A, containing a list of important books consulted. He has purposely used footnotes rather sparingly. Without tagging every statement with the authority on which it is based, he has tried in the text to indicate what may reasonably be accepted as fact or approximate truth, and what must be regarded only as probability or guesswork.

On such a subject no one could hope to write a book that

would be free from error. In some cases doubtless the so-called authorities have themselves been misinformed. Fuller knowledge, it is hoped, will in the future correct the errors and fill in some regrettable gaps in the author's work. And yet some facts about the naming of places can never be known, because it is impossible to subpœna the dead.

The author has, for the most part, refrained from any criticism of the names selected by the early settlers of Pennsylvania. On this point the reader will form his own judgment. If he thinks that our forefathers have not generally been very successful and happy in the naming of places, and that the list of names given in the index of this book is only another proof of the poverty of the average human intellect, he should remember that the colonists and pioneers were of necessity much engrossed with more pressing concerns, and that the particular names at which one may be inclined to cavil may have been to them objects of respect and love, or become dear to them by long familiarity and association.

The relative amount of space devoted to the discussion of the names of counties and county seats, and to pertinent historical and biographical comment, has been determined by the fact that in Pennsylvania the county is the most important geographical and political unit, and that the county town is of almost equal consequence as the seat of justice and the centre of the public business of the county. In Pennsylvania the counties and the municipalities—cities and boroughs—are of far more importance than the civil subdivisions known as townships, which are useful mainly in maintaining roads, in providing means of education for rural communities, and in administering justice in minor misdemeanors and disputes.

The average size of the county towns and their total population of nearly three and a half million inhabitants have also had weight in settling the difficult question of proportion. The county seats discussed in Part I and the hundred and thirty-one large towns included in Part II contain sixty per cent. of the population of Pennsylvania. The political importance of the counties and county seats, and the large proportion of the population centered in the county towns and the other large incorporated places seem to justify the amount of space given to Parts I and II.

The author tenders his heartiest thanks to all who have assisted him in his labors.

State College, Pennsylvania,
      March 14, 1925.

CONTENTS

CHAPTER I

INTRODUCTION

THE early settlers in the American provinces had a unique opportunity. The colonists themselves made the map of their own province, and chose the names of their counties, cities, villages, and townships, retaining a few aboriginal names for such prominent natural features as mountains, lakes, and streams.

Nearly all the names discussed in this book were adopted during the two centuries between 1682 and 1882. We must remember that Pennsylvania was settled rapidly. Though it was next to the last of the thirteen original colonies to be established, it was, even before the outbreak of the Revolutionary War, the third province in point of population and wealth. For nearly a hundred years Pennsylvania has ranked second only to New York in respect to property and population.

Why is it worth while to study place names? Perhaps a sufficient answer is found in the fact that the subject is one of unusual geographical, historical, ethnological, and linguistic interest. It is a cause for regret that men and women who are otherwise well-informed should be so generally ignorant of the history and the meaning of the names that they use every day.

It is a mistake, however, to suppose that most people are not interested in names, that they do not care to know their origin and meaning, or that they have no sense of their fitness or beauty. Any one who is reputed to have some knowledge of the derivation of personal and local names finds, in the number of inquiries that he constantly

11

receives, abundant evidence of a fairly widespread interest in the subject. Many of the names discussed in this book were finally adopted only after much anxious thought and general discussion. Often a spirited meeting of the citizens of a given community was held for the sole purpose of selecting a name. Frequently a vulgar, ugly, meaningless, or inappropriate name has, by common consent, been discarded for what appears to be a more seemly designation.

There is undoubted dignity and value in an attractive name. The writers of books realize this fact and give time, thought, and ingenuity to the task of finding a captivating title. The founders of towns have often been no less anxious to find apt and pleasing names. Our local patriotism revolts at the use of an undignified or contemptuous nickname of the place in which we live, almost as much as our personal pride resents any unwarranted liberties that thoughtless people may take with our own names. King Solomon's maxim, ''a good name is rather to be chosen than great riches,'' applies to places as well as to persons.

So few people really know anything definite or conclusive about place names that a writer with a fondness for the marvelous or the sensational may easily impose on the credulity of the public. Mr. Sabine Baring-Gould, in his *Family Names and Their Story,* has an interesting chapter on ''Name Stories,'' in which he relates a number of amusing fables that people have invented in order to explain their own names. These fabulous explanations are all the more diverting because men who are otherwise intelligent put them forth quite seriously and expect others to accept them as satisfactory statements of fact. Similar ridiculous ''name stories'' are current about the origin of common place names. A few of these specimens of folk etymology, which have been offered to the writer in all seriousness, are perhaps worth repeating.

The following explanation of the village named Tamanend is given by a local historian: "There is a tradition among the old residents that about the time of the Wyoming Massacre a noted Indian chief, Taman by name, an ally of the British, was foremost in the war upon the defenseless frontier. Afterward, when the avengers of these butcheries made war upon the savages, Taman was brought to bay at Hawk's Curve, near the site of the village. Here he was captured and immediately hanged; hence the name Taman's end, or Tamanend." Alas for the name and the fame of St. Tammany![1]

Here is an explanation of the name Bellefonte which points to a German rather than a French origin. An old Pennsylvania-German farmer put a bell on one of his cows and turned the drove loose to pasture on the wooded hills surrounding the village. The cows came home, but the bell was lost. Not until the autumn, when the farmer was hunting among the hills, was the bell found. "Ya wohl! there, among the bushes, wass that *bell fount!*" And, of course, the town was christened Bellefonte[2] to commemorate the event!

"How did Tyrone get its name?" I once asked a good lady who had lived there all her days. "Have you never heard?" she said. "I thought every one knew. It was this way: the first pioneer who came into this region with his wife camped near where the town now stands. He had two horses, a gray and a roan, which he turned out to pasture in the evening. The roan seemed so restive that the careful wife urged her husband to 'tie roan.' They settled here and accordingly named the place

[1] See Tamanend, page 287.
[2] See Bellefonte, page 142.

Tyrone."[3] And the good, trustful soul who expected me to believe this story bore an Irish name!

A correspondent volunteered this explanation of the Indian name Loyalhanna. "An Indian who had become old and useless as a warrior and hunter was abandoned by his tribe. He was the last of the Indians who dwelt in the ravine. His faithful daughter Hannah, with her bow and arrow, supported him in the extremity of his age. When all others had forsaken him, she alone was faithful. Among the settlers she came to be known as 'Loyal Hannah,' and they called the place Loyalhanna[4] out of respect for her."

A traditional explanation of the good old Huguenot name Ligonier relates the extraordinary adventure of a hunter who shot at a buck that was leisurely scratching his ear with his hind foot. The bullet killed the animal, perforating at the same time both the *Leg an' ear*. From that occurrence the place, it is alleged, was called Ligonier.[5]

Another correspondent, a gentleman of unquestioned intelligence, thus attempts to explain the Delaware Indian name Masthope: "I cannot refrain from giving you the origin of the name Masthope, a small station on the Erie Railroad in Pike County. When the *Constitution*, or 'Old Ironsides,' was building, a party was sent out to find a mast tall enough for the man-of-war. They searched far and wide, but apparently in vain. Finally, well nigh discouraged, they went far up the Delaware River as a last hope. Here their diligence was rewarded, and they were able to send back word that the mast could here be procured. Hence the name Masthope."[6]

---

[3] See Tyrone, page 186.
[4] See Loyalhanna, page 284.
[5] See Ligonier, page 266.
[6] See Masthope, page 285.

The local names in a newly settled region, as will be seen in the following chapters, usually come from four principal sources: (1) aboriginal place names, which are preserved because they have become familiar, or are thought to be appropriate or euphonious; (2) place names which are borrowed from the old world, usually from the country or locality whence the colonists came, and which they have thus transplanted out of love for their ancestral home; (3) names of persons—great men of the past or present, or merely local celebrities, often the founders of towns, who thought that they had a right thus to perpetuate their own names; (4) invented names, which may owe their origin to some plant, animal, mineral, or industry, to some prominent geographical feature, to an historic event or circumstance, or to mere caprice. It is worth while to consider briefly each of these four sources.

1. The Indian place names of Pennsylvania would be a suitable subject for a separate treatise, and it is to be hoped that some Pennsylvanian will before long perform for his State the same service that Dr. William T. Beauchamp has rendered our sister state in his *Aboriginal Place Names of New York*. The extent to which Indian names prevail in the United States is shown by the fact that half the states in the Union, nearly three hundred lakes, and more than a thousand rivers and streams bear aboriginal names. The importance and the intrinsic interest of these names are attested by the fact that busy statesmen like Lewis Cass, Albert Gallatin, James Madison, and Thomas Jefferson have all been students of aboriginal place names.

Many a wordy battle has been waged over the correct form and meaning of Indian names; yet few scholars now living are experts in the languages of the aborigines.

The present writer has no knowledge of the Indian tongues, and has therefore been obliged to lean wholly upon the authority of others. Fortunately, however, a very large number of the aboriginal names in Pennsylvania have been explained by the Moravian missionaries, who lived long and familiarly with the Lenni-Lennape, or Delaware Indians, spoke their dialect fluently, and were such keen and capable students of languages that we can in many cases rely upon the soundness of their explanations of the older Indian place names in Pennsylvania. Considerable light has also been shed on this subject by more recent investigations.

It seems necessary, however, to point out that in their present pronunciation and printed forms the many beautiful and sonorous Indian place names with which we have become so familiar, and which we pronounce so glibly, were wholly the work of white men. The Indians had no written language. Their spoken tongue was a succession of syllables not always distinctly enunciated. Their names of places were first picked up by pioneer settlers, traders, hunters, and so-called interpreters, none of whom were critical students of language, and most of whom were men of meager learning, densely ignorant of all that goes to make up modern scholarship. It is but natural, therefore, that their attempt to pronounce these names or to write them down should produce results that are both misleading and grotesque. Yet such men were, for the most part, responsible for the present form of these Indian names. If we add to this the fact that in Pennsylvania not only the English, but also the French and the Germans attempted to give these spoken names a written form, we can readily see that our so-called Indian names must make but a slight and sorry approximation to the actual names used by the aborigines.

So much it seems necessary to say by way of caution. The author approaches this part of his subject with fear and trembling, sure of this fact only, that all these names once had a definite meaning, and hopeful that in many cases he has been able to discover by diligent inquiry what the meaning was. The signification of Indian names is usually quite commonplace and prosaic. However sonorous they may seem, they are not essentially poetical.

2. Some borrowed place names, like Lebanon, Bethlehem, Sharon, or Mount Carmel, are taken from the Bible. Others are drawn from classical antiquity; for example, Troy, Athens, Tarentum, and Etna. Most borrowed place names, however, are simply transferred from the native land of the colonists. Thus the nationality of the early settlers in a given region is often evident from the names that they have brought from their old homes. The English settlers in the three original counties, for instance, naturally borrowed such English names as Chester, Bristol, Darby, and Birmingham. The prevalence of names like Merion, Radnor, Haverford, and Bryn Mawr is characteristic of "the Welsh tract."

This same phenomenon is often apparent within the restricted limits of a single county. Lancaster County, which was originally settled by English Quakers, Welsh Episcopalians, Irish Presbyterians, and German Mennonites and Moravians, furnishes a good illustration. The names of the townships and villages often show whence the first settlers came. The townships of Lancaster, Warwick, Salisbury, and Little Britain mark the English settlements. In like manner the Welsh have given their names to East and West Lampeter, Caernarvon, and Brecknock Townships. The Scotch-Irish gave their settlements such names as Leacock, Drumore, Colerain, Rapho, and Donegal. The settlers of German

2

extraction bestowed their own names on Manheim, Lititz, New Holland, and Strasburg.

3. The names of great men from many nations have been applied to Pennsylvania places: Kossuth, Bismarck, Homer City, Lamartine, Ulysses, Mozart, and Calvin may be cited as examples. The great men of England are represented in such names as Pittsburgh, Wilkes-Barre, Wesley, and Bessemer. Scores of places perpetuate the name and memory of men prominent in colonial affairs, in the war of the Revolution, and in the government of the State and nation: familiar examples are Pennsburg, Franklin, Morrisville, Saint Clair, Waynesburg, Mifflintown, Washington, Lincoln, Scottdale, Wilkinsburg, and Cameron. Purely local celebrities have given their names to such important places as Scranton, Pottsville, Bloomsburg, Wellsboro, Montrose, and Chambersburg.

No one can make much progress as a student of local names, particularly of place names in the United States, without some knowledge of family names. Although it is not a part of the author's purpose to write a dissertation on surnames, it may here be helpful to point out that with respect to their origin most family names readily fall into five or six great classes, and to mention these divisions, giving under each half a dozen surnames that have been applied to places mentioned in Parts I and II:

(*a*) Surnames indicating rank, office, or occupation: Franklin, Butler, Mercer, Norris, Potter, and Snyder.

(*b*) Local or territorial surnames[7]: Blair, Crawford, Luzerne, Montgomery, Ridgway, and Washington.

(*c*) Family names of personal characteristic: Allen, Armstrong, Cameron, Sharp, Sullivan, and Swoyer.

---

[7] A "territorial surname" is a family name that has been derived from a place name.

(*d*) Patronymic surnames, which usually contain some such addition as *Mac, O,* or *-son:* McConnell, McKean, McKee, Dickson, Jefferson, and Kane (originally O'Kane).

(*e*) Surnames derived from personal or baptismal names: Archbald, Gilbert, Lawrence, Titus, Adams, and Edwards. The last two are probably only shortened patronymic forms.

To these five classes we should perhaps add a sixth, containing surnames which were originally diminutives or nicknames. The family names Wilkins and Rankin will serve as illustrations.

4. Invented names that refer to the plant life of a region are Peach Bottom, Ryeland, Forest City, Grassflat, Castanea, and Hazleton. The prevalence of some particular type of animal life is shown by names like Catfish, Panther, Turkey City, Bruin, Doe Run, and Turtle Creek. Mineral resources are indicated by such names as Carbondale, Ganister, Petrolia, Bitumen, Kaolin, and Natrona. Particular industries have resulted in names like Milton, Quarryville, Steelton, Old Forge, Glassport, and Slatington. Prominent geographical features are responsible for such names as Doublinggap, Chalkhill, Springglen, Outcrop, and Delaware Water Gap. Names like Warriors Mark, Torpedo, Canoe Camp, Fallentimber, and Burnt Cabins commemorate some important event. Mere caprice has produced such inventions as Pen-Mar, Windber, Rough and Ready, Decorum, and Bird-in-Hand.

I

STATE, COUNTIES, AND COUNTY-SEATS

CHAPTER II

PENNSYLVANIA, THE KEYSTONE STATE

H OW did Pennsylvania get its name? And how did it afterwards happen to be nicknamed "The Keystone State"?

To the first question can be given a definite and final answer, for we have the evidence of William Penn himself. The name Pennsylvania means "Penn's forest land." The oft-repeated statement that the wilderness province was named Pennsylvania in honor of its illustrious proprietor is simply not true. William Penn modestly interprets the name as "the high or head woodlands," and explains that it was given in honor of his father.

Pennsylvania

On March 14, 1681, as soon as King Charles II had signed the grant that made William Penn the master of a province about three hundred miles by one hundred and sixty in extent, William Penn wrote to his friend, Robert Turner, as follows:

"After many waitings, watchings, solicitings, and disputes in Council, this day my country was confirmed to me under the great seal of England, with large powers and privileges, by the name of *Pennsylvania*;[1] a name the king would give it in honor of my father.[2] I chose New Wales, [that] being, as this, a pretty hilly country; but Penn being Welsh for *a head* (as Penmanmoire in Wales, and Penrith in Cumberland, and Penn in Buck-

---

[1] Spelled Pennsilvania in the charter.
[2] Sir William Penn, the famous English admiral, who rendered valuable service to the Stuarts during the tempestuous days of the Commonwealth.

23

inghamshire, the highest land in England), [they] called
this Pennsylvania, which is the high or head woodlands;
for I proposed, when the secretary, a Welshman, refused
to have it called New Wales, *Sylvania,* and they added
Penn to it; and though I much opposed it, and went to
the king to have it struck out and altered, he said it was
past, and would take it upon him; nor could twenty
guineas move the under-secretary to vary the name; for
I feared lest it should be looked on as a vanity in me, and
not as a respect in the king, as it truly was, to my father,
whom he often mentions with praise.''

Thus Pennsylvania received its sonorous and appropriate name. The founder suggested *Sylvania,* ''forest
land,'' and to this the king prefixed *Penn.* Who can
gainsay the will of a king? The pious proprietor was
anxious to disclaim the responsibility for the apparent
vanity lurking in the name of Pennsylvania, but in spite
of his protest and his genuine modesty, may we not suppose that he afterwards became reconciled to the name
and was even secretly pleased that the king was arbitrary
and stiff-necked in this choice of a name? Pennsylvanians at least should be thankful. New Wales would
have been a poor substitute.

There are a score of Penn Townships in Pennsylvania,
but it is a singular fact that no county in Pennsylvania
or in the United States bears the name of
Places Penn. Michigan, North Dakota, and Penn-
Named sylvania have post-offices named Penn.
for Penn Missouri and West Virginia have each a
Pennsboro. There is a Pennsville in New
Jersey and also in Ohio. Port Penn is in Delaware. In
Pennsylvania the following post-offices contain the name
of Penn as a prefix, in honor either of William Penn or
of some member of his family: Pennhurst, in Chester

County; Penn Run, in Indiana County; Pennsburg, in Montgomery County; Penns Creek, in Snyder County, named for John Penn; Pennsdale, in Lycoming County; Penns Park, in Bucks County, situated within the original park, or town square laid out by direction of William Penn; and Pennsville, in Fayette County. Mount Penn borough is in Berks County. William Penn is in Montgomery County.

Pennsbury Manor, laid out by Penn as a sort of country capital soon after he came to his wilderness province, and containing a tract of more than eight thousand acres beautifully situated along the Delaware, about four miles above the present town of Bristol, does not now enjoy even the dignity of being a post-office. Here Penn erected a country-seat sixty feet long by forty deep, "with offices and outhouses at the side, fronting upon a beautiful garden, which extended down to the river." This mansion, which was then regarded as a marvel of spaciousness and magnificence, was the abode of Penn and his family for only a brief period in 1700-1. Being unoccupied, it gradually fell into decay, and it was taken down shortly before the Revolutionary War.

When, and why, and by whom was the popular name, "The Keystone State," first applied to Pennsylvania?
"The Keystone State" These questions cannot be answered as definitely and positively as one might wish. Certainly the nickname "Keystone State" has been generally current for more than a century. A published address of the Democratic Committee in 1803 contains the following sentence: "As Pennsylvania is the *keystone* of the Democratic arch, every engine will be used to sever it from its place." This, says Doctor Egle, was "probably the first

instance in which the comparison of the Commonwealth
to the keystone of an arch was used."[3]

Pennsylvania was apparently called "The Keystone
State" because of its central position among the states
when the Federal Constitution was adopted. If the thirteen original states are named in the order of their
geographical position from northeast to southwest, Pennsylvania will stand seventh, thus occupying a central
position, with six states to the north and east, and six
to the south and west. Thus Pennsylvania became the
keystone of the Federal arch.

Many people will be surprised to learn from Doctor
Egle's statement that the conception of Pennsylvania as
the Keystone State is at least one hundred and twenty-
two years old. But, in point of fact, the idea is consider-
ably older. The earliest indication that Pennsylvania
was regarded as the Keystone State dates back to 1784.
On the walls of the American Philosophical Society in
Philadelphia hangs a drawing about twelve inches by
nine, tinted with water-colors, representing the thirteen
American states in the form of a stone arch, with Pennsylvania in the keystone position. The arch spans a
waterfall and is surmounted by a figure of Hercules.
This interesting picture undoubtedly goes back to the
time of the French alliance during the American Revolution. It was presented in 1784 by the French Chargé
d'Affaires, M. Marbois Francois de Barbé (afterwards
Marquis de Marbois) to Charles Thomson, then secretary
of Congress.

Our ancestors were rather fond of symbolizing ideas.
For instance, when General Washington entered Trenton
on April 21, 1789, he passed under an arch supported by
thirteen pillars as symbolizing the thirteen states. "On

[3] Egle's *History of Pennsylvania*, p. 235.

the bridge over the creek which passes through the town was erected a triumphal arch, highly ornamented with laurels and flowers, and supported by thirteen pillars, each entwined with wreaths of evergreen.''[4] Witness also the symbolism that appeared in the early efforts to find a national flag or emblem. Most of us are familiar with the colonial device attributed to Benjamin Franklin, —the picture of a snake severed into thirteen parts, with the initials of one of the colonies on each segment and with the motto, ''Join or Die!'' beneath it. This graphic bit of symbolism appeared in the *Pennsylvania Gazette* at the outbreak of the French and Indian War in 1754.

It is reasonable to suppose that during or even before the American Revolution the arch and its keystone may have been popular symbols of union and strength. At a time when the new nation was groping about for an apt emblem of its national life, it was both natural and appropriate to use an arch and a keystone to symbolize the union and the strength of the thirteen confederated states.

The peculiar appropriateness of this symbol of the arch and the keystone was destined to give it wide popularity. The size, the population, the wealth, the resources, and the political importance of Pennsylvania, as well as the leading part that the State played in the struggle for freedom, and the fact that both the Declaration of Independence and the Constitution of the United States were written within its borders, all contributed to make ''The Keystone State'' a popular name for Pennsylvania.

About 1800 the symbolism of the arch and the keystone was actually given material form in a bridge built in the new capital city of Washington; and a good many people

---

[4] John Marshall's *Life of Washington*, vol. II, p. 142.

have erroneously considered the existence of this bridge as evidence of the *origin* rather than a proof of the *popularity* of the appellation "The Keystone State."

General Peter Force, author of the *American Archives* and once mayor of Washington, has been cited[5] as authority for the statement that about 1800, when Pennsylvania Avenue in Washington was extended across Rock Creek to Georgetown, a stone bridge with a single arch was erected out of some stones which had remained unused in the construction of the first Capitol; and that on the exposed side of the thirteen arch stones were carved the initials or abbreviations of the thirteen states, Pennsylvania being represented conspicuously as the keystone of the arch. "From this circumstance," it has often been erroneously alleged, "Pennsylvania obtained the name and has since been widely known as 'the Keystone State.'"

The name has become so generally popular, even outside of Pennsylvania, that ten different states now have a post-office called Keystone.[6]

---

[5] *A History of the Origin of the Appellation Keystone State* (Philadelphia, 1874), p. 20. This curious book, in spite of its promising title, throws very little light on the subject.

[6] Pennsylvania, as province and state, has had four different capitals,—Upland (or Chester), Philadelphia, Lancaster, and Harrisburg. Each of these names will be discussed in its proper place.

CHAPTER III

THE THREE ORIGINAL COUNTIES

IT is impossible to give the exact date for the formation of the three original counties of Philadelphia, Bucks, and Chester. Perhaps they had been planned by William Penn before he sailed from England. Suffice it to say that shortly after his arrival, probably in November, 1682, he divided his province into the three counties of Philadelphia, Buckingham (which was later called Bucks), and Upland (which was soon changed to Chester); for in November of this year he appointed a sheriff for each county.[1] These three counties were represented in the first provincial Assembly, which met at Upland December 4, 1682, and remained in session four days, ratifying the code of laws drawn up in England, and formally annexing the three counties of Delaware to Pennsylvania.

The county of Philadelphia included the newly planned city of Philadelphia and the surrounding region; Bucks County lay to the north without any definite limits except the Delaware River to the east; and Chester County extended westward from Upland, or Chester, "without certain boundaries." The fixing of boundaries was a matter of detail that could not be attended to immediately.

Fully a year before, in September, 1681, Penn had sent out three commissioners, William Crispin, Nathaniel Allen, and John Bezan, directing them to select a site for a city on the Delaware, where "it is most navigable, high, dry, and healthy." Crispin died on the voyage, and his

---

[1] Scharf and Westcott's *History of Philadelphia*, vol. I, p. 101.

place was taken by a fourth commissioner, William Heage. Penn further specified that the new city was to cover 10,000 acres, and that the building plots were to be spacious, with "ground on either side for gardens, orchards, or fields, so that it may be a green country town, which will never be burnt and always be wholesome." In making these special provisions Penn doubtless had in mind the London plague of 1665 and the great London fire of 1666.

Although he may have contemplated making Upland the chief town of his province, he was wise enough to give his agents liberty to select any site they thought best. They passed by Upland as unsuitable, and chose the site of the Indian camp at Coanquannock, "the grove of tall pines." In July, 1682, Thomas Holme, the newly appointed surveyor-general, in accordance with modified instructions received from Penn, laid out the city of Philadelphia.

Exactly when Penn selected the name Philadelphia for his "great towne" is not known. There can be no doubt that Penn himself chose the name, but **Phila-** he does not mention it in the proposals he ad-**delphia** dressed to prospective settlers. As a close student of the Bible he must have been attracted by the name of the Lydian city of Philadelphia, the seat of one of the seven early Christian churches. As he was educated in theology and in the classical languages, but had no extensive knowledge of profane history, it was natural for him to make the mistake of supposing, as so many have done since his day, that the name of the Biblical city of Philadelphia must have had its origin and meaning in the abstract Greek noun *phila-*

delphia, which occurs five times[2] in the Greek text of the Epistles of the New Testament, and which in three instances is translated "brotherly love" in the Authorized Version. In Philadelphia, mentioned in the Apocalypse, Penn saw the ready-made name of a city that must have taken his fancy because he thought that it was identical in meaning with the common noun *philadelphia,* which stood for an idea dear to his heart; and there is no evidence to show that he knew the real origin and etymological derivation of the name of the Lydian city.

He was sincerely desirous that his new town should actually become "the city of brotherly love." The sentiment implied in this name doubtless appealed to him as peculiarly appropriate for the capital city of the Quaker commonwealth. This name, he hoped, would be prophetic and significant of the feeling that would prevail among the inhabitants. The name of Philadelphia appears in a land warrant executed July 10, 1682.[3] In the address of August 12, 1684, which Penn sent out from England to the Quaker meetings in Pennsylvania, he said: "And thou, Philadelphia, the virgin settlement of this province, *named before thou wert born,*[4] what care, what service, what travail has there been to bring thee forth, and preserve thee from such as would abuse and defile thee."

The name of Penn's "great towne" was apparently suggested by that of the little Lydian city of Philadelphia, which really signifies "the city of Philadelphus," but which Penn evidently thought meant "the city of brotherly love." This ancient city in Asia Minor—now the

---

[2] The textual references are Romans 12: 10; 1 Thessalonians 4: 9; Hebrews 13: 1; 1 Peter 1: 22; and 2 Peter 1: 7. In the first three passages *philadelphia* has been translated "brotherly love" in the Authorized Version; in the last two references the word is translated "love of the brethren" and "brotherly kindness" respectively.

[3] Egle's *History of Pennsylvania,* p. 1017.

[4] The italics are ours.

dilapidated and almost deserted Allah-Sehr, "the city of God"—was founded and named by Attalus II, known in history as Attalus Philadelphus, king of Pergamus from B. C. 159 to 138, who was surnamed or nicknamed *Philadelphus*, "brother-loving," from the fraternal love he displayed toward his brother Eumenes, whom he had succeeded to the throne.

"Fair Philadelphia next is rising seen,
  Betwixt two rivers plac'd, two miles between."

Philadelphia County was named for its chief town and county-seat.   The present city includes the whole of
Phila- Philadelphia County.   In 1854 the nine munic-
delphia ipal corporations, or "incorporated districts"
County of Northern Liberties, Kensington, Southwark, Spring Garden, Penn, Moyamensing, Richmond, West Philadelphia, and Belmont, and the six boroughs of Germantown, Frankford, Manayunk, Bridesburg, Whitehall, and Aramingo, together with certain unorganized districts and villages, were consolidated with the city of Philadelphia.   As many of the names of these earlier districts and towns are still frequently used, it seems worth while at this point to comment briefly upon the most important of them.

Although it was at first intended that the original city should cover 10,000 acres, the quadrilateral actually laid out by the surveyor-general between the Schuylkill and the Delaware Rivers contained only 1,280 acres.   Penn had provided that for every five hundred acres of country land purchased from him, the buyer was to receive, as a bonus, ten acres in the "great towne."   The great reduction in the actual area of Philadelphia when the town was laid out made this arrangement impossible.   In order that Penn's promise might be kept, at least in a modified form, the so-called "Liberties," or areas of free land, were established, and some of the purchasers thus secured their extra assignment of land in the Western Liberties beyond the Schuylkill, while others received their bonuses in the **Northern Liberties,** lying north of the city. The Northern Liberties became an incorporated district in 1819.

The founder of **Kensington,** which was incorporated as a separate municipal district in 1820, was Anthony Palmer, a rich ship captain and merchant, who came to Philadelphia from Barbados in 1709, bought extensive tracts of land north of the city, became prominent in the affairs of the colony, lived in considerable style, and was a conspicuous figure as he drove through the city with his coach and four, or sailed down the Delaware in his handsome pleasure barge. About twenty-five years after buying his land he laid out a town, which he called Kensington, after the English parish which is now a part of London.

The populous district of **Southwark** in southern Philadelphia, which was incorporated in 1794, was named after Southwark in London. The English Southwark was literally the "South Work" (called *Suth-geweorc* in the Saxon Chronicle), having been named from an earthwork made to defend the southern approach to London Bridge.

Spring Garden, at first used as the appropriate designation of a private estate, gradually won its way into use as the name of a village in the northern suburbs. The district was incorporated in 1813.

The district—formerly the township—known as **Penn** was, of course, named for the founder of the colony. **Richmond** was probably named for Richmond in Surrey, England. **Olney** was named for the English town of that name in Buckinghamshire. **West Philadelphia** took its

3

name from its location to the west of the older municipality.

Belmont, the "beautiful hill," was so named from the
historic country-seat of the Peters family.   Belmont
Mansion, which gave its name to this district, was a
notable estate in colonial days, beautifully situated on
the west bank of the Schuylkill, and still standing in
Fairmount Park.   It was built in 1743 by William Peters,
whose son, Richard Peters, named for his uncle, the
Reverend Richard Peters, secretary to the proprietary
government and rector of Christ Church in 1762, was
secretary of the Board of War in 1779 and throughout
the remainder of the Revolution.   In point of fact, if not
in name, Richard Peters the younger was our first Secretary of War, and by his energy, enterprise, and resourcefulness in securing funds, supplies, and munitions,
he contributed in no small measure to the ultimate
triumph of the colonial patriots.   For thirty-six years
he was judge of the United States district court for
Pennsylvania.

Several Indian names given in the early days to districts, boroughs, and villages are still in use.   **Moyamensing** means "the place for maize," or "maize land."
Proud says that Maniyunk, according to a Swedish
manuscript, was the native name of the Schuylkill.
Heckewelder explains **Manayunk** as being a corruption
of the Delaware Indian word *Mene-iunk,* which means
"where we go to drink."   **Passyunk** is said to signify "a
level place, a valley, a place below the hills."   **Kingses-
sing** means "a place where there is a bog."   **Tacony,**
which took its name from the Tekony or Tekone Creek,
signifies "forest, or wilderness."[5]

Roxborough was originally Rocksburrow, according to

---

[5] See Tunkhannock, page 136.

Doctor Oberholtzer,—"perhaps because of the fox-burrows among the rocks."

Germantown is the oldest German settlement in the United States. Soon after Penn received his grant of Pennsylvania there appeared in London a little pamphlet entitled *Some Account of the Province of Pennsylvania in America.* Almost simultaneously a German translation was published in Amsterdam. Copies of this and other pamphlets were sown broadcast in Holland, southern Germany, and Switzerland. Shortly before the Quaker colony was planted in Pennsylvania, George Fox, revered as the founder of the Society of Friends, William Penn, Robert Barclay, and George Keith had all made missionary journeys into Germany. The Quakers undoubtedly did everything in their power to attract the persecuted German sects to their colony in the new world. Their efforts soon bore fruit. A company of German Mennonites and Quakers from Frankfort, Kriegsheim, and Crefeld, the places visited by the Quaker missionaries, organized the "Frankfort Company," bought 25,000 acres of land six miles northwest of the Philadelphia settlement, and arrived at Philadelphia on board the *Concord* on October 6, 1683.

Their settlement at Germantown under the leadership of the learned Dr. Francis Daniel Pastorius was the beginning of a mighty Teutonic migration that brought fully 100,000 Swiss and German settlers to Pennsylvania before the outbreak of the American Revolution. Philadelphia then had only eighty houses—"such as they were," to use Penn's apologetic phrase. The Quakers and the Mennonites were kindred spirits, and it is noteworthy that the persecuted Germans came into their heritage in Pennsylvania almost as soon as their Quaker brethren. They were destined to play an important part in the development and the prosperity of the new commonwealth. The German settlements in Pennsylvania, from the very beginning, were an essential part of Penn's "holy experiment."

It was appropriate and natural that this first German settlement in the new world should be called Germantown. A little later, when **Frankford** was settled, it took its name from the "Frankfort Company," which had been organized to promote the German colony in Philadelphia County. The ancient city of Frankfort-on-the-Main was literally the "ford of the Franks."

Although Chester was at first used as a sort of impromptu capital for convening the first colonial Assembly, Philadelphia soon became the seat of the provincial government, and remained the capital of the province and state of Pennsylvania until 1799, when Lancaster became the state capital. Philadelphia was the capital of the United States from 1790 to 1800.

Bucks County

Bucks County was named for the English shire or county of Buckingham, generally abbreviated Bucks. This name was appropriate for two reasons: the Penns were an old Buckinghamshire family and had been seated there for generations; and many of the Quakers who had come over with Penn on the *Welcome* had migrated from Buckinghamshire. At first the Pennsylvania county was called Buckingham, and twenty-five years after it was formed Oldmixon speaks of it as Buckingham County; but the abbreviated name Bucks was always the more usual and popular form, and its use gradually became general.

The name Buckingham is commonly explained as meaning "the home of the men of the beech forest." Certainly the beech was long the predominant tree in the forests of Buckinghamshire. Yet it seems more likely that the name signifies simply "the home of the Buccings," the progenitor of this family or clan either being called Bucca, or having the *buck* as his totem.

Bucks County has had three different county-seats, Bristol, Newtown, and Doylestown. The little settlement at what is now Bristol, laid out in 1697, was **Bristol** first called Buckingham. About 1700 the name was changed to New Bristol. The present name first appeared in 1702. In 1705 Bristol was designated as the permanent seat of justice for Bucks County, the courts before that year having been held in Falls and Middletown Townships. The name Bristol was borrowed from that of the English city, then the chief seaport in the west of England. William Penn's grandfather, Giles Penn, belonged to Bristol, and his father, Sir William Penn, was buried in the beautiful church of St. Mary Redcliffe at Bristol. It should be remembered also that in 1696 William Penn married his second wife, Hannah Callowhill, daughter of a rich Quaker merchant of Bristol. These facts may have furnished a reason for this choice of name. The name Bristol is first mentioned in the Saxon Chronicle in 1087 as *Bricgstow*, "the place of the bridge" over the Avon.

In 1724 the county-seat was removed to a more central location at Newtown, where it remained eighty-eight years. When Newtown Township was laid **Newtown** out, shortly after the formation of Bucks County, there was reserved, near the middle of it, a townstead of 640 acres, on which now stands the borough of Newtown. The name Newtown occurs in land conveyances as early as 1683. Just when the townstead began to be built up is not known. As to the origin of the name, tradition tells us that in passing through this part of the Bucks County wilderness with his surveyor-general, Thomas Holme, Penn remarked, "Here I will lay out my *new town.*"

In 1812 the seat of justice was removed to Doylestown, then a village with less than one thousand inhabitants.

Doyles-town In 1778 the place was first called Doyle's-town, when there were only two or three log houses at the cross-roads. In July of this year the Continental army encamped here for several nights just before the battle of Monmouth. Doylestown took its name from William Doyle, who settled there about 1735, and kept a tavern at the cross-roads as early as 1742. The Irish surname Doyle signifies "dark stranger."

To explain the name of the town and county of Chester, a very pretty story has obtained wide currency. "When William Penn first arrived at Upland, **Chester and Chester County** now old Chester, turning round to his friend Pearson, one of his own society, who had accompanied him in his ship *Welcome,* he said: 'Providence has brought us here safely. Thou hast been the companion of my perils. What wilt thou that I should call this place?' Pearson replied, 'Chester, in remembrance of the city from whence I came.' Penn also promised that when he divided the territory into counties, he would call one of them by the same name." [6]

It is too bad that one must spoil this story by pointing out that it is probably fiction rather than history. It appeared for the first time in Clarkson's *Life of Penn,* which was published more than a century after Penn landed at Upland, or Oplandt, where the Swedes and the Dutch had alternately held sway. It is doubtful whether any person named Pearson came over on the *Welcome.*

---

[6] Mr. Joseph J. Lewis, in the West Chester *Village Record,* 1824.

The report for the year 1704 of the Vestry of St. Paul's Church, Chester, to the Society for the Propagation of the Gospel in Foreign Parts contains this significant statement: "The people of Chester County showed very early zeal to have the Church of England worship settled among them. This county is so called because most of the inhabitants of it came from Cheshire in England." From this contemporary evidence we may fairly conclude that soon after his arrival Penn changed the name of Upland to Chester, and gave the same name to the new county in deference to the wishes of the English settlers in the town, most of whom had come from the neighborhood of Chester in England.[7] The name Chester is a corruption of the Latin word *castra,* "a camp."

Chester County has had two county-seats, Chester and West Chester. Chester is the oldest town in Pennsylvania, the Swedish settlement at Upland dating from 1645. The borough of Upland, in Delaware County, still preserves the ancient name of this place. Near Chester is the famous "Caleb Pusey House," erected in 1683, said to be the oldest building in Pennsylvania. Chester also has the oldest city-hall now in use in the United States.[8] Until a comparatively recent time Chester was a very small place. Oldmixon, in 1708, says that Chester did not contain "above one hundred houses." As late as 1820 the population was less than seven hundred; and in 1850, less than two thousand. Its present size is due to the recent growth of large manufacturing interests.

Chester remained the county-seat for more than a century after Penn's arrival. In 1786, after the most violent opposition, the seat of justice was finally removed to its present location in West Chester. The people in the

[7] Ashmead's *History of Delaware County,* p. 21.
[8] Erected in 1724.

West   western part of the county had long clamored
Chester   for a more central location of the county-seat.
          The new county town was called West Chester
because of its situation some sixteen miles northwest of
old Chester.

The two county names, Bucks and Chester, have been
very little used elsewhere in the United States. Virginia
alone has a Buckingham County. There are two other
Chester Counties, one in South Carolina, and one in
Tennessee; and New Hampshire has a county named
Cheshire.

A word should be said about "the three lower
counties," which now form the state of Delaware, but
                    which were once a part of Pennsyl-
"The Three   vania. These three counties were
Lower Counties" conveyed to William Penn by the
                    Duke of York on August 2, 1681, and
united with Pennsylvania in December, 1682. The Dutch
district of Hoorn-Kill—"the Horn stream," so named
by David Pieterzen de Vries for his native town of
Hoorn on the Zuyder Zee—was divided by the English
into the counties of Sussex and St. Jones.

The English parish of St. Jones is in the county of
Kent. In 1683 St. Jones County became Kent County.
Sussex and Kent Counties in Delaware were named for
the English counties of Sussex and Kent. The English
name New Castle was probably first applied to the old
Swedish and Dutch town about 1665. In March of that
year William Cavendish (1592-1676) was created first
Duke of Newcastle-on-Tyne; and as the new Duke was
just then prominently before the public, it may be sur-
mised that the town and the county of New Castle may
have been named for him. The ultimate source of the
name was the Northumbrian city of Newcastle.

CHAPTER IV

COUNTIES NAMED FOR ENGLISH SHIRES

TWELVE Pennsylvania counties bear the names of English shires. Two of these, Bucks and Chester, have been discussed in the preceding chapter. Three others, York, Bedford, and Huntingdon, were probably not named for English shires directly, but for English noblemen; and they will therefore be discussed in separate chapters. Besides the two original counties of Bucks and Chester, the seven counties of Pennsylvania that were named directly for English shires are Lancaster, Cumberland, Berks, Northampton, Northumberland, Westmoreland, and Somerset.

In 1712 the region that is now Lancaster County was erected into the township of Conestoga, then a part of Chester County. The new township took its name from its chief stream, the Conestoga Creek. The meaning of the Indian name Conestoga is not known with certainty. It has been variously interpreted as meaning "crooked stream," "great maize field," "people of the cabin poles," or "at the place of the immersed pole." This last meaning is probably the correct one. The name has become widely known because it was early applied to that great carrier of overland freight, the Conestoga wagon, which Benjamin Rush aptly styled "the ship of inland commerce." The same word has furnished the name *stogie* for the rude cigar that the driver puffed as he trudged along the highway beside his team.

On May 10, 1729, nearly half a century after the three original counties were formed, the Council and Assembly

Lancaster established the new county of Lancaster.
County Among the early settlers, John Wright, who
had come from Chester to the Susquehanna
in 1726 and established Wright's Ferry where Columbia
now stands, was undoubtedly the leading spirit, and
one of the prime movers in the formation of the new
county. For twenty years he was a justice of the
peace for Chester and Lancaster Counties, and for
many years a member of the provincial Assembly. It
was natural and proper that he should name the county
of which he was perhaps the foremost citizen. Through
his influence it was called Lancaster County from his
native shire of Lancaster,[1] now the most populous county
in England. At the time of its formation Lancaster
County covered a vast territory: the counties of York,
Cumberland, Berks, Lebanon, Dauphin, and Northumberland
have all been taken from Lancaster County. Virtually,
all the counties to the west were once a part of
Lancaster County.

There were three contestants for the county-seat,—
Postlethwait's, the Indian Field or "Gibson's Pasture"
(the present site of Lancaster), and Wright's Ferry.
The last-named place seemed at first to be the strongest
competitor: Robert Barber, the first sheriff, a neighbor
of John Wright, felt so sure of this location that he had
built, near his residence, a strong wooden building intended
for the county jail. John Postlethwait's tavern
near the Conestoga Creek, in what is now Manor Township,
became the temporary seat of justice; and Gibson's
Pasture was finally selected as the site of the permanent
county-seat. When this location was chosen, probably

---

[1] Rupp's *History of Lancaster and York Counties*, p. 240; also Clare's *Brief History of Lancaster County*, p. 109.

the only building standing in what is now the city of Lancaster was "a log tavern, with the sign of a hickory-tree, kept by George Gibson."

James Hamilton, who was later governor of Pennsylvania from 1748 to 1752, and from 1759 to 1763, laid out **Lancaster** the town of Lancaster in March, 1730, on a tract of land two miles square; yet, for some reason, he did not dispose of any lots until 1735. On May 1, 1730, the governor signed the document approving the site selected, designating the place as "the townstead of Lancaster." Thus the county-seat formally received its name, which was taken from the county town of Lancashire in England. The Anglo-Saxon form of Lancaster was *Luneceaster,* "the *castra,* or camp, on the Lune."

For a period of fifty years, from 1770 to 1820, the little town of Lancaster was a place of vast importance, out of all proportion to its size. Here George Ross, one of the Pennsylvania signers of the Declaration of Independence, began to practice law in 1750. Here lived Frederick Augustus Muhlenberg, third son of the founder of Lutheranism in America, Heinrich Melchior Muhlenberg, and first Speaker of the national House of Representatives in 1789. In September, 1777, when General Howe occupied Philadelphia, the seat of the state government was temporarily moved to Lancaster.

Situated on the main highway leading from Philadelphia westward to the newer settlements on the frontier, colonial Lancaster became a bustling place of business with a multitude of quaint shops and taverns. "The portraits of half the kings of Europe," says one writer, "of many warriors and statesmen, and of numerous things, animate and inanimate, made the streets an outdoor picture gallery." Lancaster was the capital of

Pennsylvania from 1799 to 1812. It has had a city charter since 1818.

Cumberland County, erected January 27, 1750, was the sixth Pennsylvania county in the order of formation. It **Cumberland** is the consensus of opinion that Cumber-
County land was named from the county of Cumberland, situated in the northwestern part of England.[2] The fact that the county-seat of the new county was called Carlisle, the name of the capital of the English county, tends to confirm the traditional explanation. And yet Cumberland County might have been named in honor of Prince William Augustus, Duke of Cumberland and favorite son of George II, who had become very popular because of his great victory over the Young Pretender at the battle of Culloden in 1746. At nearly the same time two American counties were named for the royal duke,—Cumberland County, Virginia, in 1748, and Cumberland County, North Carolina, in 1754.

The name Cumberland appears in the Saxon Chronicle as *Cumbra-land*, ''the land of the Cymry,'' as the ancient Welsh called themselves, the term *Cymry* signifying ''compatriots, or fellow-countrymen.''

New Cumberland, in Cumberland County, which was founded by Jacob Haldeman in 1810 and for a while called Haldeman's-town, has its present name from the same source.

When Cumberland County was organized, Shippensburg, which, with the exception of York, is the oldest Pennsylvania town west of the Susquehanna, **Shippens-** was designated as the temporary seat of
burg justice. As early as 1730 about a dozen families had settled in this neighborhood.

[2] Egle's *History of Pennsylvania*, p. 612.

Seven years later Edward Shippen obtained title to 1,312 acres of land and laid out the town which has since borne his name. This Edward Shippen was a grandson of the Edward Shippen who was the first mayor of Philadelphia, and who was distinguished for having "the biggest person, the biggest house, and the biggest coach in the city." He was himself elected mayor of Philadelphia in 1744; his son, Edward Shippen, was chief justice of Pennsylvania from 1799 to 1805; and his granddaughter, Peggy Shippen, was the wife of Benedict Arnold.

In spite of the protest of the Scotch-Irish settlers who lived in the western part of the great area of old Cumberland, "the mother of counties," and who pas-

Carlisle sionately preferred Shippensburg, the governor was pleased to fix the permanent seat of justice in the extreme eastern part of the original county, at Le Tort's Spring, where Carlisle now stands. In 1735 James Le Tort, a French Protestant trader with the Indians, had built his cabin at the spring which took his name.

On this site Nicholas Scull, then surveyor-general of the province, in pursuance of instructions issued by the proprietary government, laid out in 1751 a town which was called Carlisle from the capital of the English county of Cumberland, and which became the permanent county-seat in the following year. In 1753 there were only five dwellings in the place. Thirty years later, Dickinson College, which is next to the oldest college in Pennsylvania, was chartered, and was named in honor of John Dickinson, then governor of Pennsylvania, in recognition of his great services to his State and country, and in gratitude for his liberal gifts to the new-born college.

The English Carlisle is a sort of prototype of its Pennsylvania namesake. Both towns are built with streets

radiating from a central square and both are surrounded
by high hills. The Roman name of the old English town
was *Lugu-vallum* ("wall with a tower"), which the
ancient Britons abbreviated to Luel. The British word
Caer means "city." Hence Carlisle designated the "city
of the tower, or fort, at the end of the wall," being situated at the western end of the great wall that Hadrian
built.

On March 11, 1752, Berks and Northampton Counties
were erected. Berks County was formed from parts of
Philadelphia, Chester, and Lancaster Counties.
Berks The population of this new county was esti-
County mated at about seven thousand. Nearly twenty
years before, Thomas and Richard Penn had
bought most of this region from the Indians. Berks
County was "named from Berkshire in England, where
the Penn family held large landed estates."[3] Berkshire
appears in Anglo-Saxon charters as *Baroc-scir*. Its
original meaning is extremely doubtful. The oldest
guess as to its etymology is that of Brompton, abbot of
Jervaulx in the thirteenth century, who informs us that
Baroc-scir was so called from a certain polled oak ("bare
oak") in Windsor Forest, at which the shire-mote assembled. The more modern guesses are not much more
convincing than that of the holy abbot.

The little village of Berks, sometimes called West
Hamburg, was named after Berks County.

In the autumn of 1748 the surveyor-general, Nicholas
Scull, laid out the town of Reading on land which had,
by repurchase, become the private property
Reading of Richard and Thomas Penn. Several years
before Berks County was erected, the Penns
named their new town Reading after the capital of Berk-

---

3 Egle's *History of Pennsylvania*, p. 378.

shire; and in 1752, when the town had about four hundred inhabitants, they made R̍eading the county-seat of Berks County. *Readingas,* the Anglo-Saxon name of the old English city, is a plural patronymic or clan name, signifying "the descendants of the Red."

The borough of West Reading, which was laid out in 1873 and incorporated in 1907, was named for the county-seat of Berks County.

Easton "The Forks of the Delaware" was the ancient name by which was designated not only the site of the present town of Easton, but the triangular tract included between the Lehigh and the Delaware Rivers. In a letter to Governor James Hamilton, written from London in September, 1751, Thomas Penn says: "Some time since I wrote to Doctor Graeme and Mr. Peters[4] to lay out some ground in the forks of the Delaware for a town, which I suppose they have done or begun to do. I desire it may be called Easton, from my Lord Pomfret's house; and whenever there is a new county, it is to be called Northampton."

Northampton County Thomas Fermor, second Baron Lemster, or Leominster, was advanced to an earldom in 1721, by the title of the Earl of Pomfret, a name corrupted from Pontefract ("broken bridge") in Yorkshire. His fourth daughter, Juliana, was married to the Quaker statesman's son, Thomas Penn, of Stoke Park, Buckinghamshire.[5] The Earl of Pomfret resided at his country-seat of Easton Neston, in Northamptonshire. Thus it is clear that Thomas Penn had a definite reason for transferring the names Northampton and Easton to the new county and county town on the Delaware.

---

[4] Mr. Richard Peters, then secretary of the provincial government.
[5] Burke's *Peerage.*

The land on which Easton was laid out was owned by
Thomas Penn. The first settlement had been made in
1739 by David Martin, who had received a patent authorizing him to establish a ferry at the forks of the Delaware. About nine-tenths of the present county of
Northampton was included in the famous "Walking Purchase" of 1737. This unique but questionable method of
extinguishing the Indian title to the lands opened up this
important region to early settlement.

The most active spirit in the formation of Northampton
County was William Craig, whom the first County Commissioners in 1753 reimbursed to the amount of £30 for
the "considerable expense" he had incurred in "procur-
ing Northampton County to be divided from Bucks
County."

The origin of the name Northampton is not definitely
known. Hampton is derived either from *Ant-ton*, "the
town on the Ant," or from *Hean-tune*, "at the high
town." The prefixes *North* and *South* were used to distinguish Northampton from Southampton. Easton originally meant the "east town or estate." The boroughs
of Northampton and Northampton Heights obviously
took their names from the county.

Lafayette College, situated at Easton, was chartered
in 1826, and named in honor of General de la Fayette,[6]
who had just then completed his triumphal tour of the
United States.

Northumberland County, formed in 1772 out of parts
of Berks, Cumberland, Bedford, and Northampton, re-
Northumber-   ceived its name, in all probability, from
land County   the English county of Northumberland.
                       There can be no doubt that the only
                       other county with this name in the

---

[6] See Fayette County, page 61.

United States—Northumberland County in Virginia—was named for the English County. No evidence can be found that Northumberland County was named for the Duke of Northumberland; such an origin of the name seems improbable. Although Sir Hugh Smithson, who was created first Duke of Northumberland in 1766, who was allowed to assume the name of Percy, and who died in 1786, was a man of considerable social and political consequence, yet there is no apparent reason why the Penns should wish to honor him.

Certainly the early settlers in Northumberland County seemed to think that it was named for the English county; for the founder of Berwick, only fourteen years after the erection of the county, apparently gave his town the name of the Northumbrian borough because it was located in Northumberland County and seated on its principal river. Etymologically, Northumberland is the ''land north of the River Humber.'' The town of Northumberland was laid out in 1772 and named for the newly formed county.

Three months after the formation of Northumberland County, Governor Richard Penn and the provincial Council ordered that ''the surveyor-general (John **Sunbury** Lukens), with all convenient speed, repair to Fort Augusta on the Susquehanna and with the assistance of Mr. William Maclay[7] lay out a town for the county of Northumberland to be called by the name of Sunbury.'' The county-seat was to be located ''at the most commodious place between the fort and the mouth of Shamokin Creek.'' Richard Penn borrowed the name of Sunbury from the English village of that name, situated on the Thames about fifteen miles southwest of London.

---

[7] See Harrisburg, pages 64, 65.

4

Etymologically Sunbury signifies "the city of the sun." The new county town grew up on the site of the populous Indian village of Shamokin[8] and about the old pioneer Fort Augusta, erected in 1756, and named, in all likelihood, for the Princess Augusta, mother of George III. In 1797, twenty-five years after it was formally laid out, Sunbury was incorporated; but it did not attain its growth until many years later, when it was greatly stimulated by the opening of coal mines and the building of the railroad. It received a city charter in 1920.

Westmoreland County, formed from Bedford in 1773, was the eleventh of the original provincial counties, and

Westmoreland County the last one organized under the proprietary government. It was named "after the county of Westmoreland in England, a name which geographically describes its situation."[9] Westmoreland has been called "the mother county of western Pennsylvania" because its extensive territory was later divided into a dozen different counties. The meaning of Westmoreland, as applied to the English county, is "the land of the western moors."

The original county of Westmoreland introduces the subject of the "three Virginia counties in Pennsylvania."

"The Three Virginia Counties" The county of Augusta in Virginia was erected in 1738, and named in honor of the Princess Augusta of Saxe-Gotha, wife of Frederick, Prince of Wales, to whom she had just borne a son destined to rule England under the title of George III. Augusta County comprised all the western and northwestern part of Virginia, including an immense territory which is now

---

8 See Shamokin, page 192.
9 Albert's *History of the County of Westmoreland*, p. 52.

in Pennsylvania. Virginia had long laid claim to the Pennsylvania land lying to the west of the meridian that formed the western boundary of Maryland. Augusta-town, a village about two miles west of the site of Washington, Pennsylvania, was made the county-seat of Augusta County.

In 1776 the Virginia Legislature enacted that the "district of West Augusta," the disputed territory which now belongs to Pennsylvania and Ohio, be divided into three counties: (1) Ohio County, a rectangle about fifty miles long and thirty miles wide, named for the Ohio, "the Great River"; (2) Yohogania County, nearly square in shape, about fifty miles in length and forty in width, taking its name from the Youghiogheny River; (3) Monongalia County, similar in shape and size to the other two, receiving its name from the Monongahela River.

Nearly all of Yohogania County and a considerable part of Ohio and Monongalia Counties were composed of what is now Pennsylvania territory. This region, according to a rough estimate, covered approximately four thousand square miles in area. The "lost county of Yohogania" took in the sites of the county-seats of Westmoreland, Washington, Fayette, and Allegheny, and the territory to the north of these counties. For four years, from 1776 to 1780, Virginia actually exercised jurisdiction over this region, appointing justices, holding courts, electing senators and delegates to the Virginia Legislature, and performing "all the functions of government, civil and military." [10]

The agitation known as "the new state project," more or less active between 1776 and 1782, aimed to have the Continental Congress form a new state in western

---

[10] James Veech's *The Monongahela of Old*, p. 253.

Pennsylvania, to be known as Westsylvania, including
the territory in dispute between Pennsylvania and Virginia, as well as parts of what are now
"West-   Ohio, Virginia, and West Virginia. In 1782
sylvania"   the General Assembly of Pennsylvania
passed a law threatening to "adjudge guilty
of high treason" any citizen of the Commonwealth engaged in promoting this project of establishing a new state.

The act creating Westmoreland County named five
commissioners to locate the county-seat and erect the
county buildings. One of these was Robert
Hannastown Hanna, a north-country Irishman, who
kept a log tavern along the historic
Forbes Trail, about three miles northeast of the site of
Greensburg. Another was Joseph Erwin, to whom
Hanna rented his hostelry. These two commissioners
prevailed on one of the others, Sloan by name, to rec-
ommend Hanna's place as the most central, convenient,
and desirable site for the county-seat. The minority,
with Lieutenant Arthur St. Clair as their spokesman, reported in favor of Pittsburgh, situated about thirty miles
farther west, representing that in the near future the
growing settlement around Fort Pitt must eventually become a place of consequence.

Hannastown, which at no time contained more than
thirty mud-plastered log cabins strung along the pack-
horse trail, was the county-seat from 1773 till July 13,
1782, when the one tragic event in the early history of
Westmoreland County erased Hannastown[11] from the
map of Pennsylvania. A band of about one hundred
Indians and Tories fell upon the settlement, attacking
the inhabitants, who were fortunate enough to make

---

[11] The present post-office of Hannastown is situated about a mile north
of old Hannastown.

their escape from the harvest fields to the shelter of the stockade fort, and burning all the houses but two.

The burning of Hannastown was the last hostile act of the American Revolution. In the attack only one person was killed, Janet Shaw, a young girl who lost her life heroically in rescuing a child that had crawled out beyond the stockade pickets. About twenty prisoners were taken, several of whom were brutally murdered, but most of whom later found their way back from their British captors in Canada.

In 1784 what was known as the "Pennsylvania State Road" was opened up along the old Forbes Trail. About this time a town was laid out on the land **Greensburg** of Christopher Truby, and named Greensburg in honor of General Nathaniel Greene, under whom had fought many a valiant Scotch-Irish soldier from Westmoreland. Greensburg became the second county-seat of Westmoreland County. The old inn at Greensburg, which furnished entertainment to the commissioners of the United States and the Pennsylvania officials who had met to settle the trouble known as the Whiskey Insurrection, had for its sign a full-length portrait of General Greene.[12]

Somerset, the last of the Pennsylvania counties to take its name from an English shire, was formed from Bedford County on April 17, 1795, and **Somerset** named for Somersetshire in England. On **County** the present site of the town of Somerset, which has a higher elevation than any other county town in Pennsylvania—about 2,200 feet above sea-level—Ulrich Bruner had laid out the village of Brunerstown in 1787.

On September 12, 1795, the four commissioners charged

---

[12] For some account of General Greene, see Greene County, pages 89-91.

with the duty of selecting a site for the county-seat reported that "Summerset—formerly called
Somerset   Brunerstown—is a fit place for the seat of
justice of said county." On the same day
Adam Schneider, who had bought Bruner's property,
plotted the town of Somerset near the centre of Somerset Township.

The Anglo-Saxon form of the name Somerset was
Sumersæte. This term, like Dorset, was a tribal name
and originally referred not to the land, but to its inhabitants. In Anglo-Saxon times the chief place in the shire
was Somerton, a royal *tun,* or estate, used as a summer
residence. *Sumersæte* designated those who originally
settled around Somerton. In the twelfth century the
Welsh called Somerset Gwalad-yr-Haf, "the land of
summer." In Latin documents Somerset appears as
Æstiva Regio, "the region of summer." And so the
commissioners who selected the site and named the town
were not entirely wrong when they spelled the name
"Summerset" in their report.

It is worth noting that the seven borrowed county
names discussed in this chapter have been used rather
sparingly as names of counties outside of Pennsylvania.
There are seven other Cumberland Counties in the United
States. Virginia, South Carolina, and Nebraska have
each a Lancaster County. There is a Berkshire County
in Massachusetts. Both Virginia and North Carolina
have a Northampton County. Virginia has a Westmoreland County, the birthplace of Presidents Washington
and Monroe. There is a Somerset County in New Jersey,
Maryland, and Maine.

CHAPTER V

COUNTIES NAMED FOR ENGLISH NOBLEMEN

THE city and county of York were probably christened in honor of a royal duke, and the town and county of Bedford received their name from the Duke of Bedford. The only other county in Pennsylvania bearing the name of an English nobleman is Delaware, which was named directly from the Delaware River.[1] Huntingdon County was named in honor of an English noblewoman, the Countess of Huntingdon. In its choice of county names Pennsylvania stands in striking contrast to its aristocratic neighbor, Virginia, thirty-nine of whose one hundred counties were named for English royalty and nobility.[2]

In October, 1741, Richard, Thomas, and John Penn ordered Thomas Cookson, then deputy surveyor of Lancaster County, which included the present territory of York County, to "survey and lay off in lots a tract of land on the Codorus, where the Monocacy road crosses the stream." They further directed that the town was to be called York, or Yorktown. The Penns were the actual owners of the site of York, which was laid out on a part of Springettsbury Manor,[3] which had been named for Springett Penn, the eldest son of the founder's son William.

Whether the Penns named York for the ancient Eng-

York

---

[1] See Delaware County, page 139.

[2] See Charles M. Long's *Virginia County Names*.

[3] Springetsbury Township, in York County, was named for this old manor, which was once the property of Springett Penn.

55

lish city of York or for James Stuart, long the Duke of York and afterwards King James II, who had been the friend and patron of both the founder and his father, Admiral Penn, is a question that cannot now be definitely answered. In the absence of any direct evidence, all that one can do is to balance the probabilities; and when one considers how much the Penn family owed to the favor and friendliness of the Duke, one is inclined to believe that the Penns chose the name of York in a desire to honor the memory of the royal patron and benefactor of their family.

In fairness, however, to those who accept the other explanation we must remember that gratitude—especially among the descendants of William Penn—was likely to be an evanescent emotion; that the Quaker, Samuel Blunston, who, as the agent for the Penns, had so much to do with starting and directing the settlements on the western side of the Susquehanna, was a native of Upper Hallam in Yorkshire; and that the English counties of Lancaster and York, like the two Pennsylvania counties, lie side by side. When we consider Samuel Blunston's close relations with the Penns, we must at least admit the probability that, with his old English home in mind, he may have suggested the name of York and York County.

Of the four other York Counties in the United States, the one in Nebraska was named for a resident family, and those in Maine and Virginia were certainly named for James Stuart, Duke of York, and afterwards King James II.

In 1749, eight years after the town of York was laid out, the new county of York was set apart from Lancaster. It embraced the territory now included in York and Adams Counties. Fully a decade before York was

York County   laid out, the proprietary government had issued permits to settlers on the western side of the river, and it has been estimated that in 1741 there were about two thousand white inhabitants in the present territory of York County.

The town of York, which has always been the county-seat, did not grow very rapidly at first: when the Continental Congress met there in 1777, it contained about a thousand people, mostly of German descent. York was incorporated in 1787.

York Haven, in York County, and York Springs, now in Adams County, both borrowed their names from the county of York.

The Celto-Latin name of York, the capital of Roman Britain, was Eboracum, which the Saxon Chronicle changed to Eoforwic. *Wic* signifies "town"; the origin and meaning of the Celtic *Ebor* are unknown. The Danes corrupted the Saxon Eoforwic into Jorvik (pronounced Yorwick), of which the modern name York is a survival.

The earliest name of Bedford was Ray's-town,[4] so called for John Wray, who, sometime before 1752, established there an important trading post for **Fort Bedford**   Indians and pioneer hunters and trappers. The old stockade fort was built probably six or seven years later. The place was called Raystown, Camp Raystown, or "the fort at Raystown," until August, 1759, when General John Stanwix formally named it Fort Bedford, apparently in honor of John Russell, fourth Duke of Bedford, then Lord Lieutenant of Ireland, and later a member of the British Cabinet and the leader of "the Bedford party."

----

[4] See Hanna's *Wilderness Trail*, vol. I, pp. 280, 281. Wray and Ray are different spellings of the same family name.

The Duke of Bedford, who was a prominent political figure in England from 1744 to 1765, is said to have presented to the commander of Fort Bedford a "beautiful silken English flag" in appreciation of the honor thus bestowed upon him. Although the Duke was proud, arrogant, and conceited, he nevertheless possessed considerable ability as an administrator and political leader. The meaning of the second syllable of Bedford is obvious; the first syllable is all that now remains of an old Saxon personal name, Bedica.

Fort Bedford was one of the most important military posts during the French and Indian War. It served as a rendezvous and a depot of supplies for colonial troops recruited from the east and the south for the relief and defense of the exposed western frontier. In 1757-8 General John Forbes had a wagon road cut from Bedford westward toward Fort Duquesne for the convenient movement of his expeditionary army of 7850 men, with its artillery and its hundreds of wagons. "Forbes Trail" soon afterwards became a great highway over which a peaceful army of sturdy settlers invaded the western wilderness. At Bedford, in 1794, President Washington reviewed the army that he had brought together to quell the Whiskey Insurrection in western Pennsylvania.

Fort Bedford may be taken as a type of the pioneer fort, which was not only a defense, but a fortified or protected enclosure for the residence of settlers. In the colonial period and particularly during the Indian wars, these pioneer forts, of which there were nearly two hundred in Pennsylvania, were absolutely necessary as a means of protecting the lives, homes, and property of the settlers against treacherous and savage foes, who spared neither old men nor women nor children.

A pioneer fort, like the one at Bedford, generally consisted of a group of cabins, with several blockhouses, surrounded by a bullet-proof stockade. First a ditch about five feet deep was dug about the area to be enclosed. In this trench were set upright a row of heavy hewn logs, usually of oak, pointed at the top, and securely fastened together. An effort was thus made to produce a substantial barrier that could not readily be burned or cut through. About five feet above the ground, on the inner side of the stockade, was built a sort of platform, on which the garrison stood and fired through loop-holes in the wooden wall. The corners of the enclosure were further defended by blockhouses, which also contained port-holes. The cabins were usually ranged along one side of the stockade, with their roofs sloping wholly inward. A large folding gate, constructed of thick slabs, made the enclosure complete. Fort Bedford was also protected on two sides by a moat about eight feet deep and fifteen feet wide.

In 1761 the Penns set apart the Manor of Bedford, containing about 2800 acres; and five years afterwards, by order of the proprietary government, John **Bedford** Lukens, the surveyor-general, laid out the town of Bedford, which received its name from Fort Bedford. During the colonial period, Bedford, like Carlisle and Chambersburg, was a very important outpost of civilization. The famous Bedford Springs are situated about a mile and a half from the town.

In 1768 the great township of Bedford was organized as a part of Cumberland County. The increasing number of settlers in this western region now **Bedford County** began to complain about the hardship of traveling all the way to Carlisle for the transaction of public business, and to clamor for the erection of a new county. In March, 1771, their petition was granted by the formation of Bedford County, which was doubtless so called for the town and township of Bedford. Within five weeks after the county was established the first Pennsylvania court for the benefit of the scattered settlers in the western part of the province was convened at Bedford, the county-seat. Arthur St. Clair [5] was the first prothonotary of the new county.

---

[5] See Saint Clair, page 229.

CHAPTER VI

COUNTIES NAMED FOR FRENCH NOBLEMEN

AT the close of the Revolutionary War, within exactly three years, from September 26, 1783, to September 25, 1786, the three Pennsylvania counties of Fayette, Dauphin, and Luzerne were formed and named in honor of three French noblemen and in grateful appreciation of the friendship and assistance of France during the struggle for American independence.

Fayette County, once claimed by Virginia as a part of Monongalia County, was erected in 1783 out of Westmoreland County, and was named in honor of **Fayette** Roche Yves Gilbert Motier, Marquis de la **County** Fayette, whose influence and bravery had been of inestimable value to the American colonies in the war just ended. No country has ever had a more disinterested friend than this enthusiastic young French nobleman, who was not yet twenty years of age when Congress commissioned him a major-general. Though he won no victories, and though he seems never to have exercised any important, independent command, or to have been in charge of any considerable number of troops, yet the value of his example, his personal sympathy, and his moral support was priceless. Not only did he serve without pay throughout the Revolutionary War, but he actually expended $140,000 of his own money in promoting the American cause. On his return to France Congress commended him to his king as ''wise in council, brave in battle, and patient under the fatigues of war.''

On May 26, 1825, by special invitation, General de la
Fayette, accompanied by his only son, George Washington de la Fayette, visited Uniontown, the county-seat
of Fayette County. The people turned out *en masse* to
greet their distinguished guest. The address of welcome
on behalf of the citizens of Fayette County was delivered
by Albert Gallatin,[1] who had been United States Senator
from Pennsylvania in 1793 and Secretary of the Treasury
from 1801 to 1814.

Fayette City, in Fayette County, and Fayetteville, in
Franklin County, were also named for General de la
Fayette. The fact that seventeen American counties and
forty-four towns bear his name is proof of his great
popularity in the United States. The name Fayette signifies "beechwood."

The first settlement on the site of the county-seat was
made about 1768 by Henry Beeson, a Quaker from
Berkeley County, Virginia. Here, in 1776,
Uniontown   he laid out a village, popularly known in
those early days as Beeson's-town. Soon
after the town-plot was surveyed, the name Union began
to be applied to the place, probably at the suggestion of
the founder. As early as 1780 this name occurs in deeds
and other legal documents.[2] Union was undoubtedly the
name with which the town was formally christened.
When old Union Township was formed in 1783, with
Union situated at its centre, it became necessary to distinguish between the township and the village by calling
the latter "the town of Union," or "Union-town."
More than half a century after the town was laid out and
named, Sherman Day wrote, "The county-seat of Fayette
is the borough of Union, usually called Uniontown."

---

[1] See Gallatin, page 263.
[2] Nelson's *Historical Reference Book of Fayette County.*

The name of Union was first applied to the place at the very time when the idea of union was becoming a part of the national consciousness. This would seem to be a sufficient reason for its use.[3] The phrase "United Colonies" was first used by the Continental Congress in June, 1775; and a year later, in the Declaration of Independence, the phrase "United States of America" appears for the first time.

What is now Dauphin County was once Paxtang Township in Lancaster County. The petitioners who asked **Dauphin** that a new county be formed from Lancaster **County** in 1785 suggested the name of Dauphin in a desire to honor the friendly court of France by bestowing upon the new county the name of the hereditary title of the eldest son of the French king. Louis XVI was then king of France, and his eldest son, Louis, the Dauphin, who was born on October 22, 1781, was not yet four years of age. He died in 1789.

Our interest lies more in the name of Dauphin than in the youthful prince. This curious title has been the subject of considerable controversy. In all probability it originated in a personal name. Among the Norsemen and in the countries that they colonized the name Dolfin or Dolphin was not uncommon. From a personal name, the original meaning of which is now unknown, Dauphin, in the thirteenth century, became firmly established as a title of nobility. The usual explanation is that the French province of Dauphiny was "so called from the dolphin assumed by the Counts of the Viennois as a symbol of the mildness of their rule." But, on the contrary,

---

[3] The author is not unmindful of the traditional explanation given by Mr. Henry Gannett that Uniontown was "so named because of its being built on two farms, the owners of which disputed as to whose name the town should bear." One can find no historical confirmation of this explanation.

the armorial device was probably assumed from the name Dolphin.

In 1349 Humbert II, Count of the Viennois, and the last of his line, sold Dauphiny to Charles of Valois on condition that the heir to the French crown should assume the arms and bear the title of the Dauphin of the Viennois. When Charles became king of France in 1364, he transferred the title of Dauphin to his eldest son. After that time the eldest sons of the French kings always bore this title.

The borough of Dauphin, once called Greensburg for General Innis Green, who laid it out about 1825, was later named for Dauphin County.

When Dauphin County was formed, the county-seat was fixed at Harris's Ferry, then a village of about a hundred houses, though both Lebanon and **Harrisburg** Middletown were then more important places in the new county. John Harris, a Yorkshireman who had come to America with a total capital of only sixteen guineas, was licensed in 1705 as an Indian trader by the provincial authorities, and allowed to "seat himself on the Susquehanna." Some years later he settled at Paxtang, now the site of Harrisburg. In 1725 the Penns granted him five hundred acres of land, on which a small settlement began to grow up. About ten years later he received a second grant of three hundred acres. Parson John Elder, of the old Paxtang Presbyterian Church, declared that "John Harris was as honest a man as ever broke bread."

His son, John Harris, Jr., the founder of Harrisburg, was born at the Paxtang settlement about 1726. In 1753 the Penns granted him the privilege of establishing a ferry across the Susquehanna, and the place was thenceforth known far and wide as Harris's Ferry. At the death of his father in 1748 he came into possession of more than seven hundred acres of land, on which the older part of Harrisburg now stands. Besides managing his ferry and a large farm, John Harris, Jr., a man of energy, industry, and resourcefulness, became prominent as an Indian trader and a keeper of military stores on the frontier during the Indian wars.

In 1785 he and his son-in-law, William Maclay, laid out a town at Harris's Ferry and called it Harrisburg. Foreseeing and firmly believing that the capital of the State might sometime be located there, he conveyed four acres of land on Capitol Hill "in trust for public use and such public purposes as the Legislature should hereafter direct."

It is worth noting that as early as 1690 William Penn seems to have had a vision of a city upon the Susquehanna: he knew that there should be such a city as Harrisburg. He then wrote: "It is now my purpose to make another settlement, upon the River Susquehannagh, that runs into the Bay of Chesapeake and lies about fifty miles west from the Delaware. There I design to lay out a plan for the building of another city in the most convenient place for communication with the former plantation on the east."[4]

The state officials were not satisfied with the name Harrisburg. The Executive Council conceived the notion that as the county was named for the Dauphin, the county-seat should be called Louisbourg in honor of Louis XVI,—a proposal which may be taken as an index of the great popularity of France at that period. In the minutes of the second court held at Harrisburg occurs the following entry: "The name of the county town, or seat of the courts, is altered from Harrisburg to Louis-

[4] Rupp's *History of Berks and Lebanon Counties*, p. 361.

5

bourg in consequence of the Supreme Executive Council of the Commonwealth so styling it.''

In 1791 the town was still officially known as Louisbourg, but the new name never came into popular use and was soon dropped. Plain-spoken John Harris is said to have remarked, ''The members of the Council may *Louisbourg* as much as they please, but I will never execute a title for a lot in any other name than Harrisburg.''

The movement to locate the state capital at Harrisburg began almost as soon as Dauphin County was formed. In 1787, more than a decade before Lancaster became the seat of government, the General Assembly resolved to build a State House at Harrisburg, but afterwards reconsidered the vote. In 1810 the law was passed by which the capital of Pennsylvania was moved from Lancaster to Harrisburg in 1812. To the four acres already set aside ''for public use'' by John Harris, who died in 1791, ten acres were added by William Maclay, who, in 1769, had married Mary, the only daughter of John Harris. William Maclay, for whom Maclay Street in Harrisburg was named, was the first United States Senator from Pennsylvania. He was associated with Thomas Jefferson as one of the founders of the Democratic party.

One of the most memorable events in the history of Harrisburg was the burning of the State Capitol in 1897. In this historic building ''Presidents Harrison, Tyler, Taylor, Lincoln, Grant, and Hayes, and Senator Daniel Webster had all spoken.''

In 1778 the court of France generously recognized the independence of the United States and made an alliance with the infant republic, declaring war against England and sending a fleet and an army to aid the Americans.

The next year France sent as its minister to the United States Anne César, Chevalier de la Luzerne, a brother of Cardinal de la Luzerne.   Chevalier was a title given by courtesy to the younger sons of certain noble families in France.   De la Luzerne remained at his diplomatic post in the United States for five years, greatly endearing himself to the American people by his friendliness, his helpful counsel, his prudence as a diplomat, and his concern for the successful outcome of the great Revolutionary struggle.

In 1783, when he returned to France, Luzerne Township in Fayette County was named in his honor; and **Luzerne County** three years later, when a new county was erected out of Northumberland, it was called Luzerne County in token of the high regard in which the people of Pennsylvania held this distinguished foreigner.   It is said that in the darkest hour of the Revolution, when the Continental army was almost destitute and the government practically without funds, the Chevalier de la Luzerne "raised money on his own responsibility to relieve the general distress." [5]

Many years later, the borough of Luzerne, which was once known as Hartseph in honor of Zachariah Hartseph, an early settler who lived there a century ago, also took its name from that of the beloved Chevalier.

Luzerne was originally a Swiss place name.   According to an old etymology the name of the Swiss lake and of the ancient city on its shore was derived from a certain watch-tower which served as a *lucerna,* or lighthouse, for vessels navigating the lake.

Wilkes-Barre was chosen as the county-seat of Luzerne County in preference to old Forty Fort, or Kingston, its only formidable competitor.   In May, 1769, Major John

[5] Pearce's *Annals of Luzerne County,* p. 157.

Durkee of Norwich, Connecticut, brought to this region about a hundred settlers from his native state. During the next month these pioneers erected a **Wilkes-** palisade fort, which they called Fort Durkee **Barre** in honor of their leader. Soon afterwards, "say, the last of June or early in July, 1769, Major Durkee compounded and originated the almost unique name 'Wilkesbarre,' and bestowed it upon the settlement and territory at and immediately adjacent to Fort Durkee."[6]

The first recorded mention of the name Wilkes-Barre occurs under date of July 31, 1769. Twenty-one months before this, Major Durkee, who was a great admirer of Colonel Isaac Barré, with whom he had served at the capture of Quebec, had named his youngest son Barré Durkee; and one year before Wilkes-Barre received its name, John Durkee's first cousin, Andrew Durkee, who was also in the Wyoming region in 1769, had christened his son Wilkes Durkee. Hence some persons contend that Major Durkee named Wilkes-Barre primarily for the two Durkee infants, and not directly for the two great liberal leaders in Parliament, Colonel John Wilkes and Colonel Isaac Barré, who had already distinguished themselves as the champions of the American colonies in the growing struggle against British oppression.

"In the spring of 1769, when the Wyoming colonists left New England, it was well known that Colonel John Wilkes, who had been a member of the British Parliament, and whose name was indissolubly connected with liberty in the minds of the American colonists and their friends, was suffering what his admirers and followers believed to be an unjust imprisonment in the King's Bench Prison, London. At the same time Colonel Isaac

---

[6] Oscar J. Harvey's *History of Wilkes-Barre*, p. 503.

Barré, who had been an officer in the English army in America in the campaigns of 1758 and 1759, and had been personally known to Major Durkee, who was also an officer in the provincial service during the same campaign, stood in the British House of Commons as the foe of America's oppressors, and was almost unrivaled as a brilliant speaker and was hardly surpassed by any of the opposition—even by Edmund Burke himself—in violent denunciation of the government. Among the admirers of Wilkes and Barré in Connecticut during the period to which we refer, it is doubtful if there was one who surpassed in earnestness and devotedness the tried and steadfast patriot, John Durkee.'' [7]

No satisfactory sketch of John Wilkes or of Isaac Barré can be given here. Without partisanship it may be said that John Wilkes was a scholar, a wit, a libertine, a demagogue, and a *poseur.* He was neither a great nor a good man. In the perspective of history it is difficult to understand why such a man had so many devoted adherents and admirers. His popularity can best be explained by the fact that he made a stubborn fight for rights that are dear to English freemen. On the whole, the political influence that he exerted upon the England of his day was no doubt salutary.

John Wilkes's right to a seat in Parliament was not denied him after 1774, and he was a member of the House of Commons from that year until 1790. In 1774 he was Lord Mayor of London. To attain these distinctions John Wilkes struggled for ten years against the insidious influence of the court and the ministry. The "friend of liberty" had fought a successful battle for the freedom of the press, for immunity from arbitrary arrest, and for the right of electors to choose their representatives

[7] Harvey's *History of Wilkes-Barre,* p. 503.

without governmental interference or dictation. By Americans he deserves to be gratefully remembered for the friendly interest he took in the preservation of their cherished rights and liberties.

Isaac Barré, who was born in Dublin of Huguenot parents, was far more admirable than Wilkes in his private character and far more influential as an outspoken friend of America in Parliament both before and during the Revolution. It was he who invented the phrase, "the Sons of Liberty," which the colonists used to such telling effect in their opposition to the Stamp Act. Isaac Barré was an officer of the British army for fourteen years, and was a member of Parliament from 1761 to 1790.

The family name Wilkes signifies "Wilke's son." Wilke or Wilk is a shortened form of Wilkin, which is a double diminutive of William. The Huguenot surname Barré is probably derived from the Old French *barre*, "a barrier, or a gateway."

The town plot of Wilkes-Barre[8] was made in 1770. After the Wyoming massacre in 1778 the Indians and Tories burnt the little settlement. Again, in 1784, during the second "Pennamite war," as the bitter contest between the Pennsylvanians and the Connecticut Yankees was called, all the houses in Wilkes-Barre but three were burnt to the ground. In 1806 Wilkes-Barre was incorporated as a borough, though it was not separated politically from Wilkes-Barre Township until 1818.

---

[8] The name of Wilkes-Barre, which is now written and printed so as to do equal honor to both Wilkes and Barré, was spelled in seventeen different ways during the first half-century of its existence.

CHAPTER VII

COUNTIES NAMED FOR PRESIDENTS

FOUR Pennsylvania counties—Washington, Adams, Jefferson, and Monroe—bear the names of Presidents of the United States.

Washington County, erected out of Westmoreland on March 28, 1781, eight years before George Washington became President of the United States, was the first Pennsylvania county formed after the Declaration of Independence and the only one organized during the Revolutionary period. At the time of its formation the struggle for independence already showed signs of ending in victory. George Washington, as commander-in-chief of the Revolutionary forces, was at the height of his military fame. He was recognized as the leader and the founder of the young republic, and was without doubt the most popular man in America.

Washington County

Five years before, when he was just entering upon his difficult and heroic leadership, his native Virginia had named a new county in his honor. For nearly thirty years, ever since he had set out on his memorable journey over the rough trails and through the vast wilderness of Pennsylvania in the autumn of 1753, to demand, on behalf of Virginia, an explanation of the French, who were beginning to build a chain of forts from Lake Erie southward to the Ohio, George Washington, as explorer, Indian-fighter, and general, had linked his name forever with the history of Pennsylvania. It was on the soil of Pennsylvania that he had served his apprenticeship as

71

a soldier in the French and Indian War; and it was in this State also that, as commander-in-chief of the Revolutionary army, he had conducted a courageous campaign against disheartening odds, and had endured, with his brave little army, the fearful winter at Valley Forge. The choice of name for the new Pennsylvania county was the most appropriate that could then have been made.

In 1775, Washington, through his agent, Captain William Crawford, had bought 2,813 acres of land in what later became Washington County. After the war was over, General Washington spent about a month—from September 1 to October 4, 1784—in Washington County, making a careful survey and examination of his Pennsylvania possessions in Mount Pleasant Township. He found that many squatters had settled upon his lands, and he was obliged to dislodge them by writs of ejectment. As soldier and as President, Washington must have spent fully ten of the most active years of his life in Pennsylvania.

It is one of the little ironies of history that only a decade after its formation Washington County became the very storm-centre of the Whiskey Insurrection, which was perhaps the most serious internal disturbance of Washington's presidential administration.

The site of Washington, the county-seat of Washington County, was once known as "Catfish's Camp" from the fact that a chief of the Delawares **Washington** called Catfish had his abode here about 1750. Catfish's Camp became a favorite resting place for travelers journeying from Redstone Old Fort—or Brownsville—to Wheeling. In 1769 David Hoge bought the three tracts of land on which the town was subsequently built. Early in 1781 he erected a log house, in which the first court of Washington County was held; and later in the same year he laid out a town, which he at first called Bassett-town in honor of his kinsman, Richard Bassett, who was a few years later distinguished as a member of the convention that framed the Constitution of the United States, and who was governor of Delaware from 1798 to 1801.

After selling forty-seven lots "in Bassett-town," David Hoge, realizing in the latter part of 1781 that the place would become the seat of justice of Washington County, called the new village "Washington-town" in all the remaining certificates of sale. The superfluous "town" was soon dropped, and Washington became the permanent name of the county-seat. David Hoge donated two lots in Washington to the great general whose name the town had taken. Even the little college that was established here in 1806 was named in honor of Washington.

Other Pennsylvania towns named for Washington are New Washington, in Clearfield County; North Washington, in Butler County; Fort Washington, in Montgomery County; Washingtonville, in Montour County; and Washington Boro, in Lancaster County.

Washington was originally an English place name in Durham and Sussex. The Anglo-Saxon form of the name was *Wassingatun*, "the town of the Wassings." The patronymic ending *ing* indicates that Wassing was a clan name. From the little Durham village the ancestors of George Washington "are believed to have derived their territorial surname." [1]

The name of Washington has perhaps more frequently been applied to places in the United States than the name of any other person. When Congress chose Georgetown in Maryland as the site of the national capital, they pat-

[1] Taylor's *Names and their Histories*, p. 291.

riotically changed its name to Washington. One of the
states of the Union also bears his name,—an honor that
has been conferred on no other President. Thirty-two
states have a Washington County, seven of them being
among the original thirteen states. Twenty-eight states
have a post-office named Washington; and of more than
a score of other post-office names, Washington forms a
part. In the United States there are 318 cities, counties,
and townships which "have thus indirectly come to bear
the name of the little Durham village."[2]

On January 22, 1800, after ten years of agitation, the
western part of York County was erected into the new
county of Adams, a name bestowed in honor of
Adams   John Adams, then President of the United
County States, who is said to have traversed this
region on his way to the new national capitol
at Washington. The name of Adams County seems to
have special appropriateness from the fact that twenty-
two years before, when the territory of the new county
was yet a part of York County, John Adams, the Massachusetts statesman, lived and labored at York for six
weeks as one of the leaders of the Continental Congress,
which met there on September 30, 1777.

Though John Adams was a staunch patriot, it cannot
be said that he was a popular President. Of the eleven
other Adams Counties in the United States, only those
in Iowa, Mississippi, Ohio, and Washington are known
to have been named for our second President. Three
others were named for his son, President John Quincy
Adams. Adamsburg, in Westmoreland County, is said
to have been named for John Adams. The surname
Adams is, of course, derived from the Hebrew personal
name Adam, which literally means "red earth."

---

[2] Taylor's *Names and their Histories*, p. 292.

About ten years before Adams County was organized, James Gettys, who has been described as "a man of brains, force of character, and resources,"

Gettysburg scenting the certainty of a new county and the possibility of securing an eligible site for the county-seat, bought a tract of land and laid out a village, which he called Gettys-town. On the erection of Adams County this little settlement was chosen as the seat of justice; and the act of Legislature authorizing the levy of a tax for the construction of the county buildings designated the place for the first time as Gettysburg. James Gettys, for whom Gettysburg was named, never dreamed that the name of the little town which he planned and plotted was destined to become famous throughout the world and memorable in history as the name of a bloody battlefield, on which the great Rebellion was to be checked and the fate of the Union decided.

On March 26, 1804, five new counties were formed out of Lycoming, and were named Clearfield, Jefferson, McKean, Potter, and Tioga. One of the

Jefferson counties carved out of the vast Lycoming
County County wilderness received the name of Jefferson in honor of Thomas Jefferson, then serving as the third President of the United States, and famous as the author of the Declaration of Independence and the founder of the Democratic party, which was at that time dominant in Pennsylvania politics and destined to remain in power during the greater part of the next half-century. The borough of Jefferson, in Greene County, was also named for our third President. Jefferson's popularity is attested by the fact that at least a score of counties in the United States and nearly two score of towns are named in his honor.

Jefferson is an English patronymic surname signifying "the son of Jeffery, or Geoffrey." Jeffrey is an old personal name corrupted from Godefroy, the French equivalent of the Anglo-Saxon *Godfrith*, "good peace."

For many years after its formation Jefferson County was little more than an excellent hunting ground for Indians and white settlers and prospectors. During a quarter of a century it was, for judicial purposes, connected with Westmoreland or with Indiana County. In 1829 Governor John A. Shulze appointed four commissioners to locate a county-seat for Jefferson County. They chose the site of Brookville because of its situation on the Susquehanna and Waterford turnpike, at the confluence of the Sandy Lick and Red Bank Creeks.

The next year the county-seat was laid out and was christened Brookville because of the numerous brooks and springs that flowed from the hills en-
Brookville circling the site.[3] The name was made by adding the French *ville,* "a town," to the English word *brook.* In those strenuous days of internal improvement the advocates of this site believed that Brookville could have ready communication by steamboat with Pittsburgh. At first the hopeful little town did not grow very fast. Only three houses were built the first year, and the population at the end of ten years was less than three hundred.

In 1836 a new county was formed from Northampton and Pike, and named Monroe in honor of James Monroe, fifth President of the United States, whose title to lasting fame rests on the Monroe Doctrine,[4] which has for a century exerted a powerful influence in shaping the

---

[3] Information furnished by Dr. W. J. McKnight, author of *A Pioneer History of Northwestern Pennsylvania* and *A Pioneer History of Jefferson County.*

[4] John Quincy Adams was probably the real author of the Monroe Doctrine.

foreign policy of our country. Sixteen states besides
Pennsylvania have honored James
Monroe County   Monroe by naming a county for him.
Monroe is a Scotch territorial surname
signifying in Gaelic "a dweller at the red bog." The
club-moss, which grows in boggy places, is the appropriate badge of the Munro clan.

Kellersville and Stroudsburg competed for the distinction of being the county-seat of Monroe County. A
popular vote decided the contest in favor
Stroudsburg   of Stroudsburg. Jacob Stroud, for whom
the town was named, was a native of New
Jersey and a veteran of the French and Indian War. He
settled at this place in 1769. A few years later he became a colonel in the Revolutionary army and was placed
in command of Fort Penn, which stood at the east end
of the little village that had begun to grow up near his
tract of four thousand acres. He was a member of the
Assembly in 1781, and later sat in the convention that
framed the State Constitution of 1790.

Jacob Stroud refused to sell building lots, and he
erected only three houses on his land before his death in
1806. Then his son Daniel laid out the town, widened
the main street, and sold lots on the wise condition that
the houses should be set back thirty feet from the street.
East Stroudsburg,[5] a namesake of the county-seat, has
grown to be almost as large and important as the older
town. The English surname Stroud or Strode means "a
dweller at the thicket."

---

[5] Both Stroudsburg and East Stroudsburg are situated in Stroud Township.

CHAPTER VIII

COUNTIES NAMED FOR PENNSYLVANIA GOVERNORS

THE counties of Franklin, Mifflin, McKean, and Snyder were named in honor of four distinguished citizens of Pennsylvania, who served their State as chief executive from 1785 to 1817, a period of thirty-two years. These governors were all natives of Pennsylvania except Franklin.

Though born in Boston, Benjamin Franklin belongs to Pennsylvania, whither he came as a lad of seventeen. When he was seventy-eight years old, Pennsylvania honored its most illustrious citizen by bestowing his name upon the new county which had been set apart from Cumberland County in 1784. In 1776 Franklin, as "Chairman of the Committee of Safety," had acted for a brief period as temporary executive of Pennsylvania.[1] After the erection of Franklin County he served as governor from October 18, 1785, to October 14, 1788. In various public offices he devoted fifty-two years to the service of his State and nation. He was clerk of the Assembly from 1736 to 1747. Then, for fourteen years in succession, he was elected a member of the Assembly, in which he was an outspoken opponent of the proprietary government. In 1775, by appointment of the Continental Congress, he became our first Postmaster-General. From 1776 to 1785 he served his country on various diplomatic missions in Europe.

Franklin County

---

[1] Jared Sparks's *Life of Benjamin Franklin*, p. 393.

The importance and the extent of his public services are attested by the fact that he helped to frame and signed the Declaration of Independence, the treaty of alliance with France, the treaty of peace with Great Britain, and the Constitution of the United States. Before he became governor in 1785, he had attained distinction as printer, journalist, scientist, educator, man of letters, patriot, statesman, and diplomat.

Three Pennsylvania towns and twenty-two American counties are named for this distinguished Pennsylvania patriot. The surname Franklin is derived from the common English noun, *frankelyn* or *franklin*, which means "free man," and which was used during the early English period to refer to important freeholders ranking next to the gentry and eligible to certain dignities. The *franklin* was a man of consequence in Chaucer's time.

The legislative act that created Franklin County designated Chambers'-town as the county-seat. A few years later this name was changed to **Chambers-** Chambersburg. Benjamin Chambers, who **burg** founded the town, and for whom it was named, was one of the first white settlers in what is now Franklin County. In 1730, at the age of twenty-one, he came to Falling Springs, where, four years later, he secured a grant of four hundred acres, on which he erected a saw-mill and a grist-mill. The brave little frontier "settlement on the Conococheague," protected by Fort Chambers, was long one of the very outposts of civilization. Here Benjamin Chambers performed the varied functions of miller, millwright, sawyer, trader, physician, colonel of militia, justice of the peace, and arbitrator of minor troubles among his contentious and turbulent Scotch-Irish neighbors. He was even sent on a mission to England to aid in settling the long-standing boundary controversy between Lord Baltimore and the Penns, which was then retarding the colonization of Maryland and southern Pennsylvania. In 1764 Colonel Benjamin Chambers formally laid out the town of Chambersburg. The surname Chambers, by metonymy, originally designated a chamberlain.

In 1789 a new county was taken from Cumberland and Northumberland, and named Mifflin in honor of General Thomas Mifflin, then governor of Pennsylvania. To this staunch patriot belongs the distinction of having served as chief executive of the State longer than any other person. He was governor more than eleven years,—from November 5, 1788, to December 17, 1799. He served two years as president of the Supreme Executive Council under the Constitution of 1776; and he was thrice elected governor under the Constitution of 1790.

Mifflin County

Thomas Mifflin was born and reared in a prosperous Philadelphia Quaker family, was well educated, and had traveled extensively in Europe. He was an eloquent speaker, a member of the Assembly, president of the Continental Congress at the close of the war, a major-general and Quartermaster-General of the Revolutionary army, one of the framers of the Federal Constitution, and president of the convention that drew up the State Constitution of 1790.

Mifflinville, in Mifflin Township, Columbia County, and Mifflinburg, in Union County, which was long called Youngmanstown for Elias Youngman (or Jungmann), who laid it out in 1783, were both named for Governor Mifflin.

About a mile from the place where old Fort Granville once stood is situated Lewistown, the county-seat of Mifflin County, on the site of the Indian village of

Poketytown, which is said to have received its name from that of an Indian chief. Mifflintown, once known as

Lewistown "John Harris's Plantation," was at first chosen as the county town; but this place was unsatisfactory to the people who lived "above the Narrows." In 1791 Samuel Edmiston, who had but recently secured possession of three hundred acres of land comprising the site finally chosen for the county-seat, laid out a village, which he named Lewistown in honor of his friend, William Lewis, an iron-master, who then owned and operated Hope Furnace, which was situated in old Derry Township, a few miles west of the new town.[2]

On March 26, 1804, were formed six new counties, one of which was called McKean County for Thomas McKean,

McKean County then governor of Pennsylvania. McKean was thrice elected governor, beginning his administration in 1799 at the age of sixty-five after serving twenty-two years as chief justice of Pennsylvania. He was the only signer of the Declaration of Independence who sat in the Continental Congress from its beginning until the close of the Revolution, a period of more than eight years. Of Irish parentage, he was handicapped in his administrative work by a somewhat arbitrary manner, an irascible temper, and an occasional outburst of violent language, which raised a spirit of antagonism against him in the Legislature. His name should be held in grateful remembrance because he was instrumental in introducing into the Con-

---

[2] Letter from Mr. G. R. Frysinger of Lewistown. Mr. Frysinger is a local historian, who has made a special study of the origin of the name of Lewistown. No reason or historical confirmation can be found for Dr. Egle's statement that Lewistown was "christened in memory of a celebrated island of the Hebrides group west of Scotland, called Lewis." (*History of Pennsylvania*, p. 944.)

6

stitution of 1790 a provision "for the establishment of schools throughout the State in such a manner that the poor may be taught gratis."

The name McKean is probably a variant of McKeon or McKeown, "son of John," the Erse form for John being *Eoin.* McKean, in Erie County, and McKeansburg, in Schuylkill County, were also named for Governor McKean.

McKean County was not organized immediately after its creation by the Legislature, but for ten years it was joined to Centre County, its records being **Smethport** kept at Bellefonte. In 1814 it was attached to Lycoming County for judicial purposes. It did not have a county-seat of its own until nearly twenty years after its formation. Then the new town of Smethport became the county-seat.

To explain the origin of the name of this town, it is necessary to record a bit of hitherto unwritten history. On December 24, 1792, a young Irish soldier named John Keating came to Philadelphia. He had been a member of the so-called Irish Brigade in the French army in 1781, and had received the cross of St. Louis for meritorious services. He had been commissioned a captain in the Ninety-second French Infantry, and had come to Philadelphia on leave, with letters of introduction to Washington. Shortly after his arrival he became the agent and manager of the "Ceres Land Company," most of the capital of which was supplied by exiled Frenchmen of the better class, who had fled from France at the outbreak of the French Revolution.

The Ceres Land Company bought of the Bingham family about 300,000 acres of forest land in northwestern Pennsylvania. Much of this land lay in the present counties of McKean and Potter, and this land company, under the guiding hand and brain of Captain John Keating, was intimately and vitally connected with the settlement, development, and early history of these two counties. According to a prominent citizen of McKean County, "it is due to the memory of John Keating to say that, from the earliest settlement of this county to the time of his death, his watchful care over it and anxiety for its progress, his sympathy with the sufferings and privations of the settlers, and his readiness to help in every possible way, partook more of the character of the care of a father over his children than that of a capitalist over a business enterprise."

Since the Frenchmen who had invested their funds in the Ceres Land Company were exiles, their financial interests were entrusted to two Dutch banking firms at Amsterdam. One of these was the banking house of Raymond and Theodore de Smeth, established in 1736. Though Theodore de Smeth died in 1772 and his brother Raymond in 1800, the business was continued after their death under the firm name of "Raymond and Theodore de Smeth." The extent of the business of this firm is evident from the fact that princes and kings were their clients, some single loans amounting to 10,000,000 francs or more. In 1782 the loans that the de Smeths had made to Catherine of Russia totaled 17,000,000 francs. Theodore de Smeth received from her the title of Baron.

As manager of the Ceres Land Company, John Keating was on intimate terms with the banking firm of Raymond and Theodore de Smeth; and in 1807, when a new town site was laid out in Keating Township for the future county-seat of McKean County, the place was called Smethport at the request of John Keating, in honor of the two Amsterdam bankers, Raymond and Baron Theodore de Smeth.[3]   Ceres Township, in McKean County, was named for the Ceres Land Company.

In 1853 a movement was set on foot to divide Union County and to call the northern division Buffalo County because it comprised the Buffalo Valley. Two **Snyder** years later, however, when the division was **County** made, the northern part retained the name of Union County, and the southern division was called Snyder County, in honor of Simon Snyder, the first Pennsylvania governor of German descent, who was chief executive from 1808 to 1817. The new county contained the old town of Selinsgrove, where Simon Snyder lived from 1784 until his death in 1819.

Born in Lancaster in 1759 of German parents, he moved, at the age of twenty-five, to Selinsgrove, which was founded and named by his brother-in-law, Captain Anthony Seling, or Selin, a veteran of the Revolutionary War. Here the ambitious young Pennsylvania-German opened a store, and began his public career as justice of the peace, in which capacity he served his pioneer community for twelve years. His first experience in a deliberative body was as delegate to the convention that drew up the State Constitution of 1790. He was a member of the Legislature for eleven years, and he was twice elected speaker of the House. Though a man of imperfect education and mediocre ability in comparison with his three predecessors, Franklin, Mifflin, and McKean, he possessed unquestioned integrity and sound judgment, and proved himself a popular, public-spirited, patriotic, and capable executive during the trying times

---

[3] For information concerning John Keating, I am indebted to his great-grandson, Mr. J. Percy Keating, LL.D., of Philadelphia; and for the essential facts about the banking house of de Smeth, to the Dutch scholar, Dr. H. T. Colenbrander of the Hague. See Coudersport, page 104.

when the United States was waging its second war for independence.

The family name Snyder is an Americanized form of the common German surname *Schneider,* which means "tailor."

The little Pennsylvania-German village of Middleburg, on account of its central location, was chosen as the county-seat of Snyder County. This town **Middleburg** was laid out in 1800 on the land of John Swineford, and was long known as Swinefordstown. About 1825, because of its location on Middle Creek, in the heart of the Middle Creek Valley, and near the centre of what was then Centre Township, its name was changed to Middleburg.

CHAPTER IX

COUNTIES NAMED FOR AMERICAN SOLDIERS

THE counties of Montgomery, Greene, Wayne, Armstrong, Butler, Crawford, Mercer, Warren, Potter, Pike, Perry, Sullivan, and Lawrence were named in honor of famous American soldiers. All the men for whom these thirteen counties were named served as officers in the American Revolution except Pike, Perry, and Lawrence, who fought in the second war with England. Seven of them—Wayne, Armstrong, Butler, Crawford, Mercer, Potter, and Sullivan—were also noted as Indian fighters; and of these seven all except General Sullivan were Pennsylvanians by birth or residence. Generals Montgomery, Armstrong, Butler, and Potter were born in Ireland; and four others—Wayne, Crawford, Perry, and Sullivan—were of Irish descent.

In 1784 the new county of Montgomery was set apart from old Philadelphia County. The petition presented to the Legislature, it is said, did not suggest a name for the proposed county. **Montgomery County** Less than nine years before, the brave and beloved General Richard Montgomery, for whom the new county was named, had fallen in the heroic but vain effort to capture Quebec. His untimely death was one of the severest blows to the American cause during the early days of the Revolution. So popular was he that at the news of his death "the city of Philadelphia was in tears; every person seemed to have lost his nearest friend." It is no wonder that

Pennsylvania sought to honor his memory by giving his name to the new county that was taken from the side of Philadelphia.

Richard Montgomery was born in Ireland in 1736. After his graduation from Trinity College, Dublin, he entered the British army as ensign at the age of eighteen, and served under Wolfe at the siege of Louisburg. In 1762 he was promoted to the rank of captain. A year or two later he returned to England, where he became intimate with some of the great liberal leaders, among whom were Isaac Barré, Charles James Fox, and Edmund Burke. In 1773 he left England forever and came to New York, where he purchased an estate and married Janet, the daughter of Judge Robert R. Livingston.

At the beginning of the trouble with England he sided with his adopted country and, offering his services to Congress, was made a brigadier-general. With his little army of less than a thousand soldiers he captured two-thirds of Canada. General Montgomery was a tall man, "of fine military presence, of graceful address, with a bright, magnetic face, winning manners, and the bearing of a prince."

Some effort has been made to show that Montgomery County was named for Colonel John Montgomery of Carlisle, who commanded a Pennsylvania regiment at the battle of Long Island, who was in command of the Pennsylvania militia at Brandywine and Germantown, and who served as a member of the Continental Congress in 1782-3.

Though there can be little doubt that the name of Montgomery County was given with the intention of honoring General Richard Montgomery, it would be a mistake to overlook the fact that this name was particularly acceptable to the large number of influential Welsh settlers then living in the new county. As early as 1717 these Welshmen had colonized and organized Montgomery Township, naming it for their native Montgomeryshire. The village of Montgomeryville in this township traces its name to the same source. It is noteworthy also that two of the most active supporters of the bill to establish Montgomery County were James Montgomery, of Lancaster County, and William Montgomery, of Northumberland. Eighteen counties in the United States and the city of Montgomery, the capital of Alabama, are said to have been named in honor of General Richard Montgomery.

The family name Montgomery is derived from Mont-Gomerie, a place near Lisieux in Normandy. In 1067 Roger de Montgomery, a Norman knight, apparently the first person who is known to have borne the name, was made Earl of Arundel, Sussex, and Shrewsbury.

In 1784 "the town of Norris," now Norristown, the county-seat of Montgomery County and the most populous borough in Pennsylvania, was laid **Norristown** out by William Moore Smith, son of Dr. William Smith,[1] first Provost of the University of Pennsylvania. On October 2, 1704, William Penn gave to his son, William Penn, Jr., the Manor of Williamstadt, containing 7,482 acres. Three days later this prodigal son of the great Quaker statesman disposed of the entire tract to William Trent and Isaac Norris, Sr. About 1712 Trent sold his share to Norris, and removed to New Jersey, where he founded Trenton.

Norristown was named for Isaac Norris, who was born in London in 1671 and came to Philadelphia in 1693. He was active in public life, serving successively as a mem-

---

[1] See Huntingdon, pages 114, 115.

ber of the governor's Council, speaker of the Assembly, justice of Philadelphia County, and mayor of the city. In 1730, six years before his death, the Manor of Williamstadt was organized as Norriton Township. It was his son, Isaac Norris, Jr., who, in 1751, suggested the prophetic Scriptural motto for the famous Liberty Bell, "Proclaim liberty throughout the land, to all the inhabitants thereof."

On the death of Isaac Norris, Sr., most of Norriton Township, which had been named for him, came into the possession of his son Charles, who died in 1766, and whose widow sold the greater part of "Norriton Plantation and Mill Tract" to Colonel John Bull, who, in spite of his name, was so staunch a patriot that the British burned one of his barns as they passed by on their way to Philadelphia. In 1776 Colonel Bull sold the Norriton Plantation, which now forms the heart of Norristown, to Dr. William Smith, whose son laid out and named the town in 1784. The "town of Norris" was incorporated as Norristown in 1812. The surname Norris is derived from the Old French *norice,* which survives in the English word "nurse."

Six counties were named for men born in New England. Franklin County[2] was established in 1784, and Adams County[3] in 1800. The other four—Greene, Warren, Perry, and Sullivan—are discussed in this chapter.

Greene County, in the extreme southwestern corner of the State, was formed from Washington in 1796, and was named in honor of General **Greene County** Nathaniel Greene, the ablest of Washington's officers. Old Greene Township was organized fourteen years earlier as a part of Wash-

[2] See Franklin County, page 78.
[3] See Adams County, page 74.

ington County, and named for General Greene when he
was at the very height of his popularity. The name of the
township was transferred to the new county. Greensboro,
in Greene County, was also named for General Greene.

Greene's services to his country are a part of American history. Born near Warwick, Rhode Island, in 1742,
the son of a blacksmith fourth in descent from Dr. John
Greene, who had come from England shortly after Roger
Williams' arrival, Nathaniel Greene was reared as a
Quaker and trained to his father's trade. His formal
education was meager and defective; he was almost
wholly self-taught. He was elected to the Assembly of
Rhode Island at the age of twenty-six. In 1776, as
brigadier-general he led the three Rhode Island regi-
ments to Boston to join Washington, the newly appointed
commander-in-chief. For his willingness to participate
in the war his Quaker brethren disowned him. Congress
made him a major-general, and he served with conspicuous valor and ability at Dorchester Heights, Trenton,
Princeton, Germantown, and Monmouth.

In the autumn of 1780 Greene took command of the
demoralized fragment of General Gates's army in the
South. In less than a year, by a series of brilliant victories and by a superb generalship that has placed him
forever in the rank of the world's great military leaders,
General Greene had driven the British from all their
strongholds in the South except Savannah and Charleston. Six months later General Wayne captured Savannah, and by the end of 1782 Greene made his triumphal
entry into Charleston. The war was practically ended,
and the South acclaimed the great New England general
as their hero and savior. South Carolina voted him
$50,000. North Carolina gave him $25,000. Georgia presented him with an estate of 24,000 acres near Savannah.

Here he settled down to a life of comparative ease after his six years of strenuous campaigning; and here, at the age of forty-four, he died of sunstroke in June, 1786.

Ten years later the new county that was taken from the side of Washington County very appropriately received the name of Greene, the great military genius who had done more than any other American soldier to help Washington bring the war of independence to a victorious conclusion. The surname Greene was first given to a "dweller at the village green."

Green Village, in Franklin County, derived its name from Greene Township, which was christened in honor of General Greene.

Waynesburg, the county-seat of Greene County, was laid out in 1796 and named in honor of General Anthony

Waynesburg Wayne, whose recent decisive victory over the Indian tribes of the northwest had made possible the permanent settlement not only of Greene County, but also of all western Pennsylvania and the great, fertile valleys beyond. Waynesburg was incorporated in 1816.[4]

Wayne County, in the northeastern corner of Pennsylvania, was formed out of Northampton on March 21,

Wayne County 1798, receiving its name in honor of General Anthony Wayne, who had died at Erie a little more than a year before. "Mad Anthony Wayne," as he was nicknamed because of the many unexpected successes that he won in hazardous expeditions, was born in 1745 in Easttown, Chester County, whence his grandfather had emigrated from Ireland some years after the battle of the Boyne. At the age of thirty he entered the Revolutionary army as

---

[4] Some account of General Wayne will be found in the discussion of Wayne County, which immediately follows.

colonel, and two years later was commissioned a brigadier-general. His services during the Revolution are so well known that they scarcely require comment. He fought at Three Rivers, Brandywine, Paoli, Monmouth, Stony Point, and Yorktown: "where Wayne went, there was a fight always; that was his business." At the close of the war he was brevetted major-general and, returning to civil life, was elected to Congress.

In April, 1792, he succeeded General Arthur St. Clair as commander-in-chief of the United States Army, with the rank of major-general. Neither General Josiah Harmar nor General Arthur St. Clair had succeeded in subjugating the warlike and unruly Indians on the western and northwestern frontiers, where the agents of the British government seemed to be constantly inciting them to new depredations and atrocities. General Wayne prudently spent more than a year in preparing his soldiers for the peculiar warfare that they would have to wage against their Indian foes. On August 20, 1794, he met a force of two thousand Indians in the wilderness at Fallen Timbers, fully three hundred miles from civilization, and there won "the most important victory ever secured over Indian foes. This victory made possible the settlement of Ohio, Illinois, Indiana, and the West. It closed a campaign similar in its objects and difficulties to that of Cæsar in Gaul." [5]

A year later, at Greenville, Ohio, General Wayne negotiated a treaty in which twelve Indian tribes participated. The service that Anthony Wayne rendered his native State in effectually breaking the Indian power and in giving permanent peace to the western frontier can hardly be overestimated. After his conquest of the northwestern tribes the colonization and development of west-

---

[5] Samuel W. Pennypacker's *Pennsylvania—The Keystone*, p. 106.

ern Pennsylvania began in earnest, and the settlements in this region grew with amazing rapidity.

"Wayne, Wayne, Anthony Wayne,
Fiery heart and cool, clear brain,
Deep in the wilds of the Northwest region
Marched at the head of his hard-drilled legion,
Pressing where two had failed before,
Bringing the choice of peace or war.
Iroquois, Ottawa, Chippeway,
Back of the fallen timbers lay;
Wyandot, Shawnee, Delaware,
Poured their shot from the sheltered lair.
Over the root-laced parapet
The legion stormed with the bayonet,
Hunting the warriors out and out;
Hard on the flank of the savage rout,
Leaping the trunks in their reckless course,
Thundered the mad Kentucky Horse,
Lunging, plunging, bridles ringing,
Pistols flashing, sabers swinging,
Till the woods were clear as a new-washed fleece
And the vanquished sachems sued for peace." [6]

As to how the surname Wayne or Wain originated, no definite information can be given. The word means "wagon." It may have been abbreviated from Wainwright, or derived from an old tavern at the sign of "The Wain."

For six or seven years after the formation of Wayne County the temporary seat of justice was located alternately at Wilsonville and at Milford, now the **Bethany** county-seat of Pike County. In 1805 the little town of Bethany, founded in 1801 by the Quaker, Henry Drinker of Philadelphia, laid out by Jason Torrey, and named for the village in Palestine, became the county-seat of Wayne County and continued as the seat of justice until 1842, when Honesdale became

---

[6] Arthur Guiterman. Quoted by permission.

the county town.   The Hebrew name Bethany signifies
"the house of dates."

Bethany was the birthplace of David Wilmot, a member of the lower house of Congress from Pennsylvania
in 1845-51, where he became famous as the author of the
"Wilmot Proviso," which started the Free-soil movement in American politics.   In 1861 Pennsylvania sent
Wilmot to the United States Senate.

The early settlers in this region, many of whom came
from New England, seem to have been particularly fond
of Biblical names: Wayne County contains the villages
of Bethany, Galilee, and Damascus, and the townships of
Canaan, Lebanon, and Salem.   After the removal of the
county-seat, the court-house at Bethany was used for an
academy, which, in 1848, was chartered as the "University of Northern Pennsylvania."   Three years later this
flourishing institution had over two hundred students.
In 1857 the old court-house burned down, and the "university" ceased to exist.

In 1827, as soon as it was definitely known that "the
forks of the Dyberry" were to be the terminus of the
                           Delaware and Hudson Canal, the town of
Honesdale   Honesdale was planned and laid out.   Hones-
                           dale very properly received its name from
Philip Hone of New York, the chief patron and the first
president of the Delaware and Hudson Canal Company.
He was a wealthy merchant, and "the courtliest mayor
New York ever saw."   The family name Hone was first
used to designate a "dweller by a large stone or rock."
Honesdale was incorporated in 1831, and eleven years
later it became the county-seat of Wayne County.

It is an interesting fact that one of "the first locomotive engines introduced and worked in America—
called the 'Stourbridge Lion,' built in England, of the

best workmanship and material, and the most approved pattern of that date—was run in 1828 for a while on a little railroad at Hone's Dale.''[7]

On March 12, 1800, eight new counties were created, mostly out of Allegheny County, five of them—Armstrong, Butler, Crawford, Mercer, and Warren—being named for officers in the Revolutionary army.

Armstrong County, composed of territory contributed by Allegheny, Westmoreland, and Lycoming, was named in honor of General John Armstrong, who **Armstrong County** was thus gratefully remembered for his exploit in capturing and burning the hostile Indian village at Kittanning in this county forty-four years before. From this important village many a warlike Indian expedition had gone forth to harass the frontier. Before daybreak on September 9, 1756, Colonel Armstrong made his attack upon Kittanning with five of his eight companies of frontiersmen, the other three having not yet crossed the last range of mountains. The Indians, asleep in a cornfield near their village, were taken by surprise. Their settlement was practically annihilated. Large quantities of powder, munitions, and supplies, which had been furnished by the French, were destroyed with the burning cabins and wigwams. Both Colonel Armstrong and Captain Hugh Mercer were wounded, but led their little army safely home.

At the beginning of the Revolution, Armstrong, who was a north-country Irishman living at Carlisle, was commissioned a brigadier-general, and saw service at the battles of Brandywine and Germantown. Armstrong—''strong in the arm''—is a surname of personal characteristic.

---

[7] Hollister's *History of the Lackawanna Valley* (Third Edition), p. 355.

Kittanning, the county-seat of Armstrong County, which occupies the site of the old Indian village that **Kittanning** Armstrong's expedition had destroyed, was laid out in 1803 by Judge George Ross.

From this place a famous Indian trail known as "the Kittanning Path" led across the mountains to Standing Stone, now Huntingdon. It was this trail that Colonel Armstrong and his little army followed in their expedition against Kittanning. Kittanning was made a borough in 1821. Kittanning is an Indian word corrupted from *Kit-hannink*, "the town on the great river," the *Kit-hanne*, or "great river," being the Allegheny.

Butler County, formed from Allegheny in 1800, was named for General Richard Butler, who served with distinction as a Revolutionary officer and per- **Butler** ished in the bloody battle on the Miami in **County** which General Arthur St. Clair was so disastrously defeated in November, 1791.[8] Richard Butler was born in 1743 in Dublin, Ireland, whence his parents emigrated to Pennsylvania. He studied law and spent most of his life in the practice of his profession at Carlisle. At the age of twenty-one he received his first military experience as an ensign in the expedition that Colonel Henry Bouquet led westward for the relief of Fort Pitt.

He entered the American Revolution as major, served with distinction at Saratoga and Monmouth, and emerged as colonel. Both Washington and Wayne, under whom he served, thought highly of his ability as an officer. He was especially familiar with Indian life, ways, and warfare, and knew several Indian dialects. The last three or four years of his life he spent in western Pennsyl-

---

[8] See Saint Clair, page 229.

vania. He was prominent in urging the formation of Allegheny County, serving as one of its judges and representing it in the Legislature. He was popular in Pittsburgh, where one of the chief taverns bore his name, and where "many a partial parent called a son after him."

When General St. Clair and his little army were sent forth to punish the hostile Indians on the Miami and the Wabash, Richard Butler was made a major-general and placed second in command. Wounded unto death in the dreadful battle, in which more than three-fifths of the American force were killed, injured, or missing, General Butler urged his comrades to leave him to his fate, and to make good their escape.

Early in 1803 the town of Butler was laid out on one hundred and fifty acres of land which John and Samuel Cunningham had donated for that purpose, and **Butler** on March 3d of that year the Legislature approved of Butler as the county-seat. The first settlement at this place had been made about ten years before. Butler Township was organized in 1804. Both the village and the township were named for General Butler. The borough of Butler was incorporated in 1817. The town now has a city charter. The family name Butler is an occupation name, being derived from the old English word *boteler,* "bottle-keeper."

Crawford County, set apart from Allegheny County in 1800, was named in honor of Colonel William Crawford, who was burned at the stake by the **Crawford** Indians near Upper Sandusky, in Wyandot **County** County, Ohio, on June 11, 1782. He was born of Scotch-Irish stock in Berkeley County, Virginia, in 1732. He served as a surveyor under Washington, who was his life-long friend, and later he became a captain and a famous Indian-fighter both in

7

the French and Indian War and in the war against Pontiac. In 1767 Captain Crawford settled in western Pennsylvania, just across the Youghiogheny River from Connellsville.[9] Throughout the Revolution he was in command of a Virginia regiment.

After the war he retired to his farm in western Pennsylvania in the hope of ending his days quietly with his family after a quarter of a century of frontier hardship and Indian warfare. In May, 1782, he reluctantly undertook the leadership of an expedition against the intractable savages in the Muskingum country, who had become justly enraged because the white settlers, about two months before, had brutally murdered nearly a hundred inoffensive Moravian Indians.

The little army of less than five hundred mounted frontiersmen under the command of Colonel Crawford marched boldly forth into the Ohio wilderness against their Indian foes. The expedition was made up largely of the undisciplined and unruly woodsmen who had participated in the wanton massacre of the Christian Indians at Gnadenhütten. On the afternoon of June 4th they were furiously attacked, but as night fell, the Americans had the advantage. The next day there was more or less desultory fighting, but no general engagement. In the afternoon, however, the enemy was strongly reinforced by mounted English soldiers called Butler's Rangers and by hordes of savage warriors. Being greatly outnumbered, the handful of Americans decided to make good their retreat under cover of darkness. As soon as their movements were detected, they were hotly pursued, and on the next day they were forced to give battle again, in which they were once more victorious.

But a few soldiers were separated from the main force,

---

9 See Connellsville, page 211.

and these were captured by the Indians. The gallant commander was among these unfortunates. All the captives were savagely murdered except Dr. John Knight and John Slover, who, after being condemned to death at the stake, escaped as it were by a miracle, to tell the terrible fate that befell their leader.

Colonel Crawford was led to a spot half a mile distant from the Indian village and stripped naked. His hands were bound behind him, and his face was painted black as a sign that he was doomed to death. One end of a stout rope was tied to the ligature of his wrist, and the other end fastened to a post. The rope was long enough to allow him to walk twice around the stake and back again. The wood for the fire was piled in a circle about the post and the victim. The Indians first shot about seventy charges of powder into Crawford's body. Then, after cutting off his ears, they lighted the faggots. They applied burning sticks to his naked flesh, "already burned black with powder." The squaws amused themselves by throwing live brands upon him until the space in which he walked within the circle of flames was a mass of coals and scorching ashes. He begged the Tory renegade, Simon Girty, to shoot him, but that "white savage" only laughed in derision.

For three terrific hours the Indians compelled William Crawford to perform his awful dance of death within the fiery circle, until his strength finally gave out. Then they scalped him, and he lay down to die. His body was burned. Thus perished the heroic soldier and pioneer whose name and fame have been worthily commemorated in the official designation of Crawford County.

Ohio, Indiana, and Michigan have also named counties in honor of Colonel William Crawford. The territorial surname Crawford, signifying "the ford by a colony of crows or rooks," is an old Lanarkshire name dating as far back as 1159.

Meadville, the county-seat of Crawford County, was named in honor of General David Mead, who made the first permanent white settlement in north-

Meadville   western Pennsylvania.   He was sixth in descent from William Mead, who had come from England to Stamford, Connecticut, in 1640. In 1770 David Mead migrated from New York into the Wyoming valley, from which he was later evicted by the "Connecticut intruders." Then he moved to the region of Sunbury, where, for a number of years, he kept a tavern. One day, in 1787, a copy of Washington's report to Governor Dinwiddie fell into his hands, and he and his brother John decided to seek their fortunes in the northwestern wilderness. The next year they pushed their way westward to the site of Milesburg, now in Centre County, and thence followed the old "Chinklaca-moose Path" into the Clearfield region as far as the mouth of Anderson's Creek, near Curwensville. From this point they cut through the wilderness a path that was long known as "Mead's Trail," leading across what is now Clearfield, Jefferson, Clarion, Venango, and Crawford Counties, to the site of Meadville.

In 1789 they returned and brought their families and a number of other hardy pioneers out over this rude pack-horse trail, and started "Mead's Settlement" in Crawford County. Here in 1793, David Mead planned a town, which he laid out two years later and called Cussewago, an Indian name said to mean "the snake with a big belly."

In 1795 David Mead, a substantial frontier farmer, miller, and lumberman, was commissioned justice of the peace for Mead Township, which then comprised all the territory now in Crawford and Erie Counties. In 1800 he was made one of the associate justices of the new county of Crawford, and the town that he had started was chosen as the county-seat and formally christened Meadville in his honor. Having seen service in the Revolutionary War, he was appointed major-general in command of the militia in this region, and in 1813 he rendered important service to his country by marching with his pioneer soldiers to the defense of Erie, where Perry's squadron, then in process of building, was threatened with destruction. David Mead was six feet, three inches in height, a man of fine presence, dignified bearing, and irreproachable character. Meadville was incorporated in 1823. The family name Mead was first given to "a dweller at a mead or meadow."

Mercer County, formed from Allegheny in 1800, was named in honor of General Hugh Mercer, who was born in Aberdeen, Scotland, in 1720, was educated as a physician at the University of Aberdeen, and served as a surgeon in the army of the Pretender, Prince Charles Edward, at the battle of Culloden in 1746. Two years later he emigrated to Pennsylvania and began the practice of medicine in what is now Franklin County, near Mercersburg, which was named for him. He took an active part in the French and Indian War, and was with Washington in the ill-fated campaign of General Braddock. He also served as lieutenant-colonel in General Forbes's expedition, and was later commandant of Fort Pitt.

When the Revolutionary struggle began, Doctor Mercer was practicing medicine at Fredericksburg, Virginia. He was made a brigadier-general on Washington's recommendation, and in 1777 fought at Trenton and at Princeton, where he fell mortally wounded. His funeral in Philadelphia is said to have been attended by 30,000 people.

Counties in six other states have been named for General
Mercer. The name Mercer, from the Low Latin *mercerius*,
means "trader, or storekeeper."

Mercer Mercer, the county-seat of Mercer County, was laid
out in 1803 by the three trustees, John Findley, William
Mortimer, and "Little Billy" McMillan, on two
hundred acres donated to the county by John
Hoge, who owned large tracts of land in that
region. Mercer was named for General Hugh Mercer.
In 1807 enough money had been secured from the sale
of lots to begin the erection of a court-house. In 1814
Mercer was made a borough.

Warren County Warren County, which received its territory from Allegheny and Lycoming, was named for the Revolutionary
patriot, General Joseph Warren, who was born
at Roxbury, Massachusetts, in 1741, and was
killed in the battle of Bunker Hill at the age
of thirty-four. Doctor Warren began the
practice of medicine when nineteen years of age. By his
marriage he came into possession of a considerable fortune. From the very beginning of the troubles with
England in 1765 until the actual outbreak of war, Doctor
Warren was an active agitator and an ardent upholder
of the rights and liberties of the colonists. He was chairman of the committee of safety in Boston; he busied
himself with the collection of military stores and the organization of the militia for the coming conflict; and on
May 31, 1775, he presided at the provincial Congress held
at Watertown and became the executive head of the pro-
visional government of Massachusetts. On June 14th,
three days before his death, he was made one of the two
major-generals of the Massachusetts forces.

At the time of its formation in 1800 Warren County
was very sparsely populated. Ten years later it had less

than a thousand inhabitants; and it was not completely organized as a county until October, 1819. Eleven other American counties were named in honor of General Warren. The family name Warren originated from residence "at or by the warren," the privileged enclosure for rabbits, hares, and partridges.

The town of Warren, which became the county-seat of Warren County, was laid out near the mouth of the **Warren** Conewango as early as 1795, on land belonging to the State, by General William Irvine and Andrew Ellicott, the two commissioners specially appointed for that purpose. Warren also received its name from General Joseph Warren. Notwithstanding its advantageous situation, the place did not really begin to grow until after the war of 1812: in 1813 there were only five houses in Warren. It was incorporated in 1832. The village of North Warren, located two or three miles from the parent town, lies on the west bank of the Conewango.

Warrensville, in Lycoming County, was also named for General Warren.

Potter County was one of the five counties taken in 1804 from the territory of Lycoming. In the bill that passed the House the name at first given to **Potter** the new county was Sinnemahoning, from the **County** river, or creek, by that name, which flows through the county. Sinnemahoning is an Indian name signifying "stony lick." When the bill reached the upper house, Senator James Harris of Centre County, one of the founders of Bellefonte, made a motion to change the name from Sinnemahoning to Potter County in honor of the Centre County soldier, General James Potter. In this amendment the lower house concurred.

James Potter was born in Tyrone, Ireland, in 1729, and came to Pennsylvania in 1741 with his father, John Potter, who nine years later became the first sheriff of Cumberland County. James was a captain and later a major in the Indian wars. In 1777 he was made a brigadier-general of Pennsylvania troops in the Revolutionary army, serving with distinction almost continuously throughout the war, and receiving a commission as major-general in 1782. In the spring of 1778 Washington wrote from Valley Forge: "If the state of General Potter's affairs will admit of his returning to the army, I shall be exceedingly glad to see him, as his activity and vigilance have been much wanted during the winter."

In 1781 he was vice-president of Pennsylvania, and in the following year he was John Dickinson's strongest rival for the governorship. After the war General Potter retired to his estate of six thousand acres in Penn's Valley, near the present borough of Centre Hall, where, in 1789, he died from injuries received in helping to raise a barn. The surname Potter originated as an occupation name.

Coudersport Coudersport, which, in 1807, was approved by the Legislature as the county-seat of Potter County, received its name at the suggestion of Captain John Keating, manager of the Ceres Land Company, in honor of Jean Samuel Couderc, senior member of the Amsterdam banking firm of Couderc, Brants, and Changuion, who looked after the interests of some of the exiled Frenchmen who had invested their funds in the Ceres Company.[10] This company, through its agent, John Keating, generously donated to the county one half of the town plot of Coudersport. In the naming of the county-seat the final

---

[10] See Smethport, pages 82-84.

letter in M. Couderc's name was dropped for the sake of euphony. The little town grew very slowly at first and contained only about fifty people in 1835, when the first court-house was built.

On March 26, 1814, less than a year after General Zebulon Montgomery Pike was killed in battle at York (now Toronto), Canada, a new county, formed **Pike** out of a part of Wayne, was named in his **County** honor. Pike County borders on General Pike's native state, New Jersey, and at the time of its organization it joined Northampton County, in which young Pike spent his youth at the home of his father, Captain Zebulon Pike, in Easton, whither the family had moved from Bucks County. At the age of twenty young Pike entered the United States Army as ensign in his father's regiment.

Shortly after the United States purchased the vast tract known as Louisiana from the French, two important exploring parties were sent out, one under Captain Meriwether Lewis and Lieutenant William Clark, to trace the Missouri to its source, and the other under the leadership of Lieutenant Zebulon M. Pike, to discover the headwaters of the Mississippi. In August, 1805, young Pike set out from St. Louis with a party of twenty picked men, and made a wonderful journey of exploration during the following nine months. The next year the intrepid young explorer was sent on a second expedition of discovery into the unknown interior of the Louisiana territory. It was during this journey that he discovered Pike's Peak. After his return to civilization in the midsummer of 1807 Captain Pike received the formal thanks of Congress. In 1810 he published an extended narrative of his two journeys of exploration.

Pike rose rapidly in military rank. He was a major at

the age of twenty-nine and a lieutenant-colonel at thirty.
He entered the second war with Great Britain as colonel
of the Fifteenth Infantry, and in less than a year was
commissioned a brigadier-general. He was only thirty-
four years old at the time of his death. Nine states contain counties named for General Pike. The family name
Pike, from the Anglo-Saxon *pic,* means "a dweller at
the point"; that is, at a pointed hill or a pointed piece
of land.

The town of Milford, which was finally selected as the
capital of Pike County, was laid out about 1796 by John
Biddis, a Philadelphian of Welsh descent.
Milford   Before the Revolution the Wells brothers had
come into this region from Connecticut, built
a saw-mill and a grist-mill, and started a ferry across
the Delaware River near the mouth of Saw Creek. There
is a Milford Haven in Pembrokeshire, Wales, and a Milford in Connecticut; and some have guessed that the
name of Milford may have been borrowed from one of
these two places. If the name was really borrowed, it
seems likely that the founder, John Biddis, appropriated
the name of the Welsh town.

There is a strong probability, however, that the name
of Milford and Milford Township originated independ-
ently from an old ford which crossed Saw Creek near its
mouth, where the Wells brothers had built their mill, and
that the juxtaposition of the *mill* and the *ford* suggested
the name Milford.

Perry County was set apart from Cumberland in 1820
and named in honor of Commodore Oliver Hazard Perry,
the hero of the battle of Lake Erie, who,
Perry County   seven months before, had died of yellow
fever in the island of Trinidad, at the
mouth of the Orinoco River. Perry was born at South

Kingston, Rhode Island, in 1785. In the spring of 1813, in the harbor of Erie, amid almost insuperable difficulties and hardships, he began to build his little squadron out of timber just cut from the forest. The total tonnage of his nine vessels was 1,671; only two could fairly be called men-of-war. The squadron carried fifty-four guns. Perry had a force of five hundred landsmen and sailors. His opponent, Captain Robert H. Barclay, had an equal force; but his six vessels, with a tonnage of 1,460, carried sixty-three guns.

In the famous battle that took place on September 10, 1813, the British had the advantage at first, and Lieutenant Perry was forced to abandon his flagship, the *Lawrence,* for the *Niagara.* By three o'clock in the afternoon Perry had won a complete victory. The British flag was hauled down, and the British squadron was surrendered to a young man of twenty-eight. Perry then sent his famous message to General William Henry Harrison: "We have met the enemy, and they are ours."

This victory made Perry one of the popular heroes of the war, and he was everywhere lionized and fêted. The rest of his short life was profitably spent in sweeping the pirates from the Algerian coast and from the West Indies. Nine counties in the United States have been named in his honor. Ten townships in Pennsylvania and the village of Perryopolis, in Fayette County, bear his name. According to Harrison, Perry signifies "a dweller by a pear-tree," *perye* being the early English form of the word.

Ten places competed for the seat of justice of Perry County, and New Bloomfield, the present county town, was finally selected by the fourth commission of "disinterested persons." Bloomfield was the name by which Thomas Barnett's tract of 418 acres, on which the town was built, had been designated in the original patent. Tradition asserts that this name was given in compliment

New Bloomfield	to the Irishman, Colonel Benjamin Bloomfield, who was born in County Tipperary in 1768, had seen military service in Newfoundland, was knighted in 1815, and made an Irish peer in 1825, with the title of Baron Bloomfield.

It seems quite as probable, however, that the first surveyor had sufficient floral justification for this name. The popular explanation is that the name of New Bloomfield owed its origin to the fact that the town was laid out in June, 1823, in a clover field that was then in full bloom. Until the new county buildings were completed in 1827, Landisburg, which was founded in 1793 by Abraham Landis, was the temporary seat of justice. New Bloomfield is the name of the post-office, though the corporate name of the town is Bloomfield.

Sullivan County, set apart from Lycoming in 1847, was named in honor of General John Sullivan, who was

Sullivan County	born in 1740 at Somersworth, New Hampshire. He studied law, and, when the Revolutionary War broke out, was practising his profession at Durham, New Hampshire. He was appointed one of the eight brigadier-generals of the Continental army, and in 1776 was commissioned a major-general. He served with credit throughout the war, participating in the battles of Long Island, Brandywine, and Germantown.

The famous punitive expedition that General John Sullivan organized and led against the Iroquois Indians in the summer of 1779 has inseparably connected his name with the history of Pennsylvania. This expedition was conceived by Washington as a means of punishing the hostile Indians in northern Pennsylvania and in New

York, whom the British had armed and hired to harass the defenseless frontier settlements by indiscriminate murder, pillage, and destruction. The most heart-rending of the border atrocities thus inflicted upon Pennsylvania by the savage allies of Great Britain was the Wyoming Massacre. On May 31st Washington instructed Sullivan, with his force of about five thousand men, to advance into the Iroquois country, to destroy the settlements of the Indians and their Tory allies, to lay waste their fields, and to capture as many prisoners as possible.

On June 18th General Sullivan's expedition set out from Easton, marching first to Wilkes-Barre, where its equipment was completed, and thence northward along the Susquehannah to Tioga Point,[11] the gateway to the fertile Iroquois country. His army penetrated and utterly desolated the lands of the Senecas, the Cayugas, and the Onondagas, killing and capturing the savages, burning forty of their towns, and destroying about 150,000 bushels of ripening corn, besides vast quantities of fruit and vegetables. Hardly a single vestige of life or of the means of sustenance was left in all the fertile region that the army overran.

In this awful visitation the Indians and the Tories experienced, to their great sorrow, the bitter punishment that the Continental army was able to inflict upon them for their wanton atrocities and barbarous massacres on the frontier. By September 30th the army had returned to Tioga Point, and on October 15th it marched victoriously into Easton. In his report to Congress General Sullivan announced that he had not suffered the loss of more than forty men "in action or otherwise since taking the command."

Five American counties are named in honor of General

---

[11] Now Athens.

Sullivan, one of them in his native state of New Hampshire. Sullivan is a name of personal characteristic, signifying "the man with the light eyes."

Laporte   Laporte, the capital of Sullivan County, the smallest county-seat in Pennsylvania, with a population of only 175, was laid out in 1850 by Michael Meylert, who named both the township and the village for his friend, John Laporte, who was speaker of the General Assembly in 1832, a member of Congress from 1832 to 1836, and the last surveyor-general of Pennsylvania, serving from 1845 to 1851. John Laporte was a descendant of one of the old exiled French families that settled in the region of Asylum,[12] now in Bradford County, at the time of the French Revolution. The name Laporte signifies "a dweller at the gateway" of a city.

Lawrence County   About 1820 the thriving town of New Castle, situated on the boundary line between the counties of Beaver and Mercer, conceived the ambitious scheme of becoming the civil centre of a new county. Twenty-nine years later this ambition was realized in the creation of Lawrence County out of parts of Mercer and Beaver. Though this county bears the name of the naval hero, Captain James Lawrence, who died on June 6, 1813, at the age of thirty-one, from wounds received in the gallant defense that his frigate *Chesapeake* made against the British frigate *Shannon* off Boston harbor, Lawrence County was named directly for the *Lawrence*, Perry's flagship in his victorious battle with the British squadron on Lake Erie.[13]

Thus the name is intimately connected with Pennsylvania history. Perry was a great admirer of James Lawrence, and when he received the news of the latter's

---

[12] See Asylum, page 304.
[13] Egle's *History of Pennsylvania*, p. 854. See Perry County, pp. 106, 107.

untimely death in the summer of 1813, he christened his flagship the *Lawrence*. When the little squadron was finished and at last confronted its foe on Lake Erie, the *Lawrence* displayed at its masthead the heroic words of Captain James Lawrence, *"Don't give up the ship."* In the fight that ensued the *Lawrence* was reduced to a mere hulk and had to be abandoned, but the memory of its gallant fight and of the hero whose name and dying message it bore into battle will live in the official designation of one of the important counties of western Pennsylvania. Nine other counties in the United States were christened in honor of Captain Lawrence. The borough of Lawrenceville, in Tioga County, was also named in his honor.

The surname Lawrence, originally a baptismal name, comes from the Latin *Laurens* or *Laurentius,* which was probably derived from *laurus*, "the laurel tree." Virgil gives a similar explanation of the name Laurentum.[14]

About 1798 a civil engineer named John Carlysle Stewart, who was engaged in resurveying the "donation lands" granted to Revolutionary soldiers **New Castle** in western Pennsylvania, discovered that the original surveyor had made the mistake of leaving an unoccupied tract of about fifty acres between two adjacent districts at the confluence of the Neshannock Creek with the Shenango. Stewart took up this tract in his own name, and in 1802 laid out a town which he called New Castle.

The traditional explanation is that Stewart had come originally from near New Castle, Delaware, and that he named his new settlement for the older American town. This tradition seems to lack historic confirmation, and

---

[14] "This plant Latinus, when his town he wall'd,
Then found, and from the tree Laurentum call'd;
At last, in honor of his new abode,
He vow'd the laurel to the laurel's god."
—Æneis, VII, lines 91-95 (Dryden's translation)

the founder's descendants are disposed to discredit it. "From the first," says a prominent citizen of New Castle,[15] who was well acquainted with the founder's daughter, "Stewart had the idea of making New Castle a manufacturing site, and the probability is that he named his town for Newcastle in England. Some of his relatives now living at New Castle are of that opinion. Stewart built a small charcoal furnace within the present city limits of New Castle and made pig iron from native ores." In its industries the Pennsylvania city certainly bears a remarkable similarity to the great Northumbrian city. New Castle, which had been incorporated in 1825, had a population of 1,563 when it became the capital of Lawrence County.

The name of New Castle, whether it comes directly or indirectly from that of the English city, has its ultimate origin in the great manufacturing city, Newcastle-on-Tyne, the county town of Northumberland, which has grown up about the ancient fortified precinct, *castellum novum,* or "new castle," which Robert Courthose, Duke of Normandy, built in 1080 to replace an older fortification that had been destroyed by his father, William the Conqueror.

The average age of the great soldiers whose names have been given to these thirteen counties[16] was less than forty-seven years. The eldest, General Armstrong, reached the age of seventy. Only one other, General Potter, attained to three score years. Warren, Lawrence, Perry, and Pike were all under thirty-five at the time of their death; and Montgomery's career was ended be-

---

[15] Ex-Congressman Oscar L. Jackson, whose great-grandmother was a sister of John Carlysle Stewart.

[16] Two other Pennsylvania counties, Washington and Mifflin, were named in honor of distinguished American soldiers. These have been discussed elsewhere: see pages 71 and 80.

fore he was forty years old. Butler, Lawrence, Mercer, Montgomery, Pike, and Warren perished in battle; Crawford was put to death by his Indian captors; and Perry died of yellow fever while on duty in the tropics. Truly war is a hazardous calling.

CHAPTER X

COUNTIES NAMED FOR WOMEN

TWO Pennsylvania counties, Huntingdon and Montour, were named for women.

In 1766 George Croghan conveyed the tract of four hundred acres, which afterwards became the site of Huntingdon, to the Reverend William Smith, D.D., a Scotchman by birth, a graduate of the University of Aberdeen, and a minister of the Church of England. In 1754, at the solicitation of Benjamin Franklin, William Smith consented to serve as the first Provost of the College of Philadelphia, which, in 1779, became the University of Pennsylvania. The tract purchased by Provost Smith was the site of the famous Indian village of "The Standing Stone," a name given because of a tall, upright stone column or pillar that long stood at the lower end of the town near the river.

On the original Standing Stone, which was a tribal totem-pole, were said to have been engraved rude hieroglyphics, or strange, cabalistic marks. Certainly the Indians regarded this stone with superstitious veneration, believing that if it should be removed their tribe would be dispersed, but that they would prosper so long as it should stand. In 1753 John Harris, Jr., of Harris's Ferry—afterwards Harrisburg—described the Standing Stone as "fourteen feet high and six inches square." The Reverend Philip Fithian, a Presbyterian missionary, who saw the Standing Stone in 1775, says that it was a "tall stone column nearly square and seven feet above the ground." Another writer speaks of it as a "tall, slim pillar of stone four inches thick by eight inches wide." Certainly these travelers did not all see the same stone. The original Standing Stone was carried away by the Indians in 1754, and a new stone set up.

In 1767 Doctor Smith laid out a town on the Standing Stone tract he had bought the previous year, and named it Huntingdon in honor of Selina Hastings, **Huntingdon** Countess of Huntingdon. A short time before, he had journeyed to England in quest of funds for his college in Philadelphia, and the Countess of Huntingdon, famous to this day for her saintly life and many charities, had made so liberal a donation to the needy little college that in gratitude for her kindness Doctor Smith named the new town in her honor. Yet the early settlers in that vicinity long persisted in calling the place by its earlier name of Standing Stone, a name that is still borne by the creek, the mountain ridge, and the valley in that region. Its Indian equivalent, Oneida, has been given to the township through which the creek flows.

The Countess of Huntingdon was the daughter of Washington Shirley, second Earl of Ferrars. She was married to Theophilus Hastings, ninth Earl of Huntingdon. In the course of her life she is said to have expended more than half a million dollars in public and private charities,—certainly no inconsiderable sum for those days. She was a devout Methodist and a close friend of John Wesley and George Whitefield. Augustus Toplady said of her, "She is the most precious saint of God I ever knew." At her death she left the bulk of her fortune to the support of the sixty-four chapels she had built. The name Huntingdon is derived from the Anglo-Saxon *Huntandun,* "the hunters' hill."

In 1787, when a new county was formed from Bedford,

with Huntingdon centrally located as its chief settlement,
the county naturally took the name of the
Huntingdon town that had been laid out twenty
County years before, and Huntingdon became the
county-seat of Huntingdon County. The
borough seal of Huntingdon very appropriately bears a
slender stone pillar, "the standing stone," as its central
figure.

Montour County, formed from Columbia County in
1850, was named in honor of Madame Montour, who has
sometimes been represented as a French
Montour half-breed, and sometimes as a white woman
County who had become an Indian by adoption and
had remained such from choice. In point of
fact, she was three-fourths Indian. In the great mass
and maze of conflicting statements that have been published about this extraordinary woman, it has been very
difficult to get at what seem to be the correct facts. A
good deal that has been written about her is undoubtedly
either fiction or guesswork. The essential facts of interest about Madame Montour appear to be these:[1]

Madam Montour's father was a half-breed Canadian
Indian, "Louis Couc, surnamed Montour," who married
a Saco Indian girl, whose Christian name was Madeleine.
They had at least three children, one of whom was
Madame Montour, born about 1682. Her first name is
generally supposed to have been Catherine, though in
colonial records she invariably appears as Madame
Montour, just as if she had no given name. According
to her own statement, when ten years old she was captured by some Iroquois and adopted into their tribe.

---

[1] See Hanna's *Wilderness Trail,* vol. I, pp. 197-206; see also Mrs. Louise
Welles Murray's *Old Tioga Point and Early Athens,* p. 107 *et seq.* Mrs.
Murray has made use of the recent researches of General John S. Clark
and Mr. Oscar J. Harvey.

As early as 1702 she was married to Carondowanna, or "Big Tree," an Oneida chief who had taken the name of Robert Hunter, colonial governor of New York. Madame Montour had three children who figure more or less prominently in colonial records,—Andrew (sometimes called Henry), Lewis, and Margaret, usually known as "French Margaret," probably her oldest child. Margaret and Andrew (or Henry) Montour, like their mother, were famous Indian interpreters and persons of distinction and influence in the Indian affairs of Pennsylvania and New York. In conformity with the Indian practice, Madame Montour seems to have retained her own name after her marriage. Sometime before 1727 she and her family had settled at the Indian village of Otstonwackin, or Otzinachson (now Montoursville, in Lycoming County), where she seems to have dwelt from time to time until her death in 1752.

She was apparently a woman of distinguished appearance, good character, and unusual intelligence, and of considerable education and refinement. Because of her extraordinary influence over the Indians, she was always treated with great consideration by the provincial authorities. This fact may have given rise to the oft-repeated statement that she was "much caressed by wealthy people of Philadelphia."

Madame Montour, besides speaking English and French, is said to have been a living polyglot of the Indian tongues, and was frequently present as interpreter at Indian conferences and treaties. She always remained friendly to the whites without losing the respect and confidence of the Indians. This fact alone, when we consider her vast influence, should entitle her to grateful remembrance. She was doubtless worthy of the honor that the people of Pennsylvania have shown her in perpetuating her name by giving it to one of their counties. The beautiful Montour's Ridge, running through Montour and Northumberland Counties, had long borne her name; perhaps it was this prominent geographical feature that suggested the name of Montour for the county it traverses. The name of Madame Montour's granddaughter Catherine was given to the town of Catherine, in Schuyler County, New York.

Danville, which became the county-seat of Montour County in 1850, was named in honor of General Daniel Montgomery, who laid out the town in 1792.

Danville   Daniel was the son of General William Montgomery, of Scotch-Irish descent, who settled in that locality during the American Revolution. When only twenty-five years old Daniel Montgomery opened a store on the present site of Danville, and soon became the trusted merchant and factor of a wide circle of patrons, to whom he was familiarly and affectionately known as Dan Montgomery.

The little settlement that grew up about Dan Montgomery's store and his father's grist-mill was at first called Dan's-town, which later, by an easy transition, became Danville. During his lifetime Daniel Montgomery was the most prominent man in that part of the State. He was a member of the Legislature in 1800, and seven years later he was elected to Congress, declining a reëlection. In 1809 he became major-general of the northern division of the Pennsylvania militia. Danville was the county-seat of Columbia County from 1813 to 1845.[2]

---

[2] See page 162.

CHAPTER XI

COUNTIES BEARING INDIAN NAMES

THE Pennsylvania counties that bear Indian names are Allegheny, Lycoming, Erie, Venango, Tioga, Susquehanna, Lehigh, Juniata, Wyoming, and Lackawanna. These ten Indian names of counties have all been borrowed from the aboriginal names of natural features.

With a population of over a million people, Allegheny County, which was erected in 1788 out of Westmoreland and Washington, is, in respect to situation, resources, and industries, second in importance only to Philadelphia. For the possession of this favored region England, France, Virginia, Pennsylvania, and the aborigines have all stoutly contended. Fifty years after the contest was over, the following paragraph of admiring eulogy was penned:

"The richest gifts of nature seem to have been bestowed by Providence upon this region; and the art of man has been most diligent in adorning the works of nature and developing her latent sources of wealth. Magnificent bridges span the noble streams. Innumerable steamboats are constantly plying to and fro. Mines are opened in every hillside. Long shafts bring up salt water from the bowels of the earth. Durable stone turnpikes run in every direction. Magnificent public edifices, beautiful villas in the midst of fertile gardens and farms, extensive manufactories rolling out their black volumes of smoke, meet the eye of the observer in all parts of the county. There are probably few regions where the respective departments of agriculture, commerce, and manufactures are so well balanced, and where each finds its own appropriate facilities to such an equal degree as in Allegheny County." [1]

Seventy-five years of growth, development, and internal improvement have followed since this word picture of the Pittsburgh region was drawn. What would Céloron de Bienville, the Marquis Duquesne, George Washington, John Forbes, Henry Bouquet, Arthur St. Clair, or Anthony Wayne now think or say of the "forks of the Monongahela," if they could be but transported thither?

Allegheny County was probably named for the Allegheny River. The original meaning of Allegheny is not known with certainty. The name has been a **Allegheny** battleground for the Indian etymologists; **County** no less than six different explanations are current. Two of these are embodied in the following quotation from Isaac Taylor: "The old etymology explains the word as 'the endless or boundless mountains,' but probably both the Allegheny hills and the Alleghewi tribe derive their name from the river, the word *oolik-hanne* meaning 'the best river' in the dialect of the Delawares." [2] If a choice had to be made between these two etymologies, one might be disposed to favor the older etymology, which derives the name from the Delaware *Eleuwi-guneu*, meaning "endless," because it seems applicable to the mountains as well as to the river.

Another explanation has been given by some Canadian Delawares: "The Allegheny mountains were called by us *Al-lick-e-wa-ny*, 'he is leaving us and may never return.' Reference is made, I suppose, to departing hunters or

---

[1] Day's *Historical Collections of Pennsylvania* (1843), p. 64.
[2] *Names and their Histories*, p. 43.

warriors, who were about to enter the passes of those rugged mountains."[3]

In an article published in the Western Pennsylvania Historical Society Magazine for April, 1925, James Mc-Kirdy of Pittsburgh, after making a discriminating study of the numerous alleged meanings and origins of the name Allegheny and reviewing the evidence for and against their acceptance, concludes that the ultimate source of this name is the tribal name Allegewi, which he identifies with Talligewi, "people of the cave country," and that Allegheny signifies "river of the cave people."

There is an Alleghany County in North Carolina and Virginia, and an Allegany County in Maryland and New York.

On February 17, 1754, shortly after Washington had performed his mission to the French at Fort Le Bœuf, Captain William Trent, with about forty soldiers, began to build, at the confluence of the Monongahela and Allegheny Rivers, a stockade enclosure which was called Fort Trent. Exactly two months later Captain Contrecœur, with about a thousand French and Indians, after capturing this unfinished fortification, enlarged and completed it, naming it Fort Duquesne in honor of the Marquis Duquesne de Menneville, then governor of New France. In the same summer Washington made an unsuccessful attempt to capture Fort Duquesne; and a year later the famous expeditionary force under General Edward Braddock, which aimed to drive the French from the forks of the Monongahela, was almost annihilated. Fort Duquesne was finally captured in 1758 by an army of more than seven thousand colonial soldiers under General John Forbes and his two capable assistants, Colonels

---

[3] *Transactions of the Buffalo Historical Society* for 1885.

Henry Bouquet and George Washington. After his victory General Forbes at once determined to erect a new stockade fort near the old site.

On November 26, 1758, General Forbes, in reporting the success of his expedition to Lieutenant-Governor William Denny, dated his letter from Fort **Pittsburgh** Duquesne, but added the words, "or now Pitts-Bourg." This seems to be the first mention of Pittsburgh on record. Even in the early days the name Pittsburgh was always more commonly used than Fort Pitt, a name that was first applied by General John Stanwix to the enlarged fort begun in 1759. In 1760 a settlement commenced to grow up around the fort, and in 1761 there were about a hundred houses. Three years later a second town was laid out by Colonel James Campbell. In 1769 the Penns set aside the "Manor of Pittsburgh," containing 5,700 acres, from which they began to sell off building lots in 1784. The placing of these building lots on the market just at the close of the Revolution gave a great and sudden impetus to the growth of Pittsburgh.

The name of Pittsburgh was given to Fort Duquesne in honor of Sir William Pitt, afterwards the first Earl of Chatham. Pitt was then a member of the English Cabinet, and though the Duke of Newcastle was nominally the Premier, Pitt was everywhere recognized as the actual head of the government. His brilliant and masterful foreign policy and his vigorous prosecution of the war resulted in France's loss of her American possessions; and it was therefore strikingly appropriate that the name of the "great Commoner," who was absolute ruler of Britain, should be given to one of the supremely important places for which the rival nations had been contending. The memory of the great Pitt is also cherished because he valiantly championed the cause of the oppressed colonies before the outbreak of the Revolutionary War. The surname Pitt means "the dweller at the pit or well."

The city of Allegheny, which was consolidated with Pittsburgh in 1907, was named for Allegheny County.

Allegheny The town of Allegheny, which was planned and designated as the county-seat, owes its existence to an act of the Legislature in 1788, reserving a tract of three thousand acres opposite the town of Pittsburgh, on the west bank of the Allegheny River, in order that lots from this "reserved tract" might later be sold to raise funds for the payment of the claims of the Pennsylvania soldiers who had served in the Revolutionary army. In 1789 a considerable part of this tract was divided and sold as building lots, on which "Allegheny-town" began to grow up; and the remainder was organized as Reserve Township. The act of Legislature designating the "town of Allegheny" as the seat of justice was, however, so vigorously opposed that a supplementary bill was passed, according to which, in 1791, Pittsburgh became the county-seat.

When Lycoming County was formed in 1795, it was as large as Connecticut and New Jersey combined, with an

Lycoming County area of about 12,000 square miles. Four different names were proposed for the new county,—Jefferson,⁴ Lycoming, Muncy, and Susquehanna. After much debate the Legislature decided to call the great northwestern county Lycoming, after the Lycoming Creek, which had for so many years separated the settled part of Northumberland County from the disputed Indian lands. From the

---

⁴ Nine years later a new county named Jefferson was formed from Lycoming. See page 75.

original area of Lycoming County have since been organized, in whole or in part, no less than seventeen counties. *Lycaumick* and *Lycomin* are earlier spellings of the name. Lycoming is corrupted from a Delaware Indian word meaning "sandy or gravelly creek."

The origin of the name of Williamsport, the county-seat of Lycoming County, has been the subject of considerable controversy. There are several **Williams-** claimants for the honor, and each claimant **port** has his partisans. The first of these is Judge William Hepburn, member of the Senate from Northumberland County, who was largely instrumental in securing the formation of Lycoming County and in determining the location of the county-seat. A history of 1876 attributes to General Samuel Stewart, the first sheriff of the county, the statement that the early settlers wished the place to be called Hepburn's Port in honor of Senator William Hepburn; but to this name he is said to have objected, suggesting as a substitute William's Port, which was finally agreed upon, and from which there has been a gradual transition to Williamsport. This is the common traditional explanation of the name; yet it happens that Michael Ross, who laid out the town in 1795 on his tract of one hundred acres, had a son William, whom he greatly loved, and for whose future he cherished the fondest hopes. Michael Ross was virtually the founder of Williamport; and at least one witness quotes him as saying that the town was named for his son.

But might not a name like William's Port have existed before any town was planned or thought of? Both the foregoing explanations are plausible enough, and either might be considered valid if it were not for an earlier claimant. A few years ago the librarian of Williamsport, O. R. Howard Thomson, published in the Williamsport *Sun* an article entitled "The Origin of the Name of Williamsport," in which he carefully reviewed all the evidence for and against the several claimants, and came to the conclusion that Williamsport was probably not named in honor either of Judge William Hepburn or of its founder's son, William Ross, but that it perpetuates the given name of William Russell, a humble boatman, who, long before the town was laid out, discovered and used a *port,* or landing place, near the site of the Philadelphia and Reading Railroad station. In support of this last explanation, Judge C. D. Eldred, a trustworthy local historian, in an article published in 1890, says:

"Among these hardy pioneers were a boat-load who landed between the mouths of the Loyalsock and Lycoming Creeks, near the present depot of the Reading Railroad. The harbor was found to be excellent because of the deep water and the low, sloping bank, which made ingress and regress easy. It was therefore called by those who landed there William's Port in honor of William Russell, the boatman. Other boats bringing recruits and supplies to the new colony were directed to land at William's Port, on the river, and in a few years the settlement was everywhere known as that of William's Port. Some ten or fifteen years later, when Michael Ross, a surveyor, had purchased a tract on the river, and proceeded to divide it into town-lots, streets, and alleys, he adopted the then well-known designation, which from usage had run the two words into one, and produced the euphonious name of Williamsport. All the old inhabitants of sixty years ago concurred in stating the facts as I have given them, respecting the origin of the name."

The large borough of South Williamsport, incorporated in 1886, was so called because of its situation across the river south of the city. This town long endured the name of Rocktown, because it presented a very rocky appearance before it had been smoothed out and improved.

Erie and Venango were two of the eight new counties created on March 12, 1800. Erie County was named for **Erie County** the great lake that forms its northwestern boundary. The original northern boundary of the State ran due west, and Pennsylvania had only about four miles of frontage on Lake Erie. The "Erie triangle" was disputed territory, the contending claimants being New York, Massachusetts, and Connecticut. Just eight years before Erie County came into existence, the United States, apparently acting on the assumption that none of the claimants had a sound title to the "Erie triangle," sold it to Pennsylvania for $150,000. By this purchase the State secured fifty miles of lake shore, and 202,187 acres of land.

The word Erie, according to the French, means *chat sauvage*, or "wild cat," which was their name for the raccoon. The earliest reference to this name is in a French map of 1651, on which Lake Erie is styled Lac du Chat, "Lake of the Cat." Charlevoix said of Lake Erie: "The name it bears is that of an Indian nation of the Huron language, which was formerly seated on its banks, and which has been entirely destroyed by the Iroquois. Erie in that language signifies 'cat,' and in some accounts this nation is called the Cat Nation. This name probably comes from the large number of these animals found in this country." Some have thought that the name was descriptive of the character of the tribe; others suppose, apparently with more reason, that the *chat sauvage*, or raccoon, was the tribal totem.

The Eries are said to have been utterly annihilated by

the Iroquois in 1654. It is more reasonable to suppose that the Eries ceased to exist as a distinct tribe,—that some were captured and others dispersed, and that those who thus escaped destruction joined themselves to other tribes. New York and Ohio have also named counties for Lake Erie.

About 1749 the French built Fort de la Presqu'isle where the city of Erie now stands. This was one of a chain of French forts extending from Quebec to **Erie** New Orleans. The fort at Erie served as a depot of supplies for all the other French forts to the south, particularly for those on the Ohio. In 1753-4 the French also constructed a portage road fourteen miles in length from Fort Presqu'isle to Fort Le Boeuf (now Waterford), the head of navigation on the Ohio River. This road afterward became known as the Old French Road. The building of this chain of forts and this portage road fired Great Britain with the determination to spare no means to dispossess the French of the Ohio Valley.

In 1795 the Legislature, ''in order to facilitate and promote the progress of settlements within the Commonwealth and to afford additional security to the frontiers by the establishment of towns,'' authorized the laying out of four towns, one at Presqu'isle, one at Fort Le Boeuf, one at the mouth of French Creek, and one at the mouth of the Conewango; and Andrew Ellicott and General William Irvine were commissioned to survey and plot the town sites. Thus Erie, Waterford, Franklin, and Warren all began their existence in the same year. Five years later the act of Legislature that formed Erie County designated Erie as the seat of justice. In 1805, when the little town on the lake had about a hundred houses, it was incorporated as a borough. During the decade from 1910 to 1920 the city of Erie nearly doubled its population.

Venango County

Venango County took its name from the Venango River, which was the name the French used for the stream that has since been more generally called French Creek. The old Indian town of Venango stood at the mouth of this stream.

At first the name was spelled Weningo, Wenango, and Vinango. The present spelling first occurs in Washington's Journal. Venango is said to be a corruption of the Indian word *innungah*, "which had some reference to a rude figure carved upon a tree, which the Senecas found here when they first came to this region."[5] Gannett says that *innungah* means "a tract of level, fruitful ground." Dr. George P. Donehoo is quoted as saying that Venango is derived from the Indian word *onenge,* meaning "a mink." The present writer agrees with Charles A. Hanna that Venango is merely a variant of Chenango or Shenango, which means "bull thistles." The name was popular in the western part of the State and is borne by townships in Butler and Crawford Counties, and also by the borough of Venango in the latter county.

About 1757 the French completed a fort at the Indian town of Venango, and called it Fort Machault in honor of Jean Baptiste Machault, who, in 1745, was Comptroller of Finance for France. Fort Machault, in 1759, was surrendered to the English, who chose a new site and erected Fort Venango. In 1787 Captain Jonathan Hart, with a company of United States soldiers, was sent up the river to erect a new fort. He chose a third site and built Fort Franklin, which was named for Benjamin Franklin, then serving as governor under the title of

---

[5] Day's *Historical Collections of Pennsylvania,* p. 636.

President of the Supreme Executive Council. Nine years later a second Fort Franklin—long known as "the old Garrison"—was erected on a new and better site.

The town of Franklin, which the State commissioners laid out for the county town in 1795 on a tract of one
Franklin thousand acres belonging to the State, took its name from Fort Franklin. The new town site was attractively situated on level, sandy ground in a pleasant, sheltered valley, surrounded by lofty hills; and yet, five years later, there were only five families living ·in Franklin. Venango County was annexed to Crawford County for judicial purposes until 1805, when Franklin actually became the county-seat.

In 1804 Tioga Township, which had been organized in 1797 as a part of Lycoming County, became the new county of Tioga. Both the township, and the
Tioga county took their name from the Tioga River,
County which flows north into New York and unites with the Cohocton to form the Chemung River. Sweeping about in a semicircle, the Chemung joins the North Branch of the Susquehanna at "old Tioga Point," which is now called Athens.

A few of the earlier forms of Tioga are Diahoga, Diago, Tayego, and Teogo. Several different explanations of this name have been given. There seems now to be little doubt that the word signifies "the forks of a stream," or "the place where two rivers meet"; that is, the ground lying between them. Heckewelder defined the word Tiaoga as meaning "gateway," explaining that in passing from the Delaware country on the south to the Iroquois country on the north the traveler entered this region as through a gate. This definition, which has long met with general acceptance, is characterized by

9

Doctor Beauchamp as "very erroneous."[6]   The Tioga River has given its name to the little borough of Tioga. New York also has a county named for the Tioga River.

Wellsboro, the county town of Tioga County, was founded by Benjamin Wistar Morris, a Philadelphia Quaker, who had met with financial reverses, **Wellsboro** and who hoped to recover his fortune by becoming the agent and manager of the Pine Creek Land Company, which owned nearly 75,000 acres in Tioga County. In 1799, when past middle life, Mr. Morris settled in this wilderness region with his wife and two children. Seven years later he laid out the town of Wellsborough, which he is said to have named for his wife, whose maiden name was Mary Hill Wells. Mrs. Morris had two brothers who, before the town was christened, had become large landowners and prominent men in the new settlement,—Gideon Wells and William Hill Wells, who was twice United States Senator from Delaware. In view of this fact, perhaps it would be only fair to say that the place was named in honor of the Wells family.

In 1806 Mrs. Morris and the Wells brothers were influential in securing the location of the seat of justice at Wellsboro, as the place has since been generally called. Mr. Morris laid out his town on the plan of early Philadelphia, generously donating to the commissioners of the new county one half of the tract of one hundred and fifty acres set apart for the original village.

Susquehanna County, which was separated from Luzerne in 1810, owes its name to the fact that within its territory the Susquehanna River first enters the State. Heckewelder's explanation of this name is the one that has generally been accepted: "The word Susquehanna, properly Sisquehanne, from *sisku,* 'mud,' and *hanne,* a 'river,' was probably, at an early date in the settlement of this country, overheard by someone while the Indians

Susquehanna County were remarking, at the time of a flood or freshet, '*Juh! Sisquehanne,*'—which is 'How muddy the river is!' " Thus Susquehanna is interpreted as meaning "muddy river." Another interpretation of Susquehanna is that it means "the long, crooked river," or to phrase it a little more poetically, "the river of the winding shore." The most recent explanation has been given by James McKirdy, who believes that Susquehanna is derived from the Delaware Indian word *saskwihanang,* signifying "the straight river," or, more accurately, "the place of the straight river." Susquehanna borough is named for the county and the river.

Montrose, the county town of Susquehanna County, owes its name to Dr. Robert H. Rose, who came originally

Montrose from Chester County, bought about 100,000 acres of land in this region, and was one of the most able and persistent supporters of the Pennsylvania title to this disputed territory. "There was not a public improvement in which he did not have a prominent part as originator or promoter." About the year 1800 the first settlement in what is now Montrose was made by Captain Bartlett Hinds, who came hither with his family from Southampton, Long Island. For the next decade or more the place was known as Hinds' Settlement. In 1812, when the present town was laid out, Doctor Rose fashioned a name for it by combining the French word *mont* with his family name *Rose.* He was a gentleman of education and literary taste, and in giving the new town the name of Montrose he doubtless also had in mind the old Scottish town famous in history and in legend. Doctor Rose and his friends offered such

favorable terms and showed such open-handed hospitality to the commissioners appointed to locate the
county-seat that the prize was easily won away from
Brooklyn, the chief competitor.[7]

Lehigh County, organized in 1812, took its name from
the Lehigh River, which separates it from Northampton,
its mother county. The explanation that
Lehigh Heckewelder gives of this interesting name is
County the one generally accepted. He informs us
that the Delawares called this river *Lechauwekink*, "where there are forks," because, at the point
where their main trail or thoroughfare from the lower
parts of the Delaware Indian country crossed the river,
numerous trails forked off in various directions to the
north and the west. The Indian name Lechauwekink
was shortened by the early German settlers into *Lecha*,
a name still used by their descendants. The form finally
adopted by the English-speaking inhabitants was *Lehigh*.
The name in its present form is unfortunately a corruption or an abbreviation of the original Indian name and
conveys no special meaning.

About 1735 William Allen, who served as chief justice
of Pennsylvania from 1750 to 1774, received from the
Penns a grant of three thousand acres of
Allentown land, which, in 1748, formed part of the
newly organized township of Allen in
Northampton County, and which included the present
site of Allentown. Chief Justice Allen was a son-in-law
of Andrew Hamilton, deputy governor of Pennsylvania
from 1701 to 1703. His daughter, Anne Allen, was married to John Penn, grandson of William Penn. William
Allen laid out a town site on his land, calling it Northampton, doubtless because it was in Northampton County.

---

[7] See Stocker's *Centennial History of Susquehanna County*, p. 269.

Under date of 1762 there is documentary reference to "the new town of Northampton."

Prior to the Revolutionary period the place grew very slowly. On the death of William Allen, his son James, a resident of Philadelphia, became owner of the town site. In 1782 James Allen bequeathed the property to his five children, who changed the name from Northampton to Allentown in honor of their grandfather, Chief Justice William Allen. The citizens of the town, however, seemed reluctant to give up the name of Northampton, possibly because the place then aspired to become the seat of justice for Northampton County. When the new county of Lehigh was created, Allentown, on being chosen as the county-seat, celebrated its new dignity by becoming incorporated under its old name of Northampton. This name it retained until 1838, when an act of Legislature again gave it the name of Allentown, which it has borne ever since. The Irish surname Allen signifies "bright, fair, handsome."

The borough of South Allentown, incorporated in 1909, owes its name to its geographical position with respect to Allentown.

Juniata County, which was separated from Mifflin in 1831, was named for the beautiful Juniata River, which flows through it from the west on its way to **Juniata** the Susquehanna. The old song entitled "The **County** Blue Juniata" has made the name of this river famous. Juniata is an Iroquois word, and there can be little doubt that it is a variant of the more common form Oneida. In various documents written before 1765 the name Juniata was spelled in more than twenty different ways. One of these forms was Choniata. The initial gutteral sound is the only thing that really differentiates this form from Oneida, when the latter is divided, as it should be, into four syllables. A. L. Guss declares that an educated Wyandot, who spoke a dialect of the Iroquois tongue, is very positive in his assertion that Juniata means "standing-stone people," or "the people of the standing rock." [8] This is the usual explanation of the name of the Oneidas, who were in the habit of setting up in each of their villages a standing stone as a national or tribal emblem. [9]

The borough of Juniata, in Blair County, which stands near the headwaters of the Juniata River, takes its name from this stream.

Mifflintown When Mifflin County came into existence, "John Harris's plantation," which afterwards became Mifflintown, competed with the Lewistown settlement for the distinction of being the county-seat. When the latter place was finally chosen, the people living in the southeastern half of what was then Mifflin County were bitterly disappointed. They felt aggrieved because, after the prize had been fairly awarded to them, it had been taken back; and they almost immediately started an agitation for the erection of a new county. Nothing daunted by defeat and disappointment, John Harris laid out his new town in 1791, and even followed out his original intention of calling it Mifflin in honor of Thomas Mifflin, who was then governor.

The agitation in favor of a new county did not meet with success until 1831, when Mifflin, or Mifflin-town, as it was variously called, became the county-seat of Juniata County. Not till many years later did the form Mifflintown come into general use; and since then the name of Mifflin has been given to another post-office in

---

[8] *History of the Susquehanna and Juniata Valleys*, vol. I, p. 33.

[9] See Huntingdon, pages 114, 115.

Juniata County. It is not unfair to say that Juniata County owes its existence to the fact that "John Harris's Settlement" was, from the beginning, determined to become a county-seat.

One of the "seventeen original townships" in the Connecticut county of Westmoreland, which was wholly within the state of Pennsylvania, was **Wyoming County** Putnam Township, so called in honor of General Israel Putnam, the Connecticut hero in the American Revolution. In 1842, when the people of this region, who were for the most part descendants of the early Connecticut settlers, petitioned the Legislature to create a new county out of Luzerne, they requested that it might be called Putnam County, for the old township of Putnam and in honor of their beloved hero; but the bitterness engendered by the "Pennamite war" still lingered, and it was apparently too early for Pennsylvania to perform a gracious act by complying with what now seems a reasonable request. In the Legislature the member from Luzerne County moved that the name of Wyoming be substituted for Putnam, and thus the new county was named Wyoming.

Originally the name Wyoming, or Wyoming Valley, had been used to designate all the territory which the Susquehanna and the Delaware Companies of Connecticut had bought of the Iroquois Indians in 1754, and which is now included in the counties of Luzerne, Lackawanna, Wyoming, Susquehanna, and Wayne. To take the name of Wyoming County from the Wyoming Valley was not inappropriate, because the county forms the northern opening of the exquisitely beautiful valley of Wyoming, famous in history, legend, and literature.

According to Heckewelder the Delawares called the

North Branch of the Susquehanna *M'chewami-sipu,* "the river of extensive flats"; and they named the valley *M'chwewormink,* "extensive plains or meadows." Neither the Moravian missionaries nor the Connecticut Yankees could be expected to pronounce or retain the first syllable of this name. The former called the region Wayomik, and the latter Waioming, which subsequently assumed the present form of Wyoming.

The borough of Wyoming, in Luzerne County, and counties in New York and Virginia, and one of the states of the great Northwest have all been named for the Wyoming valley.

In 1786, eleven years after its organization, the name of Putnam Township was changed to Tunkhannock Township, and about four years later a **Tunkhannock** settlement was begun where Tunkhannock borough now stands. Half a century after the town was started, Tunkhannock was incorporated as a borough, and in 1842 it became the seat of justice of the new county of Wyoming. Neither the county nor the county town was destined to bear the name of Putnam.

The township and the village of Tunkhannock were named for the Tunkhannock Creek. This name is usually explained as being a corruption of *Tank-hanne,* "a small stream." The earliest form of the name was *Tenkghanacke,* which Doctor Beauchamp[10] very plausibly identifies with Tagh-ka-nick, an Indian name in New York, and with Taconic in Massachusetts and Connecticut. Tenkghanacke, Taghkanick, and Taconic are all apparently the same Algonquin word dressed up in different forms. The common interpretation of this name is "forest, or wilderness." In all likelihood this was the

---

10 *Aboriginal Place Names of New York,* pp. 49 and 262.

original meaning of Tunkhannock. Zeisberger says that it means "full of timber."

Lackawanna County

Lackawanna County is the youngest county in Pennsylvania, having been established on August 13, 1878. It was named for the Lackawanna River and valley. Lackawannock seems to have been the form at first generally used. The Delaware Indian name from which Lackawanna is derived is *Lechauhanne,* and signifies "the stream that forks." Obviously the name is meant to designate the confluence of two rivers. The streams that thus come together are the Lackawanna River and the North Branch of the Susquehanna.

Scranton, which became the county-seat of Lackawanna County in 1878, has had eight different names.

Scranton

Here once stood the old Indian village of Capouse, so called for a chieftain of the Monseys, whose wigwams disappeared in 1771. After the Wyoming Massacre not a living soul was left upon the site of Scranton. Until 1798 the place was called Deep Hollow. For forty years thereafter it endured the name of Slocum Hollow, though the Slocums tried in vain to name it Unionville.

When the two brothers, George W. and Selden T. Scranton, came here from New Jersey in 1840, there was nothing but a village of five old weather-beaten houses. The Scrantons and their partners, William Henry, Sanford Grant, and Philip Mattes, being attracted by the abundance of iron ore and antbracite coal, organized the firm of Scrantons, Grant, and Company, and decided to build a forge here. After meeting frequent discouragements and overcoming many difficulties, they at last successfully solved the hard problem of how to manufacture iron with anthracite coal as a fuel.

Even then they were so far from a market for their iron that assured success did not come until the Delaware, Lackawanna, and Western Railroad was built.

In 1845 the Scrantons renamed the place Harrison, in honor of William Henry Harrison, ninth President of the United States. Their next name was Lackawanna Iron Works. Being in straits for funds, they negotiated a loan of $10,000 from their cousin, Joseph Hand Scranton, of Augusta, Georgia, who, in 1847, bought out Sanford Grant's interest and came north to help the new firm.

Joseph H. Scranton soon assumed command of the enterprise. He and his two cousins were the real founders of Scranton. The post-office of Scrantonia was established in April, 1850, and named in their honor. Less than a year later the name of the town and the post-office was changed to Scranton.

The great city which has grown up so rapidly is a fit monument to the enterprise, perseverance, and resourcefulness of the three men whose name it bears. The Scrantons were sixth in line of descent from the Puritan, John Scranton, who landed in Boston in 1637, and a little later founded the Connecticut plantation of Guilford, which he named for his native town of Guilford in England.

CHAPTER XII

COUNTIES NAMED FOR NATURAL FEATURES

BESIDES the ten counties bearing Indian names, nine other counties are named for natural features. The six counties of Delaware, Beaver, Clearfield, Schuylkill, Clarion, and Elk were named for streams. Centre County received its name because of its geographical location. Carbon was so called because it is one of the great anthracite counties. The name of Forest refers to the natural appearance and condition of this county before its settlement.

In 1786, when Chester ceased to be the county town of Chester County, the people in the eastern end immediately started a movement for the establishment **Chester** of a new county. Chester, it seems, was not happy unless it could be a county-seat. In 1789 the agitation resulted in the formation of the little county of Delaware, and old Chester [1] was once more restored to its accustomed dignity as a county town.

Delaware County was named directly for the Delaware River, which forms its southeastern boundary. This important stream, which the Dutch called the **Delaware** Zuydt (or South) River to distinguish it **County** from the North River, was named in honor of Thomas West, twelfth Baron de la Warr, governor and first captain-general of Virginia, who spent his time, his energies, and his money in establishing the Virginia colony. Lord de la Warr "passed the capes" of the Delaware in 1610. In that year Captain James

---

[1] See Chester, page 38.

139

Argall sailed into the bay and named it and the river in honor of Thomas West, Lord de la Warr,[2] "the lord of the Weir."[3]

When New Amsterdam became New York in 1664, the Zuydt River became generally known as the Delaware. The Lenni-Lennape[4] Indians, dwelling upon the banks and tributaries of this river, were thenceforth called the Delawares. Lord Delaware's name has also been bestowed upon the state of Delaware and upon counties in New York, Ohio, Indiana, and Iowa.

About twenty-five years after the organization of Delaware County, many of the inhabitants began to clamor for a new county-seat with a more central location. In 1847, after three decades of agitation, the much-mooted question was submitted to the decision of a popular vote, which resulted in a victory for those who demanded a change in the seat of justice. The next year the Legislature approved of the removal of the county-seat to its present location at Media.

Media The county Poor Farm was the site selected for the new county town. An additional tract of forty-eight acres, adjoining the Poor Farm, was purchased. When the new county buildings were being erected in 1850, only twelve houses stood on the present site of Media. The first name suggested for the town was Providence, because it was in Providence Township. The name Media, which was proposed by Minshall Painter, was given to the village because of its central location, the Latin adjective *medius, media,* meaning "central": the very name of the county town was intended to be a memorial of the victory of those who had

---

[2] Pennypacker's *Pennsylvania—The Keystone*, p. 19.

[3] *War* and *wer* were early English forms of the word now spelled *weir*.

[4] See Lenape, page 284.

so persistently contended for a more central location.

The name of Media was not adopted without some dissent. One opponent, who favored "Pennrith," the Welsh word for "red hill," thus expressed his disapproval: "To say that it was called after the ancient country of Media would place us in a purely ridiculous position. To derive it from the Latin adjective, converting it into a noun as the name of a place, would give it, if it were etymologically defensible, an origin so feeble as to ally it very closely to contempt." To-day Media is no mean town, and no one thinks that it has a ridiculous name.

Centre County, which came into existence in 1800, was so named because of its situation in the very centre of **Centre County** the State. The counties of Mifflin, Huntingdon, Northumberland, and Lycoming contributed territory for the new county. Old "Centre Furnace," a place well known before 1800, formerly in Mifflin County, may have suggested the name.

Bellefonte, which was chosen by the Legislature as the county town, had been laid out five years before by James Harris and his father-in-law, Colonel James Dunlop. The older and larger village of Milesburg, because of its situation at the head of navigation on Bald Eagle Creek, was a strong competitor for the seat of justice. There is a tradition that the proprietors and partisans of Bellefonte, in their eagerness to secure the coveted prize, resorted to the trick of loading a flatboat with secondhand furniture, towing it up Spring Creek as far as Bellefonte, and hurrying a messenger to the state capital at Lancaster with an affidavit that the first boat of the season, loaded with freight, had arrived at Bellefonte. This information seemed to indicate that Bellefonte was actually at the head of the navigable waters, and probably helped to influence the doubtful vote in its favor.

Thus the people of Bellefonte very early demonstrated their political craftiness. Later the little Centre County capital, always politically active, furnished the State with three capable governors, Andrew Gregg Curtin, James Addams Beaver, and Daniel Hartman Hastings. Governor William Fisher Packer, who preceded Curtin, the "great war governor," was born in Howard Township, Centre County.

Bellefonte   The name Bellefonte, which is the French for "beautiful spring," was bestowed upon the town because of the unusually large spring that has ever since supplied the place with an abundance of pure water. According to a well authenticated tradition this name was suggested to Mr. and Mrs. James Harris by Charles Maurice, Duke of Talleyrand-Périgord, later Prince of Benevento, who was a political exile in the United States in 1794-5. In his published memoirs Talleyrand speaks of his travels in central Pennsylvania and of his visit to Colonel John Patton's country-seat at Centre Furnace, whither he had come with letters of introduction from George Washington. Mrs. Summerville, a granddaughter of James and Anne Harris, neither of whom knew any French, had often heard her grandmother speak of Talleyrand's visit to their home at "Willow Bank," and of the fact that he had suggested the name of Bellefonte.[5]

Beaver County   One month after Centre County was created, eight new counties were formed in the western part of the State by the Act of March 12, 1800. One of these was Beaver County, taken from Washington and Allegheny, and named for the Big Beaver River, or Creek, which was so called

---

[5] Information furnished by Mr. John P. Harris and former Judge Ellis L. Orvis of Bellefonte.

because of the great number of beavers once found on its banks and in its waters.

Beaver County, in its modern aspect, has been celebrated by no less a writer than Rudyard Kipling, who asks his reader to "imagine a rolling, wooded English landscape, with the softest of blue skies, dotted at three-mile intervals with fat little, quiet little villages, or aggressive little manufacturing towns." [6]

The Legislature designated "the town on the site of Fort McIntosh" as the county-seat of Beaver County.

Beaver This fort had been built in 1778 by General Lachlan McIntosh, and named for him. In 1791 Governor Mifflin approved an act of Legislature, which provided for the laying out of a town on public lands known as the "Beaver Reservation," situated near the mouth of the Beaver River, at or near where the old French fort stood. In 1792-3 Daniel Leet surveyed and laid out two hundred acres in town lots and one thousand acres in "out-lots" for Beaver-town, which took its name from Beaver County or the Beaver River. Ten years later this new town, which became the seat of justice in 1800, was incorporated under the name of Beaver.

Clearfield County, one of the six new counties formed by the Act of March 26, 1804, was, according to Morse's

Clearfield County *American Gazetteer* of 1810, "named from a stream running through the county into the western branch of the Susquehanna."

This stream, the Clearfield Creek, which is mentioned on Nicholas Scull's map of 1770, empties into the Susquehanna about a mile and a half east of Clearfield. The first recorded literary reference to the name of

_____
[6] *From Sea to Sea*, vol. II, p. 158 (extract from a letter written at Beaver).

Clearfield occurs in an entry that the Reverend John Ettwein made in his journal while he was removing Zeisberger's flock of 241 Christian Indians from Wyalusing to the region of the Beaver River in western Pennsylvania. Under date of July 14, 1772, Ettwein made this entry: "Reached Clearfield Creek, where the buffaloes formerly cleared large tracts of undergrowth, so as to give them the appearance of cleared fields. Hence the Indians called the creek 'Clearfield.' " Clearfield Township, in the adjoining county of Cambria, was also named for Clearfield Creek. Sherman Day, without discriminating between the creek and the county, says that the name Clearfield had its origin in the fact that "clear fields, or open patches of prairie, apparently the site of some ancient cornfields, were found in this vicinity."

The place chosen for the county-seat was the site of Chingleclamouch's Old Town, which, during the first half of the eighteenth century, was the most con-

Clearfield   siderable Indian town on the West Branch of the Susquehanna. Chingleclamouch (or Chinklacamoose, to use a later and commoner form), signifying "at the quiet hill," was the name of a famous Indian who once dwelt here. The latter part of his name still survives in that of Moose Creek, which flows into the Susquehanna near the northwestern boundary of the present borough of Clearfield. On the site of this old Indian town Abraham Witmer, in 1805, laid out the town of Clearfield and named it for the county, donating one building lot for the county court-house, one for a jail, one for a market-house, and three for an academy, besides giving his bond for the payment of $3,000, "one-half thereof to be applied for the use of an academy or public school in said town, and one-half for the purpose of erecting public buildings."

The founder of the town of Clearfield was the same Abraham Witmer who, in 1799, erected his own enduring monument in the beautiful stone bridge that still spans the Conestoga Creek at Lancaster.

Schuylkill County, formed in 1811 out of Berks and Northampton, was named for the Schuylkill River, which flows through its territory.   This name, **Schuylkill** which means "hidden stream," was given **County** to the river by the early Dutch explorers because they passed by its mouth at first without seeing it.

Orwigsburg, which was laid out and named by Peter Orwig in 1796, was the county town of Schuylkill County from 1811 until 1851, when the seat of **Orwigsburg** justice was removed to Pottsville, a site chosen by popular vote after about twenty years of agitation.

Pottsville, the present county-seat of Schuylkill County, was named for John Pott, whose grandfather came from Germany to America in 1734 in the **Pottsville** same ship that brought over the little colony of Schwenkfelders, though he was not a member of that sect.   John Pott came to this region about 1816 and bought a large tract of land.   In 1822 he kept the White Horse tavern, which was a stopping place for stages on the Sunbury road.   He also built a small charcoal furnace and a mill, and laid out a town, which he named Pottsville.   In 1824 there were only five scattered dwellings in Pottsville; in 1840 the population was 4,345. The rapid growth was due to the opening of anthracite coal mines.   Pottsville was recently incorporated as a city.

It should be added that Samuel Potts, son of John Potts, whose name is properly connected with the early history of Pottstown, in Montgomery County, and who was of English descent, also held large tracts of land in Schuylkill County at an early date, and that much of this land is said to have come into the possession of John Pott. Some have even maintained that the city now called Pottsville was named in honor of this English family long before John Pott laid out a town. There can be no doubt that John Potts, the founder of Pottstown, has often been confused with John Pott;[7] but it is a well established fact that John Pott, the grandson of Wilhelm Pott, the German, was the founder of Pottsville.[8]

Clarion County Clarion County, established in 1839, received its name from the Clarion River, which flows westward through this county into the Allegheny. Until 1817 this stream had been called Toby's Creek, and sometimes Stump Creek. In that year a survey was made for a state road extending from Bedford to Franklin and passing through the town of Indiana. The traditional explanation of the origin of the name of the Clarion River runs as follows:

The three viewers appointed to lay out the new state road encamped along Toby's Creek. As they lay in their tent in the evening, "they were struck by the clear sound of the distant ripples." The course of the stream was then lined by a dense forest of giant trees, which "condensed and reflected the murmur, giving it a silvery mellowness," which it no longer possesses since the timber has been cut down. One of the surveyors, Daniel Stanard, remarked that the sound of the river was like the notes of a distant clarion. "Why not call it the Clarion River?" asked his assistant, David Lawson.[9]

---

[7] See Pottstown, page 228; also Gannett's *Origin of Certain Place Names in the United States.*

[8] Information furnished by Mr. D. G. Lubold of Pottsville.

[9] Davis's *History of Clarion County,* p. 99.

The new name slowly but steadily gained in favor; the old pioneer names, Toby's Creek, dating from 1758, and Stump Creek, bestowed somewhat later, had nothing to commend them to a civilized community. In 1819, when the law known as the "Olean Road Act" was passed, the new name of the Clarion River received something like official sanction by being mentioned in the bill. Three years later another act of Legislature designated the stream as "Toby's Creek, otherwise called Clarion River." Thenceforth, while pioneers and lumbermen naturally showed their partiality for the old names, the constantly growing number of new settlers evinced a preference for the more poetic designation, which eventually won its way to general acceptance.

The commissioners appointed to select a site for the county-seat passed by such aspirants as Callensburg, Shippensville, and Strattonville, and chose a **Clarion** place that then had but a single habitation. The site they selected was centrally located on the Bellefonte and Meadville pike, about a mile east of the point where this road crossed the Clarion River. They decided that the county town, which John Sloan laid out and plotted in 1839, should also be called Clarion. The village, whose origin was purely political, grew so rapidly that within a year it had a population of eight hundred, and in 1841 it was incorporated as a borough.

Carbon County, formed from Northampton and Monroe in 1843 after twenty-seven years of agitation, received its name from the fact that it was known to be **Carbon** underlaid with rich deposits of anthracite coal, **County** which has formed its chief source of wealth. The pioneers in the Lehigh coal industry of Carbon County were Josiah White, Erskine Hazard, and George F. A. Hauto, who, in 1818, organized themselves into "The Lehigh Coal and Navigation Company," and two years later bought fifty-four acres of land where Mauch Chunk now stands. In 1824 this firm sent 9,541 tons of coal down the river. This was then thought to be an enormous quantity, but the next year, which marked the turning point in favor of the use of anthracite coal, more than 28,000 tons were marketed. The future of the Mauch Chunk region was assured.

But where could a town be built? The proprietors well knew that the narrow gorge or ravine opposite Bear Mountain was no suitable site for a growing town. They had tried in vain to buy land about a mile above, at the mouth of the Nesquehoning Creek, but the owner, believing that the land contained coal and that the company must inevitably accept his terms, asked a prohibitive price. The company was finally compelled to locate its town in the narrow ravine, where almost every available inch of building space is now occupied. Not until 1832 did it begin to sell any of its own small tract for building lots.

The town of Mauch Chunk, which became the county-seat of Carbon County, not without keen competition on

Mauch Chunk

the part of Lehighton, took its name from the curiously-shaped and imposing hill on the opposite side of the Lehigh River, called by the Indians *Machk Tschunk*, or "Bear Mountain." In 1824 the population was 734. In 1850, when Mauch Chunk was incorporated, the new town of East Mauch Chunk was laid out on the opposite bank of the Lehigh. It has since grown to be larger than the overcrowded parent town.

In 1843 Elk County was created out of Clearfield, Jefferson, and McKean. In all probability it received its name from Elk Creek, which flows into the Clarion River at Ridgway, though Sherman Day maintains that the county derived its name directly from Elk Mountain, in the southern part of the county. Though this mountain is also mentioned in Lippincott's *Gazetteer,* one can find no conclusive evidence of its existence. In the last analysis, of course, the origin of the name can be traced to the great herds of elks which once frequented these wilds. In 1832 Judge Geddes, in the report of a survey, noted that a ''few elks still remain'' in this region. As late as 1852 a drove of twelve or more elks were found near Ridgway by two hunters, who killed seven. In the early days the county contained several favorite wintering places for elks, one of which was in the neighborhood of Portland Mills.

Elk County

The commissioners appointed for the purpose of locating a county-seat selected Ridgway, the only other competitor being Saint Marys. In 1817 Jacob Ridgway, the famous Philadelphia merchant, who ranked second only to Stephen Girard in wealth and prominence, and was then one of the few American millionaires, bought 80,000 acres of land in McKean County and 40,000 acres in what later became Elk County. In 1833 his agents laid out on his land, in what is now Ridgway Township, a town which they called Ridgway in his honor. Jacob Ridgway died almost at the very time when the town that bears his name was chosen as the county-seat. There is no evidence to show that his son and heir, John Jacob Ridgway, who spent nearly all his life in Paris, had anything to do with the founding or the naming of the town. The family name Ridgway, according to Baring-Gould, was derived from an early English provincial word, *ridgeway,* commonly applied to the old Roman roads.

Ridgway

Forest County was created out of Jefferson on April 11, 1848, by a joint resolution of the two houses of the Legislature. No other county in the State has **Forest** been established in this way. In this instance **County** the joint resolution was a parliamentary safety device designed to prevent defeat. Cyrus Blood, born in New Hampshire in 1795, educated in Boston, principal of the Chambersburg Academy in 1818, and later head of the Hagerstown Academy and a professor in Dickinson College, migrated into this wilderness region with his family in 1833, bought a large tract of land, started the hamlet long known as Blood's Settlement, and became obsessed with the idea of establishing a new county. He was the pioneer settler and founder of Forest County. He chose the name Forest because the whole county was then one vast, unbroken, primeval forest. Wisconsin is the only other state that has a Forest County named for the forests within its territory.

Cyrus Blood was a surveyor and carefully laid out a town somewhat after the elaborate plan of Washington. This place he called Marion or Marion **Marienville** Centre, a name which was changed to Marionville when the hamlet of five or six houses became the county-seat of the little county of "old Forest." Marionville, or Marienville, as it is now called, was named for Cyrus Blood's eldest daughter Marion, and remained the seat of justice until 1866. It is now a village of about twelve hundred people. By an act of Legislature passed October 31, 1866, the territory of Forest County was nearly doubled by the annexation of the townships of Tionesta, Kingsley, Green, Hickory, and Harmony from the eastern end of Venango County, and the borough of Tionesta was selected to supersede Marienville as the county-seat.

The village of Tionesta, which was incorporated in 1850, took its name from the "Tionesta Creek," a designation first used in a map made about 1795 by **Tionesta** Ennion Williams, a surveyor. Tionesta is a modification of the Iroquois word *Tiyohweno-isto*, which signifies "it penetrates the island" (as an arrow penetrates an object).[10] The name refers to the way in which the swift current of the Tionesta rushes upon Hunter Island, which lies in the Allegheny River at the confluence of the two streams.

---

[10] Interpretation given by Messrs. James Mooney and J. N. B. Hewitt of the Bureau of American Ethnology.

CHAPTER XIII

COUNTIES NAMED FOR PROMINENT PENNSYL-VANIANS

FOUR counties—Bradford, Blair, Fulton, and Cameron—were named in honor of prominent citizens of Pennsylvania.

Very few Pennsylvanians know that their State ever contained a county named Ontario. On February 21, 1810, Ontario County was formed from Ly-**"Ontario** coming and Luzerne. The name first sug-**County"** gested for the new county was Morris, apparently in honor of Robert Morris, the financier of the American Revolution. The Legislature, however, chose Ontario, an Indian word borrowed from New York and signifying "beautiful lake."

On March 24, 1812, a new Legislature changed the name of Ontario County to Bradford in honor of Wil-liam Bradford of Philadelphia, the second **Bradford** attorney-general of the United States, whom **County** Washington, in January, 1794, appointed to succeed Edmund Randolph. William Brad-ford was born in Philadelphia in 1755, and was the son of Colonel William Bradford, printer and patriot, and great-grandson of William Bradford, the first printer in Philadelphia and New York, who early put to the test the freedom of the press in his keenly contested legal controversy with the Quaker magistrates who had ac-cused him of seditious libel.

Young William Bradford was graduated from Prince-ton College with distinction at the age of seventeen,

152

attained the rank of colonel in the Continental army at the age of twenty-two, and was appointed attorney-general of Pennsylvania at the age of twenty-five. In 1791, when he was not yet thirty-six years old, he was made one of the justices of the Supreme Court of the State. This position he resigned three years and a half later, to become Washington's attorney-general. He possessed marked literary ability, was an eloquent speaker, and was distinguished for his attractive and lovable personality. His brilliant career was cut short by death on August 23, 1795, when he was not yet forty years of age.

As attorney-general of Pennsylvania and as one of the three representatives appointed by the State to support its interests before the Congressional commission specially appointed to settle the long-standing controversy over disputed land titles between the Pennsylvania and the Connecticut claimants in the Wyoming region, William Bradford performed his difficult duties with calmness, fairness, and sound judgment; and it was in recognition of his services in bringing this bitter controversy to a peaceful and satisfactory conclusion that the Legislature thought it proper to honor him by giving his name to one of the counties formed from the disputed territory. The surname Bradford is derived from the English town of Bradford on the Avon, which means *"at the broad ford."*

Towanda, the county-seat of Bradford County, was laid out in 1812 by William Means, and was for some **Towanda** years variously styled Meansville and Williamston in honor of its founder. When the village was incorporated in 1828, it took the name Towanda from Towanda Township, one of the original divisions of Bradford County. This township was named for Towanda Creek, which empties into the

Susquehanna from the southwest. Towanda—or To-
wandee, as it was written a hundred years ago—is, according to Heckewelder, a corruption of Tawundeunk,
"where we bury the dead." Here the Nanticoke Indians
are said to have interred the bones of their dead. Doctor
Beauchamp says that Tonawanda, a somewhat similar
word, signifies "swift water."

In 1846 Blair County was formed from Huntingdon
and Bedford. 'It was named for the Honorable John
Blair, of Blair's Gap, and is the only county in
Blair   the State named for a purely local celebrity.
County   His father, Captain Thomas Blair, a native of
Scotland, was instrumental during the Revolutionary period in clearing the upper Juniata valley of
Indians and Tories. After the war Captain Blair settled
in Blair's Gap, built the old Blair homestead, which is
still standing, and became a man of considerable property and influence. Here John Blair was born and lived
all his life.

He was elected to the Legislature, where he showed
himself a warm friend of internal improvement. He was
president of the Hollidaysburg and Pittsburgh Turnpike
Company, which built the macadamized road through the
gap in 1820, and ten years later he was active in promoting the Pennsylvania Canal and the Portage Railroad, which carried the canal-boats across the mountains.
In his day he was known as one of the most prominent
and public-spirited citizens in central Pennsylvania.[1]
Blair Township, in Blair County, and the borough of
Blairsville, in Indiana County, were also named for him.
He died fourteen years before Blair County was created.

---

[1] Information concerning John Blair furnished by his great-granddaugh-
ter, Miss Susan Walker Hetherington of Dubuque, Iowa.

The Scotch surname Blair is the Gaelic equivalent of the English name Field.

Hollidaysburg, the county town of Blair County, is one of the oldest settlements in the central part of the State. **Hollidays-** It received its name from two cousins, **burg** Adam and William Holliday, who emigrated from the north of Ireland about 1750, settling first in Manor Township, Lancaster County, and later at Chambersburg. At the close of the French and Indian War, in true pioneer fashion, they loaded their families and their worldly goods upon pack horses and boldly pushed their way westward across the mountains. In 1768 they each took out a warrant for a thousand acres of land. Hollidaysburg now stands on what was Adam Holliday's tract.

As Adam drove the first stake into the ground, he is said to have remarked to William, ''Whoever is alive one hundred years hence will find a considerable town here.'' Hollidaysburg was laid out about 1790, and was incorporated in 1834,—fully fifteen years before either Altoona or Tyrone was thought of. According to Harrison, Holliday or Halliday was a ''name given to one born on a holy day.''

Fulton County was separated from Bedford in 1850. The petition presented to the Legislature proposed the **Fulton** name of Liberty for the new county. When **County** the bill to establish the county had been approved by the House, it was discovered that it could not pass the Senate unless at least two of its opponents could be prevailed upon to favor it. Senators William F. Packer of Lycoming County, and Charles Frailey of Schuylkill County, out of personal friendship for John Pott and Representative Samuel Robinson of Bedford County, both active in advocating

the passage of the bill, consented to vote for it, provided
that they might have the privilege of naming the new
county.   Senator Packer made a motion to amend the
act by substituting the name of Fulton for Liberty, and
this amendment was seconded by Senator Frailey.

Thus the new county was voted into existence, and
named in honor of Robert Fulton,[2] one of the most distinguished citizens of Pennsylvania, whose fame and
genuine service to humanity should not be minimized
because others before him had made more or less successful attempts to apply steam to navigation.   There
can be no doubt that Fulton's *Clermont,* rude and imperfect though it was, was the first successful modern
steamboat, and that Robert Fulton made navigation by
steam practicable.   In view of the fact that Fulton
County was settled almost wholly by Scotch-Irish, it
seems appropriate that it should bear the name of an illustrious Pennsylvanian of Scotch-Irish descent.   The
surname Fulton is variously explained as meaning "the
fowls' enclosure," or "Fula's estate," or as a contraction of Fullerton, "the fowler's place."

McConnellsburg, which became the county-seat of
Fulton County, was laid out in 1786 by Daniel McConnell,
McConnells-
burg
Sr., for whom it was named. Long before
he founded the village, Daniel McConnell
kept a tavern "in the Big Cove" for the
entertainment of wagoners and pack-
horse pioneers.   McConnellsburg became an important
stopping place for overland travelers on the great highway connecting eastern Pennsylvania with the more
recent settlements in the region of Pittsburgh.   The new
Lincoln Highway now runs through the town.   McCon-

---

[2] See Fulton House, page 263.

nellsburg was incorporated in 1814. The patronymic surname McConnell signifies "the son of conflict."

Cameron County, formed in 1860 out of parts of Clinton, Elk, McKean, and Potter, was named in honor of Simon Cameron, then United States Sena-
Cameron tor for Pennsylvania. Simon Cameron, of
County Lancaster County, began his career as printer and editor in Doylestown and Harrisburg, and later became wealthy as a banker and as a builder of railroads. Long the "Czar of Pennsylvania politics," he filled various important public offices. He was adjutant-general of Pennsylvania and served his State in the United States Senate for eighteen years. He was a prominent candidate for the presidential nomination at the Republican convention that selected Abraham Lincoln. He became Lincoln's first secretary of war, resigning the appointment in January, 1862, to become minister to Russia. The village of Cameron, in Cameron County, is also named for him. Cameron is a Scotch family name of personal characteristic, signifying in the Gaelic "the man with the crooked nose."

Emporium, which became the seat of justice for Cameron County in 1861, is the Latinized form of the Greek word for "market, or centre of
Emporium trade." For several years the place was called Shippen because it was located in Shippen Township, which was named for Edward Shippen, one of the early settlers, who came into this locality in 1810. The name Emporium, which was assumed by the county-seat at the time of its incorporation in 1864, is said to date back as far as 1785. In that year, according to tradition, an agent of the Holland Land Company, coming up the Driftwood branch of the Sinnemahoning Creek by boat, encamped with his com-

panions at its confluence with Portage Creek, now in the eastern end of the town. Here he shaved off the bark from the side of a large tree and carved thereon the word *Emporium* in prophetic anticipation of the future importance of the place.[3]

---

[3] J. Beers and Company's *History of the Counties of McKean, Elk, Cameron, and Potter,* p. 879.

CHAPTER XIV

THE OTHER COUNTY NAMES

SIX counties—Indiana, Cambria, Lebanon, Columbia, Union, and Clinton—received their names from miscellaneous sources that do not admit of convenient classification.

In 1803 Indiana County was formed from Westmoreland and Lycoming. Old Wheatfield Township in Westmoreland County—so called because its prairie-like stretches of cleared land were readily available for wheat-fields—was created as early as 1779 and contributed sixteen of the twenty-three townships now in Indiana County. It comprised all the early Scotch-Irish settlements, including Fergus Moorehead's famous pioneer house, which was built about 1778, several miles from the present town of Indiana.

Indiana County is commonly said to have derived its name "from its first denizens." This explanation is not very enlightening. It is a little more accurate **Indiana** and definite to point out that in all likelihood **County** the name of the county was suggested by that of the Territory of Indiana, which Congress formed from the Northwestern Territory on May 7, 1800, almost three years before the Pennsylvania county was established, and which received its name "from one of the old ante-Revolutionary land companies."[1] Captain William Trent was one of the organizers of the Indiana Land Company, and it was he who gave the name of

---

[1] Harper's *Encyclopedia of United States History*, vol. V, p. 29.

Indiana to the territory comprised in this grant, which appears as "Indiana" in Hutchins's map of 1778.

As to the ultimate source of the name, Dr. Isaac Taylor points out that "it is one of the curiosities of the nomenclature that the name of one of the United States should have to be explained by the Greek corruption of the Persian form of a Sanskrit word meaning a river." India received its name from the Indus River, and the American Indians were so called because Columbus thought that he had reached India.

Indiana In 1805 the three commissioners, Charles Campbell, Randall Laughlin, and John Wilson, chose the present site of Indiana for the seat of justice, formally accepting the 250 acres which George Clymer of Philadelphia, one of the Pennsylvania signers of the Declaration of Independence, had donated for that purpose. In the same year the county town was laid out and christened Indiana, for Indiana County. The town has had a wholesome growth from the beginning and was incorporated as a borough as early as 1816.

Cambria County Cambria, nicknamed "the mountain county," occupying the plateau between Laurel Hill and the summit of the Allegheny Mountains, was formed in 1804 out of the three townships of Frankstown,[2] in Bedford County, organized in 1775 and named for Frank Stevens, a well-known Indian trader; of Conemaugh, in Somerset County, established in 1801 and christened for the Conemaugh River;[3] and of Cambria, in Somerset County, created in 1798 and settled almost entirely by Welsh immigrants. Cambria Township has given its name to the county. Cambria or Cumbria, which is etymologically akin to

[2] See Frankstown, page 309.
[3] See East Conemaugh, page 189.

Cumberland, is an ancient poetic name for Wales, "the land of the Cymry, or Cumbri," a word usually interpreted as meaning "compatriots."

An act of Legislature passed in 1805 designated Ebensburg, in Cambria Township, as the county-seat of Cambria County. A Welsh settlement was
Ebensburg made here about 1796; and a little later a town was laid out by a minister and leader of the Welsh immigrants, the Reverend Rees Lloyd, and named Ebensburg in honor of his eldest son Eben, who died in childhood.[4] Ebensburg became a borough in 1825.

Lebanon County, formed out of Dauphin and Lancaster in February, 1813, after two decades of agitation, is one of two Pennsylvania counties that have
Lebanon a Biblical name.[5] Most of its territory was
County comprised in old Lebanon Township, organized in 1729 as one of the seventeen original townships of Lancaster County. The new county took its name from this township.

Just why the name Lebanon was given to the township which eventually became Lebanon County is not positively known. It is reasonable to suppose, however, that the abundance of cedars which clothed the ridge of hills lying between Lancaster and Lebanon Counties may have suggested the "cedars of Lebanon" to the pious German settlers in this region. The Hebrew word *Lebanon,* "white mountain," probably refers to the white chalk cliffs or to the snow on the mountains of Palestine.

At the time of the erection of the new county, Lebanon, which was and still is the chief town, became the seat of justice. About 1750 George Steitz laid out the village of Lebanon, which long bore the nickname of Steitztown

---

[4] Information given by Mr. John M. McCormick of Johnstown.
[5] See Philadelphia, pages 30, 31.

II

in honor of its founder.   The city of Lebanon, like the
county, took its name directly from old
Lebanon   Lebanon Township.   The two old settlements
of Lebanon and North Lebanon gradually
grew together and were consolidated in 1869.

Columbia County was separated from Northumberland
in March, 1813.   Fifteen years before, on the evening of
April 25, 1798, Joseph Hopkinson's song,
Columbia   *Hail Columbia,* was sung for the first time
County   in the Chestnut Street Theater, Philadelphia,
by the popular young actor, Gilbert Fox.
This song at once attained wide currency as a patriotic
protest against the undiplomatic and highly repre-
hensible conduct of Citizen Adet, the French minister,
who had had the hardihood to issue an address to the
citizens of the United States designed to incite them
against their own government.   As a result, the name
Columbia became immensely popular as a poetic designation for America.   Though this name had become generally current before *Hail Columbia* was written, there can
be no doubt that the famous song helped to popularize
it; and this great increase in its popularity may partly
explain the fact that seven counties and twenty-three
towns in the United States are now called Columbia.[6]

This name is derived from Columbus, the Latinized
form of Columbo, the Italian name of the great explorer,
believed to have had its origin, through the Irish monks
in northern Italy, from St. Columba, "the dove."

Danville,[7] named for its founder, General Daniel Montgomery, became the first county-seat of Columbia County.
From the beginning, the people in the eastern end were
very much dissatisfied with its selection, justly complain-

[6] See Columbia, page 210.
[7] See Danville, page 118.

ing that it was as great a hardship for them to journey to Danville on the western boundary in order to transact public business as it had been to go all the **Danville** way to Sunbury before the new county was created. A movement was therefore set on foot to make Bloomsburg the county town. Finally, after much agitation, the Legislature in 1845 consented to submit the question to a popular vote; and in October of that year the citizens of the county decided that the seat of justice should be removed to Bloomsburg.

Bloomsburg, the present county-seat, was laid out in 1802 by Ludwig Eyer, and was long called Eyersburg and Eyertown in his honor. When the **Bloomsburg** village was large enough to become a post-office, the townsfolk, though they liked the benevolent old German who had founded the village, protested against its being called Eyertown. It was located in Bloom Township, and when someone suggested that for this reason it be called Bloomsburg, the name instantly met with general approval. Bloom Township had been organized as part of Northumberland County in 1797 and named in honor of Samuel Bloom, who was then one of the County Commissioners. In 1870 both Bloomsburg and Bloom Township were together organized as "the town of Bloomsburg,"—the only incorporated *town* in Pennsylvania, all the other incorporated places being either cities or boroughs.

Both Union and Columbia Counties were formed from Northumberland on the same day, March 22, 1813. **Union County** Union County was so named, to use Henry Gannett's phrase, "as an expression of the sentiment which actuates the American people." [3] The name is so popular that there

See Uniontown, page 62.

are seventeen Union Counties in the United States and twenty-five Union Townships in Pennsylvania. When Snyder County was formed in 1855, what is now Union narrowly escaped being renamed Buffalo County.[9]

The act of Legislature establishing Union County decided that the most suitable location for the county-seat was at Longstown, the name of which it changed **New** to New Berlin, because practically all the **Berlin** settlers in this region were Germans. The newly chosen county-seat, which had been laid out in 1792 by George Long, did not contain more than half a dozen houses. Lewisburg was then more than twelve times as large.

In 1855, when Union County was divided, the people were allowed to select their own county-seat; and Lewisburg, receiving two hundred more votes **Lewisburg** than its rival, Mifflinburg, became the new county town. About 1772 a German named Lewis Derr—or Ludwig Doerr, as he generally signed his name—had bought 320 acres of land, built a mill, and established an Indian trading post where Lewisburg now stands. Lewis Derr's house and store were known far and wide, and became a favorite stopping place for travelers. In March, 1785, six months before his death, he laid out a town, which for a number of years was indifferently called either Lewisburg or Derrstown for its founder. The former name eventually won its way to general acceptance. Lewis means "famous warrior."

Both Clinton County and its county-seat, Lock Haven, owe their existence to Jeremiah Church, an enterprising and eccentric speculator from New York. In 1833 Jerry Church, as he was generally called, bought a large cornfield along the Pennsylvania Canal and the West Branch

---

[9] See Snyder County, page 84.

of the Susquehanna, and in the following year he laid
out a town, which was christened Lock
Lock Haven Haven because the canal had a *lock* here,
and the river furnished an excellent
harbor, or *haven,* for rafts. After Lock Haven was
started, the proprietor, feeling the need of a stimulus
that would make his town grow into a place of some size
and consequence, conceived the scheme of making it the
capital of a new county.

Jeremiah Church seems to have taken pride in being
what is colloquially known as a "character," and about
ten years after laying out his town he published an amusing little book entitled "A Journal of the Travels, Ad-
ventures, and Remarks of Jerry Church." This book
gives the following account of his attempt to form a new
county:

"I now undertook to divide the counties of Lycoming
and Centre, and make a new county, to be called Clinton.
I had petitions printed to that effect, and sent
Clinton   them to Harrisburg to have them presented to
County   the Legislature, and then went down myself to
have the matter represented in good order. My
friend, John Gamble, was our member from Lycoming
at that time, and he reported a bill. The people of Williamsport, the county-seat of Lycoming County, and of
Bellefonte, the county-seat of Centre County, then had
to be up and doing something to prevent the division;
and they commenced pouring in their remonstrances and
praying aloud to the Legislature not to have any part of
either county taken off for the purpose of making a new
one, for it was nothing more or less than some of Jerry
Church's Yankee notions.

"However, I did not despair. I still kept asking every
year for three successive years, and attended the Legis-

lature myself every winter. I then had a gentleman who
had become a citizen of Lock Haven, by the name of John
Moorhead, who harped in with me,—a very large, portly-
looking man, and rather the best borer in town, and a
very clever man. We had to state a great number of
facts to the Legislature—and perhaps something more—
in order to obtain full justice. We continued on for
nearly three years longer, knocking at the mercy-seat;
and at last we received the law creating Clinton County.''

Thus, after six years of persistent lobbying, Clinton
County was formed in the midsummer of 1839. In the
end success came only as the result of a bit of strategy.
In the petitions that were presented to the Legislature
year after year, Eagle was the name suggested for the
proposed county, apparently in honor of the famous
Indian chief, Bald Eagle, who once ruled this region:
the Bald Eagle Creek, which flows through this county
into the Susquehanna, the Bald Eagle valley, the Bald
Eagle range of mountains, and Bald Eagle Township all
take their name from old Wapalanné, or ''Bald Eagle.'' [10]
When one bill after another for the creation of Eagle
County was voted down, the name of Clinton was ''substituted as a ruse to mislead the opponents of the new
county movement.'' The scheme succeeded, some members of the Legislature voting for the formation of
Clinton County without realizing that only a new name
had been used in the old bill which they had opposed for
several sessions.

Jerry Church was so elated over his success in securing the establishment of the new county that he fails to
tell us just why he chose the name of Clinton; but there
cannot be much doubt that this name was given in honor
of DeWitt Clinton, governor of New York and projector

---

[10] See Milesburg, page 266.

of the Erie Canal. DeWitt Clinton was one of the great men of Jerry Church's native state, and was a prominent political personage and even a "presidential possibility" only a few years before Church came to Lock Haven. He was a member of the United States Senate, was mayor of New York for ten years, was thrice elected governor of New York, and had been nominated for the Presidency in 1812 in opposition to Madison.

George Clinton, who served seven terms, or twenty-one years, as governor of New York and was twice elected Vice-President of the United States, was the uncle of DeWitt Clinton; but George Clinton died in 1812, and the founder of Clinton County was far more likely to be attracted by the fame of the great contemporary advocate of internal improvements, who, in 1826, inaugurated the opening of the Erie Canal with imposing ceremonies. In five other states counties are named for DeWitt Clinton. *Clint* is an Old Norse word for "headland"; and Clinton was originally a place name signifying "the farmstead by the headland or crag."

Lock Haven was, of course, made the county-seat of Clinton County. Jerry Church's dream had come true. He donated a suitable site for the court-house, and he immediately sold more than one hundred and fifty building lots in the new county town. Lock Haven began to grow rapidly; it became a borough in 1840, and thirty years later it received a city charter.

CHAPTER XV

COUNTIES AND COUNTY-SEATS—
A FINAL WORD

A FINAL word about the counties and the county-seats, mainly by way of summary and conclusion, may be worth while before we pass on to the discussion of the names of cities and towns with a population of five thousand or more.

Of the twelve Pennsylvania counties that bear the names of counties in England, nine were named directly for the English shires, and three for members of the English nobility. Three counties were named in honor of French noblemen. Four were named for Presidents of the United States, and four for governors of Pennsylvania. Fifteen counties bear the names of distinguished American soldiers, one of whom was governor of the State, another of whom was our first President, and a majority of whom were Pennsylvanians by birth or residence. Four counties were christened in honor of other prominent Pennsylvanians. Two counties were named for women. Ten bear Indian names, taken from natural features. Nine other counties were also named for natural features. Seven obtained their names from miscellaneous sources.

Fully one third of these names are unique. The following twenty-three county names occur nowhere else in the United States:

Berks	Cambria	Clearfield
Blair	Centre	Dauphin
Bucks	Clarion	Huntingdon

Indiana	Luzerne	Schuylkill
Juniata	Lycoming	Snyder
Lackawanna	McKean	Susquehanna
Lebanon	Mifflin	Venango
Lehigh	Montour	

At the end of the first hundred years of its history Pennsylvania had twelve counties; the other fifty-five were all created during its second century. Within the decade extending from 1795 to 1804 twenty-one new counties were established, ten of them being formed in the year 1800. Since 1817 only seventeen counties have been organized. At least one county was born in every month of the year except July, October, and December; thirty-five counties celebrate their birthday in March.

It is noteworthy that fully half a dozen counties came into existence simply because certain towns were ambitious to remain or to become county-seats. Thus the citizens of Chester, when that old town ceased to be the capital of Chester County, were not content until the new county of Delaware was created, with Chester as its county town. In like manner, Danville, the abandoned county-seat of Columbia County, was not satisfied until it had become the county-seat of the newly formed county of Montour. Juniata County owes its origin to the persistence of the people of Mifflintown, who were bitterly disappointed because their town did not become the county-seat of Mifflin County. In a similar way the ambition of Allentown resulted in the formation of Lehigh County. The county of Lawrence would hardly have been formed if New Castle had not yearned to be the capital of a county. Lackawanna County seems to have been organized largely for the accommodation of the great and growing centre of population at Scranton.

Pennsylvania would hardly seem to us to be the same

state if its map were marked with the county names that have been rejected,—if instead of Lycoming we had Muncy County; if for Potter we had Sinnemahoning; for Bradford, Ontario or Morris; for Lebanon, Hamilton; for Union, Buffalo; for Clinton, Eagle; for Wyoming, Putnam; and for Fulton, Liberty.

Not all the projects for the formation of new counties have been successful. Politicians and promoters have seen visions of a dozen or more new counties which have never been created. Of these the following "dream counties" are perhaps the most noteworthy:

1. In 1824 an effort was made to form *Penn County* out of a part of Berks, with Kutztown as its county-seat. The attempt was renewed in 1838, when the bill to create the county of Penn resulted in a tie. The effort was revived again in 1847 and 1849. Apparently Penn Township was to furnish the name for the new county.

2. In 1838 a proposal was made to erect a new county out of parts of Berks and Schuylkill, to be called *Windsor,* from Windsor Township, in Berks County. This project was revived in 1850.

3. In 1845 an agitation for the formation of *Jackson County* from parts of Chester, Berks, and Montgomery was started. The new county was to be named for President Jackson. The effort was renewed in 1847.

4. In 1845 an attempt was also made to erect *Conestoga*[1] *County* out of parts of Lancaster, Berks, and Chester, with Churchtown as its county-seat.

5. In 1847 the bill to form *Madison County* from parts of Berks, Chester, and Montgomery was defeated in the Legislature by a vote of 42 to 36. The new county was to be named after President Madison. This project was revived in 1854 and again in 1855.

---

[1] See Lancaster County, page 41.

6. An effort to form *Lee County* out of a part of Berks, with Bernville as the county-seat, was voted down in 1852. Berks County seems to have been a storm-centre of ambitious schemes for the formation of new counties.

7. In 1853 a project was set on foot to erect *Anthracite County* out of the anthracite coal region in the eastern part of Schuylkill and the southern part of Luzerne.

8. In 1858 Titusville was ambitious to become a county-seat, and an agitation was begun for the creation of *Marion County* out of parts of Warren, Crawford, and Erie. The new county was to be named in honor of General Francis Marion. This project was revived as late as 1870.

9. The last of these new-county projects was an act passed by the Legislature in the nineties, forming *Quay County* out of parts of Luzerne, Carbon, and Schuylkill, with Hazleton as its county-seat. The new county was to bear the name of Senator Matthew Stanley Quay. This bill was vetoed by Governor Daniel H. Hastings.

Sixteen county-seats bear the same name as the county; but five of these—Philadelphia, York, Bedford, Lebanon, and Huntingdon—were founded before the formation of the county.

The following twenty-two county-seats were named for early settlers or pioneers, original owners of the land, or prominent citizens of the locality:

Allentown	Hollidaysburg	Pottsville
Bloomsburg	Laporte	Ridgway
Chambersburg	Lewisburg	Scranton
Danville	Lewistown	Stroudsburg
Doylestown	McConnellsburg	Wellsboro
Ebensburg	Meadville	Williamsport
Gettysburg	Montrose	
Harrisburg	Norristown	

The following sixteen county towns bear the names of great men, those printed in italics being named for distinguished foreigners:

Bedford	*Huntingdon*	Washington
Butler	Mercer	Waynesburg
Coudersport	Mifflintown	*Wilkes-Barre*
Franklin	*Pittsburgh*	*York*
Greensburg	*Smethport*	
Honesdale	Warren	

Ten county-seats have borrowed place names, all of them being of British origin except the two Biblical names printed in italics:

Carlisle	New Castle	Sunbury
Easton	*Philadelphia*	West Chester
Lancaster	Reading	
Lebanon	Somerset	

Six county-seats have Indian names:

Erie	Mauch Chunk	Towanda
Kittanning	Tionesta	Tunkhannock

Nine county towns obtained their names from their location or some geographical feature:

Beaver	Clearfield	Media
Bellefonte	Clarion	Middleburg
Brookville	Lock Haven	Milford

The names of the remaining four county-seats—Emporium, Indiana, New Bloomfield, and Uniontown—do not fall into any convenient classification.

The following fifteen names of county-seats are not duplicated elsewhere among the post-offices of the United States:

Bloomsburg	Honesdale	Mauch Chunk
Coudersport	Indiana	Mifflintown
Ebensburg	Kittanning	Stroudsburg
Emporium	Lock Haven	Tunkhannock
Hollidaysburg	McConnellsburg	Wilkes-Barre

II

THE LARGER TOWNS

CHAPTER XVI

TOWNS WITH BORROWED NAMES

MORE than a score of large towns[1] have appropriated place names from Palestine, England, Ireland, Wales, Belgium, Germany, Italy, and Sicily, and from Connecticut, Kentucky, New Jersey, New York, and Rhode Island.

Although **Altoona,** in Blair County, is popularly known as "the Mountain City," its name has no direct or indirect etymological relation to the Latin adjective *altus,* signifying "elevated, lofty." Two very different explanations of the origin of this name are current. The one which seems to be most natural and reasonable runs as follows:

"The locomotive engineer who ran the first train into Altoona in 1851 was Robert Steele, who died several years ago, aged nearly ninety years. He was then the oldest continuous resident of the city. He was much respected, and had long been one of the private pensioners of Andrew Carnegie. Mr. Steele is authority for the statement that Colonel Beverly Mayer, of Columbia, Pennsylvania, who, as a civil engineer of what was then the Pennsylvania Central Railway, had laid out the tracks in the yards of the newly projected city, named the place Altoona after the city of Altona in Schleswig-Holstein, which became a part of Germany in 1862."[2] The German Altona, which lies on the right bank of the

---

[1] To this list should be added Bristol, already discussed on page 37, and Northampton, explained on page 48.
[2] Letter from Colonel Henry W. Shoemaker, Litt.D., Chairman of the Pennsylvania Historical Commission. Quoted by permission.

Elbe immediately west of Hamburg, is an important railway and manufacturing centre with a population of nearly 200,000. The etymological derivation of the name Altona is not known with certainty.[3]

The popular explanation derives the name of Altoona from Allatoona, said to be a Cherokee Indian name. In 1849 David Robinson sold his farm to Archibald Wright of Philadelphia, who transferred the property to his son, John A. Wright, who laid it out in building lots, became one of the founders of Altoona, and was responsible for the naming of the town. According to his own statement, he had spent considerable time in the Cherokee country of Georgia, where he had been especially attracted by the beautiful name of Allatoona, which he had bestowed upon the new town in the belief that it was a Cherokee word meaning "the high lands of great worth."[4] In the Cherokee language there is a word *eladuni*, which means "high lands," or "where it is high"; but to a Cherokee, Allatoona and *eladuni* are so different that the former could hardly be derived from the latter.[5]

Ashland, in Schuylkill County, was surveyed and laid out in 1847 by Samuel Lewis. The village was named Ashland after Henry Clay's famous estate near Lexington, Kentucky. Clay was then at the height of his great popularity. His home was styled Ashland either from the number of ash trees on his land, or from the town of Ashland in Boyd County, Kentucky, which was certainly called Ashland because of the abundance of ash timber in that region. Clay's popularity is shown by the fact

---

[3] For several conjectural etymologies, see Taylor's *Names and their Histories.*

[4] Africa's *History of Blair County,* p. 135.

[5] Opinion of Mr. James Mooney of the Bureau of American Ethnology.

that twenty-six post-offices in the United States bear the name that he bestowed on his Kentucky home.

Bangor, in Northampton County, is a namesake of the old Welsh seaport town of Bangor in Caernarvonshire, situated some sixty miles west of Chester. About 1866 R. M. Jones, a Welshman expert in all matters relating to slate, followed the slate strata westward from the Delaware River with a view to discovering an advantageous location for a quarry. In the belief that near the site of Bangor an almost inexhaustible supply of high-grade slate could be secured, Mr. Jones formed a company, which bought up the land, opened the quarries, and started a town. The borough of Bangor and the great slate industry that surrounds and supports it are the fruits of this venture. Bangor, which was incorporated about 1875, was settled mainly by Welsh slate workers, and received its name because its chief industry and its natural features were similar to those of the Caernarvonshire Bangor, the centre of the great slate quarries of Wales. Bangor, once the seat of a great mediæval monastery, is said to mean literally "the white choir."

Berwick, in Columbia County, was laid out and named in 1786 by Evan Owen. In choosing this name the proprietor expressed the attachment he still retained for his former English home, Berwick-on-Tweed, in the county of Northumberland.[6] The new town of Berwick was then in Northumberland County, and, like its English prototype, it stood on the banks of a great river. Berwick was incorporated in 1818. The name Berwick is a corruption of Aberwick, signifying "river-mouth town."

Bethlehem, in Northampton County, was named on

[6] Battle's *History of Columbia County*, p. 191.

12

Christmas Eve, 1741, for the birthplace of Christ in Judea. Here the Moravian Brethren had begun their settlement on the Lehigh River by erecting a log house. In this rude building they entertained their great leader and bishop, Count Nicholas Ludwig von Zinzendorf, who had but recently arrived from Germany by way of New York. On Sunday, December 24, 1741, the little company of Moravians "assembled in the first house, celebrated the Holy Communion, and kept the vigils of Christmas eve. At the close of this latter service, between nine and ten at night, the Count led the way into the adjoining stable and began to sing, with deep emotion, a German hymn in which occurred the following lines:

> *'Nicht Jerusalem, sondern Bethlehem,*
> *Aus dir kommet was mir frommet.'* [7]

This incident gave to the settlement its present name." [8] Bethlehem early became the great centre of Moravian influence, educational work, and remarkable missionary activity among the Indians and the widely dispersed white settlers. Bethlehem was incorporated as a borough in 1845; and twenty years later South Bethlehem, which has in more recent years grown much larger than the mother town, was also made a borough. In 1910 the boroughs of Bethlehem and South Bethlehem were combined and incorporated as the city of Bethlehem.

It is noteworthy that Bethlehem, whose name commemorates the birthplace of the Prince of Peace, has become famous throughout the world as one of the most important American centres for the manufacture of munitions of war.

---

[7] "Not from Jerusalem, but Bethlehem,
   Cometh that which helpeth me."
[8] Bishop Edmund de Schweinitz, in Fritts's *History of Northampton County*, p. 192.

The Hebrew name Bethlehem, which means "the house of bread," apparently refers to the great fertility of the valley surrounding the ancient Judean town and once producing an abundance of grain, olives, figs, and grapes.

The city of **Bradford**, the great oil town of McKean County, was at first called Littleton, in honor of Colonel Levitt C. Little of Boston, the agent of the United States Land Company, which, in 1836, had bought about 160,000 acres in McKean County at six and a quarter cents an acre. The next year Colonel Little built the first log house on the present site of the city. In 1838 the plan of the town was drawn up by Mr. Leech of Boston according to Colonel Little's directions. In 1850 the United States Land Company sold the Littleton tract of 50,000 acres to Daniel Kingsbury, who named the place Bradford. Why he chose this name is not positively known. Some have guessed that the name was bestowed in honor of William Bradford, who succeeded Edmund Randolph as attorney-general of the United States in 1794.[9] A far more plausible explanation is offered by a prominent citizen of Bradford,[10] who asserts that Daniel Kingsbury gave the town and the township this name because his ancestors had come from the town of Bradford in England.[11]

Carrick, in Allegheny County, is redolent of the flavor of the old sod, being a namesake of Carrick-on-Suir in County Tipperary, Ireland. Dr. John H. O'Brien, a practising physician, moved to Baldwin Township in 1846, and when steps were taken later to establish a

---

[9] For the etymology of Bradford, see Bradford County, page 153.
[10] The late Mr. Lewis Emery, Jr.
[11] Mr. F. H. Newell of Washington, D. C., consulting engineer with the United States Reclamation Service, who is a grand-nephew of Daniel Kingsbury, says: "I have never learned the real reason why my uncle changed the name of the place from its original designation of Littleton to Bradford."

post-office in the neighborhood, he was asked to suggest a name. As a matter of sentiment he proposed Carrick, the name of his native town. In 1904, when the citizens of the place petitioned the courts for a borough charter, the name of Carrick was adopted by a very large majority of the voters.[12] Carrick is the Anglicised form of the Celtic *carrig*, "a rock." According to Dr. Isaac Taylor, more than six hundred Irish names contain this word.

Charleroi, in Washington County, which was laid out about 1890, was named for the Belgian town of Charleroi, which has long been noted for its glass manufactories. An extensive plate-glass plant was the first important industry of the Monongahela Valley town, and this fact suggested the appropriation of the name of the Belgian city. The original Charleroi seems to have been a punning substitute for Charnoi: in 1666 the Spaniards captured the village of Charnoi, fortified it, and renamed it Charleroi—"Charles the king"—in honor of Charles II of Spain.

Darby, in Delaware County, was so called for old Darby Township, a transplanted English name first appearing as "Derbytown" in 1698. Our ancestors were none too particular in their spelling, and two or three centuries ago the form Darby was used quite as frequently as Derby. For instance, in *The New World of Words,* published in 1671, Darby and Darbyshire are given instead of Derby and Derbyshire, and in the certificates brought over by the early Quakers who settled in this locality in 1682, the name was almost universally spelled Darby. The English Derby is situated on the

---

[12] Data furnished by Mr. J. Boyd Duff, solicitor for the borough of Carrick; facts vouched for by Mr. Charles A. O'Brien, son of Dr. John H. O'Brien, and solicitor for the city of Pittsburgh.

Derwent, and the author of the old book mentioned above regards Derby as a contraction of Derwentty, "because it standeth on the river Derwent." A far more probable explanation of the name is that it is derived from an old personal name *Deor,* meaning "wild beast, or deer," and the Norse *by,* "a town."

Etna, in Allegheny County, has from its beginning been noted for its manufacture of iron and steel. General William Wilkins[13] once owned the town site, and the large frame house that he occupied was the first building within the present borough. David Anderson bought the land from him and laid out a town, which early received the name of Stewartstown in honor of David Stewart, a prominent citizen. About 1832 two iron manufacturers, H. S. Spang and his son, came to Stewartstown from the region that is now Catharine Township, in Blair County, where they had operated an old charcoal furnace known as the "Etna Furnace." It is highly probable—but not certain—that they brought with them the name of Etna, which seems to be an appropriate designation for a town with flaming furnaces, rolling mills, and steel works. The town was incorporated as Etna in 1868.[14] The name Etna was borrowed from the great volcano in Sicily, whose Greek name, Aitna, comes from the root *aith,* meaning "to smoke or burn." Etna may be "an adaptation of an old name derived from the Phœnician *attuna,* 'a furnace.'"

In 1763 the old town of **Hanover,** in York County, was laid out by Richard McAllister, who kept a tavern here in the midst of a hickory forest. At first the place was called McAllister's-town, but it was more generally known by the nickname Hickory-town. In this region

13 See Wilkinsburg, page 236.
14 Information furnished by Mr. Grayson M. Metz of Pittsburgh.

were a good many German settlers, the most influential being Michael Danner, or Tanner, who had been appointed one of the commissioners to lay out York County in 1749, and was made one of his Majesty's justices of the peace in 1755. To please the German settlers, but without any thought of complimenting the reigning house of Hanover, the town was, at the suggestion of Michael Danner, who owned a large tract of land southeast of the site, formally christened Hanover for his native Hanover in Germany.

The new town lay so close to the Maryland line that it long remained a region of disputed jurisdiction; and as a result so many fugitives from justice resorted thither that the place was long known as "Rogues' Resort," or "Rogues' Harbor." Hanover was incorporated in 1815, and celebrated its centennial anniversary with appropriate ceremonies in the autumn of 1915. Hanover literally means "the high shore," the old German city having originally been confined to the cliff on the right bank of the Leine.

In 1800 **Jersey Shore**, in Lycoming County, was one of the many Waynesburgs then in Pennsylvania. The first settlers, Reuben Manning and his nephew, Thomas Forster, had migrated from Essex County, New Jersey. "As the settlement grew, it came to be called Jersey Shore because Manning and Forster were Jerseymen." [15] At first the term Jersey Shore was merely a derisive nickname given by the Irish settlers dwelling in the Nippenose bottom across the river. The traditional explanation of the origin of the name is that these Irishmen usually referred to the shore on which the Jerseymen had settled as "the Jersey Shore." The nickname finally prevailed, and the act that incorporated the borough in

---

[15] Meginness's *History of Lycoming County*, p. 486.

1826 directed that "the place shall be called and styled
Jersey Shore."

The name of **Kingston**, in Luzerne County, was borrowed from that of Kingston in Rhode Island, whence
some of the "first forty" of the early settlers had migrated. "Forty Township" was one of the five original
Connecticut townships; it received its name from the
famous Forty Fort, which was situated within its limits.
In 1771 Forty Township was named Kingstown Township; and three years later occurs, for the first time, the
present form, Kingston. The town of Kingston in Rhode
Island, which is now divided into North and South Kingston, was originally called King's Town or Kingstown, a
name which was first used about 1665, and which had its
origin in "the King's Province," as this region was once
styled during the troublesome contest between Connecticut and Massachusetts for the possession of the Nar-
ragansett country.

Mount Carmel, in Northumberland County, was named
for the mountain in Palestine. No special reason can
be given to explain why it received this Biblical name.
In 1832 Felix Lerch, of Northampton County, leased a
two-story log tavern "on the northern side of the turnpike," near the site of the Commercial Hotel. This tavern
then bore the legend "Mt. Carmel Inn, 1824." [16] It was
a busy hostelry and a regular stopping place for stage-
coaches plying between Danville and Pottsville, and between Sunbury and Reading.

According to tradition the idea of laying out a town
was conceived by Albert Bradford, owner of the old
Mount Carmel Inn property, who applied the name of
the tavern to the town. The earliest town plot bears the
title, "Plan of the town of Mt. Carmel in the Middle coal

---

[16] Bell's *History of Northumberland County*, p. 657,

region, Northumberland County, Penna., 1848.'' Five
years later, when the Mount Carmel post-office was established, the place contained only half a dozen houses.
In 1854 Mount Carmel Township was organized. The
village of Mount Carmel became an incorporated borough
in 1862. The Syrian Mount Carmel is believed to have
taken its name from an altar to Karm-el, ''the vineyard
god.''

New Brighton, in Beaver County, was begun about
1830 on land which David Townsend had bought the year
before. It was named New Brighton because it lay just
across the Beaver River from ''old Brighton,'' which
received its name from the great English seaside resort
situated fifty miles south of London. Old Brighton is
now called Beaver Falls. New Brighton was incorporated
in 1838. The name of the English city of Brighton is a
shortened form of ''Brighthelm's town.'' Brighthelm
was a Saxon bishop, who is said to have founded the English city in the tenth century.

New Kensington, in Westmoreland County, was apparently named directly for the London district of Kensington. There is no evidence to show that it received its
name from the Philadelphia Kensington; but there is a
tradition that the name of Kensington was bestowed on
the town by some Englishmen who were interested in
its early settlement. After the place was named, it was
discovered that there was another Kensington in Pennsylvania, and the prefix *New* was added to prevent confusion.

Plymouth, in Luzerne County, took its name from
Plymouth Township, one of the five townships formed
by the Susquehanna Company in accordance with a resolution passed by the directors on December 28, 1768. ''Its
name was derived from Plymouth in Litchfield County,

Connecticut.''[17]   The Connecticut town was doubtless named for Plymouth in Massachusetts, the oldest settlement in New England. The Pilgrim Fathers called their town Plymouth because the *Mayflower* had sailed from Plymouth in Devonshire, which lies at the mouth of the River Plym. To the early Pennsylvania settlers the little village of Plymouth was known as Shawneetown because it was near the site of an old Shawnee Indian village.

Rochester, in Beaver County, was called East Bridgewater in 1834 because it was situated opposite Bridgewater. A year later another town, named Fairport, was started. The name Rochester was given to the two adjoining settlements about 1838. Ovid Pinney, who came to Fairport shortly before this time and laid out a large addition to the town, is said to have called the place Rochester for his native city in New York,[18] which was named in honor of its founder, Colonel Nathaniel Rochester. The township of Rochester was organized in 1840. A more recent and reliable authority declares that the name Rochester was first used by a storekeeper named Mitchell Hammond. The ultimate source of the name is, of course, the ancient English city of Rochester in Kent, called by the Saxon Chronicle *Hrofesceaster,* ''Hrof's settlement.''

The city of **Sharon,** in Mercer County, was named for Sharon in Palestine. A village was laid out there in 1815 by William Budd, and four years later the post-office of Sharon was established. No one knows why or by whom this Biblical name was given; possibly it was chosen merely because it was considered poetic and euphonious. Until 1836 Sharon was nothing more than a hamlet at the cross-roads, with a tavern, a store, and a smithy. It

[17] Pearce's *Annals of Luzerne County,* p. 215.
[18] Richard's *History of Beaver County,* p. 477.

owes its rapid growth and present prosperity solely to the great iron industry established there. Sharon was incorporated in 1841. The Hebrew word *Sharon* means "a plain."

Tarentum, in Allegheny County, was laid out and named in 1829 by Judge Henry Marie Brackenridge and his wife Caroline, who owned the land on which the town was built. No one now seems to know just why Judge Brackenridge bestowed this classical name upon his town.[19] He was a scholar and a student of ancient history and the classical languages, and he may have been especially attracted by the name of the ancient city in southern Italy which the Romans called Tarentum, and which the Greeks had previously named Taras from the small stream on which the old Greek colony was planted. Tarentum was incorporated in 1842.

Tyrone, in Blair County, derived its name directly from old Tyrone Township, which was once a part of Bedford County, and which originally embraced territory now contained in about half a dozen townships in Huntingdon and Blair Counties. This region was early settled by emigrants from the north of Ireland, who appropriated the name of their native county of Tyrone. The Irish name (which is properly pronounced *Teer-áwn*) is a corruption of Tir-Eoghain, "the land of Owen, the young warrior," who was the son of Niall, the ancestor of the important clan of the O'Neills. The Pennsylvania town is of comparatively recent origin, the first house having been built there in 1850 by Jacob Burley, a descendant of John Burley, who came from England in 1635 and settled in Norwich, Connecticut. Tyrone became a borough in 1857.

---

[19] Judge Brackenridge's grandson, Mr. Henry Morgan Brackenridge of Pittsburgh, has been unable to ascertain any special reason why this name was adopted.

To this list of borrowed place names are added for convenience two others of a somewhat different origin.

Freeland, in Luzerne County, is surrounded by land owned almost exclusively by coal-mining companies. Before the discovery of coal the land upon which the town has been built was the farm of Joseph Birkbeck. This particular tract was not, like those surrounding it, underlaid with coal. In 1868 A. Donop bought most of the Birkbeck farm, laid out streets, and divided the tract into town lots, for which he found a ready sale. The Donop plot became generally known as "free land"; that is, land that could be purchased, as distinguished from the coal companies' land, which was not for sale and not available for building sites. Mr. Donop preferred to name his new town Freehold, a name that it retained until the establishment of a post-office in 1874. The postal authorities objected to this name because of the nearness and importance of Freehold in New Jersey; and the place then adopted its nickname, Freeland.[20]

Homestead, in Allegheny County, was laid out in 1871 by a Pittsburgh corporation called the Homestead Bank and Life Insurance Company. The town took its name from this company. It happened, however, that one of the farms which the company bought belonged to Abdiel McClure, who lived in a fine old farmhouse locally known as "the McClure homestead," embowered in a clump of trees. Many believe that this stately old homestead suggested the name of the town, and one might wish to confirm so pretty and plausible an explanation. One of the sons of Abdiel McClure, however, declares that his father's old homestead had nothing whatever to do with the name. Why the company that laid out the town

---

[20] Explanation given by Mr. D. S. Buckley, editor of the **Freeland** *Tribune.*

chose Homestead as a part of their corporate name is not known.[21] Possibly it was because they were dealing in building lots.

---

[21] Facts furnished by Mr. M. P. Schooley of Homestead.

CHAPTER XVII

TOWNS THAT HAVE INDIAN NAMES

CONSHOHOCKEN and West Conshohocken, in Montgomery County, derived their name from an Indian word meaning "pleasant valley."

East Conemaugh, in Cambria County, dates back to a time when it was necessary to use the prefix East to distinguish this town from the older borough of Conemaugh, which was consolidated with Johnstown about thirty years ago. The Conemaugh River, which became famous at the time of the Johnstown flood in 1889, has given its name to East Conemaugh. The name is derived from the Indian *Connemach,* which signifies "otter creek." Both Cambria and Somerset County have a Conemaugh Township.

Lehighton, in Carbon County, which was laid out in 1794, by Colonel Jacob Weiss and William Henry, took its name from the Lehigh River, on which it is situated. The name Lehighton is a barbarous combination of the Indian form *Lehigh* [1] with the Early English *tun* or *-ton,* meaning "town." Here flourished an old Moravian settlement as early as 1745.

Mahanoy City, one of the great coal towns of Schuylkill County, became a post-office in 1839. The name Mahanoy, which is usually pronounced with a primary accent on the first syllable, and a secondary accent on the last, was derived from the language of the Delawares, the word *mahoni* meaning a "lick," a term used in pioneer days to denote saline deposits where deer congre-

[1] For an explanation of this name, see Lehigh County, page 132.

gate. Mahanoy City is situated in Mahanoy Township.
The first name of **Monongahela,** in Washington County, was Williamsport. In 1796 Joseph Parkinson laid
out the town and named it for his son William. When a
post-office was established, the name adopted was Parkinson's Ferry, because Williamsport in Lycoming
County had already become a flourishing town and a
post-office. In 1837 the name Monongahela City was
adopted. This is still the name of the corporation, though
the post-office is now simply Monongahela. The name of
the city was borrowed from the Indian name of the river,
Monongahela being a corruption of *Menaun-gehilla,* which
signifies "river with the sliding banks," or "high banks,
which break off and fall down."

Monessen, in Westmoreland County, a large and comparatively recent industrial city, first incorporated as a
borough in 1899, owes its growth and its name to the
large iron and steel industry that began operations here
in 1897 as the National Tin Plate Company of Pennsylvania. The name Monessen is a curious hybrid com-
pound, formed by combining the first syllable of
Monongahela [2] with Essen, the name of the greatest iron
town in Germany, the home of the famous Krupp works.
The original meaning of the name Essen has been lost;
it has no connection with *eisen,* the German word for
iron. The plant first established at Monessen was the
nucleus for a dozen other large industrial concerns, five
of which are steel and iron mills.

Nanticoke, in Luzerne County, received its name from
a tribe of Indians. *Nentigo* is the form used by Heckewelder. The Nanticokes, who were once seated on the
eastern shore of Maryland, are "the seashore settlers,
or the tide-water people." The first settlement at Nanti-

[2] Explained above.

coke, which owed its beginning to the water power furnished by the falls, was made about a century ago. The town did not begin to grow rapidly until after 1825, when the first coal was mined there.

The name of **Punxsutawney,** in Jefferson County, was derived from the "punkies," or gnats that annoyed the early settlers. The best explanation of the name is found in the journal of the Reverend John Ettwein, a native of Würtemberg and a Moravian missionary, who became a bishop in 1784. In 1772 Ettwein undertook to transplant a colony of 241 peaceful and christianized Delaware Indians from Wyalusing, where the "land had been sold from under their feet" by the Iroquois, to the region of the Big Beaver River.[3]

Under date of July 19, 1772, his journal contains the following significant entry: "In the evening all joined me, but we could hold no service because the *ponkies* were so excessively annoying that the cattle pressed into the camp to escape their persecutors in the smoke of the fire. These vermin are a plague to man and beast by day and night. In the swamp through which we are now passing their name is legion. Hence the Indians call it *ponsetunik,* 'the town of the ponkies.' The word is equivalent to *living dust and ashes,* the vermin being so small as not to be seen, and their bite being as hot as sparks of fire or hot ashes. The brethren here related an Indian myth,—that a hermit and sorcerer, who had long been a terror to all Indians, had been killed by one who burned his bones, but the ashes he blew into the swamp, where they became living things, and hence the *ponkies.*" The Moravians called the place Ash-town, and sometimes the early settlers spoke of it as Gnat-town. The word *punky* has found its way into the English lan-

---

guage; the *Standard Dictionary* contains this definition: *"Punky* (Northeastern United States): a species of minute, annoying gnats."

Shamokin, the metropolis of Northumberland County, was laid out in 1835 by John C. Boyd. Five years earlier Jacob Graeff, of Reading, had acquired an interest in the site and had made an unsuccessful attempt to start a town. At first the post-office was given the prosaic name Coal, which in 1840 was changed to Shamokin, presumably from the Shamokin Creek, which flows through the town. This stream had received its name from the old Indian village that once stood at its mouth, on the present site of Sunbury, eighteen miles west of the borough of Shamokin. The Delawares, according to Heckewelder, called this village *Schachamekhan,* which signifies "eel stream." Another form of the name was *Schahamokink,* or "the place of eels." A. L. Guss believes that Shamokin is derived from *Sachem-okhe,* "the place where the chief lived." Dr. George P. Donehoo derives Shamokin from *Shumokenk,* "where horns are plentiful." The famous Oneida chieftain, Shikellamy, the father of Logan, ruled over his dusky subjects in the Indian town of Shamokin from 1728 to 1749.

The site of **Shenandoah,** now the largest town in Schuylkill County, was a wilderness in 1862. In that year the Philadelphia Land Company, in the belief that extensive coal mines would soon be opened here, had a town laid out by P. M. Schaeffer, who named the place Shenandoah, presumably from the Shenandoah Creek, which flows through the town. Doctor Beauchamp[4] says that Shenandoah is an Iroquois word meaning "great plains," declaring that Boyd's derivation of the name

---

[4] *Aboriginal Place Names of New York,* p. 57.

from *Schind-han-dowi,* "spruce stream," though ingenious, is without foundation.

Tamaqua, in Schuylkill County, laid out in 1829 by the Lehigh Coal and Navigation Company, was named for the Tamaqua Creek, the west branch of the Little Schuylkill. The name is derived from *tamaque,* the Delaware Indian word for "beaver." The Tamaqua is sometimes called the Beaver Creek.[5]

---

[5] To this list of eleven large towns bearing Indian names should be added that of Juniata, in Blair County, explained on page 134.

CHAPTER XVIII

TOWNS NAMED FOR INDUSTRIES AND GEO-GRAPHICAL FEATURES

OF the twenty-seven large towns whose names originated either in some important industry or in a local characteristic, Ambridge, Millvale, Old Forge, Phœnixville, and Steelton had their beginning in the manufacture of iron; Carbondale, Coaldale, Minersville, and Nanty Glo are coal towns; Glassport started with the making of glass, and Oil City with the production of petroleum; Milton marks the site of a pioneer grist-mill; Renovo was christened for railroad repair shops; Beaver Falls found its name in the falls of the Beaver River; Middletown was a half-way stopping place between two important colonial towns; Marcus Hook, Midland, Schuylkill Haven, Summit Hill, and Turtle Creek received their names from geographical features or location; Bellevue, Dormont, Mount Pleasant, and Woodlawn pay tribute to the natural beauty of their outlook; and Avalon, Forest City, and Hazleton commemorate the plant life found in these localities.

The industrial town of **Ambridge,** in Beaver County, owes its existence solely to the American Bridge Company. In 1901 the corporation bought of the community known as the Harmony Society [1] the land on which it began to construct its Ambridge plant in January, 1902. During the following year the company tried to handle its extensive railroad business through the station at

---

[1] For information concerning Economy, Harmony, and the Harmony Society, see pages 291-294.

Economy, located about three-fourths of a mile west of its works. From the first it was apparent that this little station could not take care of the company's freight, and the Pennsylvania Railroad Company viewed with favor the proposal that a station be established opposite the central part of the plant. On March 1, 1903, the new station was opened and received the name Ambridge from *Am. Bridge* Co., the abbreviated designation of the great industrial concern. The name was adopted by the railroad company at the suggestion of Charles S. Besterling, traffic manager of the American Bridge Company. The borough of Ambridge, incorporated in 1905, comprises the old village of Economy and the new town of Ambridge, which has been built up rapidly on land bought of the Harmony Society by the Ambridge Land Company, a corporation in no way connected with the bridge manufacturers.[2]

The first settler in what is now **Avalon**, an attractive residential borough in Allegheny County, was an Irish trader named John Taylor, who built his cabin here in the latter part of the eighteenth century. From his son James, who was born here in 1803, Captain John Birmingham bought a tract of land and built a log house near the junction of Ohio and Harrison Avenues. "The surrounding land was principally an orchard, and the products were apples, cherries, and other fruits." From this fact one of the streets was called Orchard Avenue. When the railroad was built, the station was called Birmingham. In 1874 the settlement was incorporated as West Bellevue. Nine years later a post-office named Myler was established here. To avoid the confusion resulting from these three names, the citizens of the town,

---

[2] Information furnished by Mr. Marshall Williams, operating manager of the American Bridge Company.

at a public meeting held in 1893, chose the name Avalon, which is an old Celtic word signifying "orchard, or land of apples."[3]

Beaver Falls, the metropolis of Beaver County, was laid out about 1800 and was at first called Brighton by two brothers named Constable, who made the survey, and whose native place was the English city of Brighton. In 1866 the Harmony Society, which had purchased the land adjacent to Brighton, greatly enlarged the plan of the town by extending it for three miles along the Beaver River. They changed its name to Beaver Falls because of the falls in the river at this point. A new name had become desirable because the people of that region had got into the confusing habit of referring to the larger town of New Brighton as Brighton, and of calling Brighton proper "old Brighton." The name Beaver Falls was geographically appropriate, and with this new name the town could no longer be confused with any other place. R. L. Baker, one of the two trustees of the Harmony Society, in christening the place Beaver Falls, simply appropriated a name that had been used for many years. This city is without doubt the most enduring monument to the memory of the famous Harmony Society.

The name of **Bellevue,** which is situated in Allegheny County on the north bank of the Ohio River, is derived from the French *belle vue,* "beautiful view." This name is said to have been given because of an unusually fine prospect obtained from a hill in this vicinity. It appears to be a purely fanciful name, given without any special reason beyond a general recognition of the natural beauty of the scenery surrounding the town.

---

[3] Facts gleaned from the *Avalon Year-Book,* published by the Avalon High School class of 1923.

The first settlement at the city of **Carbondale**, in Lackawanna County, was made by William and Maurice Wurts
of Philadelphia, who opened coal mines here in 1824.
The name, obviously chosen to indicate a valley or dale
containing coal, was probably given by some officer of
the Delaware and Hudson Company. Tradition says that
the name was suggested by Washington Irving, who was
a warm personal friend of Philip Hone [4] and other prominent directors of this company. About 1825 a shipment
of tools for the use of laborers on this company's new
railroad was consigned to Carbondale,—apparently the
first instance on record of the use of this name. In 1843
Sherman Day mentions Carbondale as a ''prosperous
borough, which has sprung up within a few years by the
magic power of anthracite coal.'' The situation, growth,
and chief industry of Carbondale indicate the appropriateness of its name. The township of Carbondale, which
was named for the town, was organized in 1831.

Coaldale, incorporated as one of the boroughs of
Schuylkill County in 1906, also owes its existence and
its name to a dale containing rich deposits of anthracite
coal.

Dormont, an attractive residential borough in Allegheny County, was incorporated in 1909, when it had a
population of only three or four hundred. The ornate
and somewhat pretentious name Dormont, from the
French *d'or mont*, ''mount of gold,'' was suggested by
Gilbert M. Brown, who became the first burgess of Dormont. The name refers to the beautiful hills on which
the town is built and to the wonderful opportunities that
they offered.

About 1885 **Forest City**, now the largest town in Susquehanna County, was a lumber camp called Pentecost

------
[4] See Honesdale, page 94.

for one of its owners, William Pentecost. The lumbermen frequently went from their camp to the neighboring town of Carbondale. In one of these visits a young woodsman, John D. Blake, in answer to some bantering remarks about the name of the place, is said to have replied, "We come from Forest City." This impromptu name seemed to strike the popular fancy; and in 1888, when the lumbering town was incorporated, it was suitably christened Forest City.[5]

Glassport, situated on the Monongahela River in Allegheny County, owes its name and its present importance to the plant established here in 1888 by the United States Glass Company. The new port on the river, where glass was made, has developed rapidly into the large borough of Glassport, which was incorporated in 1902.

Hazleton, the second city in Luzerne County, gets its name from Hazel Township, which in turn was named from Hazel Creek. This stream, which flowed through Hazel Swamp, was noted for the abundance of hazel bushes growing along its banks. The first settlement was made about 1836, and twenty years later, when the town was incorporated, the attorney who drew up the legal papers erroneously spelled the name Hazleton, which has become fixed as the corporate name of the town.

The borough of **West Hazleton,** in Luzerne County, was so named because of its geographical situation about five miles west of Hazleton.

The name of **Marcus Hook,** a large industrial borough in Delaware County, is very old, having been used by the early Dutch settlers along the Delaware. In the patent to the "Marcus Hook tract" of one thousand acres signed by Sir Edmund Andros in 1675, the name appears as "Marreties Hoeck." The first half of the name is appar-

ently in the possessive case; that is, Marretie's Hook or
Maarte's Hook. This possessive form seems to have been
corrupted into Marcus. No one definitely knows who
Marretie or Maarte was. The traditional explanation is
that he was an "Indian chief who probably resided at
this place." The word Hook, from the Dutch *hoek,* signifies a "corner, point, or spit of land." In 1682, the
English, by order of the court, changed the name of
Marcus Hook to Chichester; but the older name had
taken root and could not be legislated out of existence.

Middletown, one of the oldest settlements in Dauphin
County, was laid out about 1755 by George Fisher on land
conveyed to him by his father, John Fisher, a Philadelphia Quaker. It derived its name from the fact that
it stands midway between the old towns of Lancaster
and Carlisle, and served as a half-way station for colonial
wagoners and stage-drivers.

Midland, an important iron town in Beaver County,
was carefully laid out in 1905 by the newly formed Midland Steel Company, and was incorporated as a borough
in the same year. The name of Midland was suggested
by J. Ramsey Speer, vice-president of this company, as
an appropriate designation both for the new business
corporation and for its new industrial town, because of
their location midway between Pittsburgh and the Shenango Valley district.[6] Six years after Midland was laid
out, the Midland Steel Company's plant was sold to the
Pittsburgh Crucible Steel Company. Since then the
growth of the town has been very rapid.

The borough of **Millvale,** which adjoins the city of
Pittsburgh in Allegheny County, has had an interesting
history. In 1844 the city of Allegheny bought a farm of
164 acres for the care of the poor. Twenty-three years

---

[6] Information furnished by Mr. J. Ramsey Speer of Pittsburgh.

later the Directors of the Poor, deciding that it would be better to secure a location farther from the city, laid out the Poor Farm in building lots. There was then much discussion in favor of a new State Constitution, which should forever forbid any legislation in the form of special borough charters. The people in the little manufacturing village of Bennett, close to the Poor Farm, were afraid that the new plan of lots would be "gobbled up" by the old. borough of Duquesne, now a part of Pittsburgh. Several citizens of the village accordingly hurried to Harrisburg, where the Legislature was in session, and on the night of February 13, 1868, secured the incorporation of the Poor Farm plan of lots into the "borough of Millvale." This name, which was chosen on the spur of the moment, was suggested by one of the party, H. B. Lyon, because the iron mills of Graff Bennett and Company were located in the valley or vale that had so suddenly become an incorporated borough.[7]

Milton, in Northumberland County, was not, as some suppose, named in honor of the great Puritan poet. Andrew Straub, the founder of Milton, was born on his father's farm near the site of Columbia, in Lancaster County, in 1748. He was a capable miller and millwright. He came to the neighborhood of Milton about 1780, and twelve years later he planned the erection of a mill near the river bank. A spring freshet diverted the course of Limestone Run, which was to furnish him with power, and he was obliged to build his mill "near where the present stone bridge is." Here Andrew Straub erected a log mill in 1792, "with a wheel outside and one run of stones." He thus became a public benefactor to his

---

[7] Information given by Mr. C. E. Theobald, solicitor for the borough o. Millvale.

pioneer community. The settlers in all the surrounding country gladly abandoned the long route to the only other mill, located at Warrior's Run, about seven miles distant, and flocked to Andrew Straub's place, which they at first called Mill-town. A village was soon laid out by Andrew Straub, and its name, at the suggestion of the surveyor, was shortened to Milton. The Milton post-office was established in 1800, and the village was incorporated as a borough in 1817.

Minersville, in Schuylkill County, was named from the fact that a large number of its people have from the beginning been coal miners. The town was started in 1830 by Titus Bennett. Like most of the large towns in the anthracite region, Minersville began its existence as three or four distinct and widely separated little clusters of frame houses. These scattered settlements have gradually merged together into one town. Minersville grew rapidly: it was incorporated in about a year after it was founded, and at the end of the first decade its population was 1,265.

As to the origin of the name of **Mount Pleasant,** in Westmoreland County, nothing more definite can be given than that it was so called because of its pleasant and commanding location. As early as 1774 the Redstone Presbytery organized the Mount Pleasant Church, which was situated about two miles from the present town; and it is probable—but not certain—that the town took its name from the historic old church. The village was incorporated as early as 1828. In the early days, when the place was a relay station on the Baltimore and Pitts-burgh pike, the fighting, thieving gang that loafed about the old inn and stables was so notoriously bad that the place was locally known as Helltown.

Nanty Glo, a coal town in Cambria County, which was

settled by the Welsh, derives its name from the Welsh phrase *nant-y-glo*, which means "the coal brook."

Oil City, in Venango County, which has grown up since 1860, lies sprawled out on both sides of Oil Creek and on both banks of the Allegheny River. It owes its name to the rise and growth of the petroleum business. The first settlement, which was called Oil City, was laid out on the western side of the creek by the Michigan Rock Oil Company about 1860. The new oil town grew so fast that it was incorporated as a borough two years later. In 1863 William L. Lay started Laytonia on the south bank of the river. A little later Vandergrift, Forman, and Company laid out an adjacent town and gave it the grandiloquent name of Imperial City. In 1866 Laytonia and Imperial City were joined and incorporated as Venango City; and five years after, the two towns of Oil City and Venango City were consolidated with a city charter under the name of Oil City.

Old Forge, in Lackawanna County, began its existence as a town about a century ago. A forge was built here in 1789 by Dr. William Hooker Smith, the pioneer physician of this region. Doctor Smith, who was the son of a Presbyterian minister, had emigrated to the Wyoming valley from New York in 1772, and had later taken part in the famous Sullivan expedition.[8] The traces of the old forge that he built just above the mouth of Ascension Brook on the rugged edge of the Lackawanna River are still plainly discernible. The iron ore turned out to be poor and scarce, and the business soon had to be abandoned. When a village was started a decade or two later, it naturally took its name from this well-known landmark.

Phœnixville, in Chester County, began as a tiny cluster of houses centering about the iron business that Benja-

---

[8] See Sullivan County, page 109.

min Longstreth started here about 1785. His property was sold by the sheriff in 1800. Within the next twelve years three other ironmasters attempted without success to carry on the enterprise. Twice were the buildings badly damaged by floods, and thrice was the dam destroyed that furnished power for the works. In 1813 Lewis Wernwag, an ingenious German of unusual mechanical ability, the most famous bridge-builder of his time, took charge of the ill-fated works, and in view of their renewed life and better prospects hopefully rechristened them "The Phœnix Iron Works" from the fabulous bird of antiquity that rose out of its ashes to new life. From the name of this reorganized company, though Wernwag met with no better success than his many predecessors, the town was called Phœnixville.

Renovo, in Clinton County, takes its name from the Latin verb *renovo,* "I renew." The town was laid out in 1862 on a tract of twelve hundred acres, one half of which was set aside as a site for the new car shops that the Philadelphia and Erie Railroad had decided to build here. It was these railroad shops, where cars were to be repaired and *renovated,* that brought the town into existence and suggested its name. Renovo became an incorporated borough in 1866.[9]

Schuylkill Haven, in Schuylkill County, was so named because it stood at the head of the Schuylkill Canal and very early became an important *haven,* or point of shipment, for anthracite coal.[10]

Steelton, in Dauphin County, is the child of the Pennsylvania Steel Company, which began to erect its extensive works here in 1865. Rudolph and Henry Kelker of Harrisburg, who owned the land adjoining the works,

[9] Information obtained from Margaret Baird's booklet, *Historical Renovo.*
[10] See Schuylkill County, page 145.

laid out the town in 1866, calling it Baldwin in honor of Matthew W. Baldwin, then head of the Baldwin Locomotive Company and one of the largest stockholders in the Pennsylvania Steel Company. The post-office established here in 1871 was called Steel Works. When the place was incorporated in 1880, at the suggestion of Major Luther S. Bent, then superintendent of the steel works, the town was formally rechristened Steelton [11] for its important steel industry.

Summit Hill, in Carbon County, was so named because it is situated at the summit of Sharp Mountain, at an elevation of nearly 1,500 feet. The town commands an excellent view of the surrounding country.

The name of **Turtle Creek,** in Allegheny County, is simply the translation of the Delaware Indian name of the stream, *Tulpewi-sipu.* This stream, on which the town has grown up, bore the name of Turtle Creek even in colonial days.

Woodlawn, in Beaver County, was named in 1877 by Mattie McDonald, wife of C. I. McDonald, who became the first postmaster. The name was a suitable tribute to the sylvan beauty of the new village site in the valley of Logstown Run. Woodlawn began to grow rapidly into a thriving industrial centre after the Jones and Laughlin Company established its steel mills there in 1906. Two years later the borough was incorporated. [12]

---

[11] Information furnished by Mr. Edgar C. Felton, president of the Pennsylvania Steel Company.

[12] Information given by Mr. J. Roy Jackson of Woodlawn.

CHAPTER XIX

TOWNS NAMED FOR PERSONS

FAMOUS men and local celebrities have given their names to more than sixty large towns.[1] Of this number the following twenty-five are called by unchanged family names: Archbald, Arnold, Ashley, Blakely, Braddock, Carnegie, Corry, DuBois, Dunmore, Duquesne, Duryea, Farrell, Kane, Latrobe, Munhall, Olyphant, Parsons, Pitcairn, Rankin, Saint Clair, Sayre, Taylor, Throop, Vandergrift, and Winton.

Far less attractive are the names of large towns that have been formed by the addition of the ubiquitous and inappropriate French *ville* to the family name: Coatesville, Connellsville, Edwardsville, Frackville, Greenville, Knoxville, Larksville, Swoyersville, and Titusville.

A variety of other additions or suffixes have been used in Crafton, Palmerton, Pittston, Johnstown, Pottstown, Dickson City, Ellwood City, Ford City, McKeesport, McKees Rocks, Scottdale, Waynesboro, Canonsburg, Johnsonburg, and Wilkinsburg.

Saint Clair, in Schuylkill County, was so called for a man's baptismal name. Lansford was the middle name of a prominent citizen. Jeannette, Coraopolis, and Saint Marys were taken from the given names of women. Wilmerding was appropriated from a woman's middle name. Clairton, Columbia, Donora, Swissvale, and Windber are the products of some modification or mutilation of family names.

Archbald, in Lackawanna County, was a mere village

---

[1] To this list should be added Luzerne, explained on page 67.

locally known as White Oak Run until about 1846, when it took the name of Archbald in honor of James Archbald, then a prominent civil and mining engineer in the employ of the Delaware and Hudson Company. James Archbald was born in Little Cambray Isle, Buteshire, Scotland, in 1793, and came to Carbondale in 1828. He had charge of most of the difficult railroad construction work that the Delaware and Hudson Company had to do in running its line across Moosic Mountain.

In 1854, when he was serving as chief engineer and vice-president of the Fort Wayne Railroad Company, he was called to Scranton, where three years later he began his fourteen years of efficient service as chief engineer of the Delaware, Lackawanna, and Western Railroad. During this period he secured direct connection with New York and practically reconstructed the whole line. The railway system that he helped to build up and the great city of Scranton, which owes so much of its prosperity to this outlet for its products, as well as the town that bears his name, are all living memorials to the life-work of James Archbald. The surname Archbald is derived from the baptismal name Archibald, which means "precious-bold." The frequent occurrence of this family name in Scotland has resulted from its erroneous acceptance as the Lowland equivalent of Gillespie, "the bishop's servant."

Arnold, in Westmoreland County, was named for Andrew Arnold, who owned the town site when the first settlement was made. In 1852, by the will of Wilson Jack, he acquired title to a considerable part of the land on which the present town stands. Arnold was set apart from New Kensington and incorporated as a separate borough in 1896.[2] Arnold means "gracious as an eagle."

---

[2] Information furnished by Mr. John McCartney Kennedy of New Kensington.

Ashley, in Luzerne County, was a coal town in 1851, and during the next twenty years bore nine names in succession,—Skunktown, Peestown, Hightown, Newton, Scrabbletown, Coalville, Nanticoke Junction, Alberts, and Ashley. The last name, which it received when it was incorporated in 1870, was bestowed in honor of Herbert Henry Ashley of Wilkes-Barre, who is ninth in line of descent from Robert Ashley, who emigrated from England to Springfield, Massachusetts, in 1638.[3] The English family name Ashley, or Ashleigh, occurring first in the time of Henry III, is a local or territorial name signifying "the ash thicket."

The borough of **Blakely,** in Lackawanna County, has taken the name of old Blakely Township, which was organized in 1818 and named in honor of the naval hero, Captain Johnston Blakely, commander of the United States sloop *Wasp* during the war of 1812. Born in Ireland and coming to America when a small child, young Blakely entered the navy as midshipman in 1800 at the age of nineteen. After capturing several prizes in the second war with England, he attained the rank of captain on November 24, 1814. Shortly after that date he was lost at sea: it is generally supposed that the *Wasp* foundered in a gale. The town of Blakely in Georgia was also named in his honor. Blakely is an English territorial family name meaning "black lea."

Braddock and **North Braddock,** in Allegheny County, as well as Braddock Township, perpetuate the name and the memory of Major-General Edward Braddock, who received his death-wound here in the dreadful battle with the French and Indians on July 9, 1755. The story of the defeat of Braddock is a familiar part of American

---

[3] Information obtained from the Reverend Horace Edwin Hayden, former secretary of the Wyoming Historical and Geological Society.

history. There can be little doubt that the disaster was caused almost wholly by General Braddock's total ignorance of the ways of Indian warfare, and by his obstinate self-sufficiency and unwillingness to listen to the advice and wise suggestions of such subordinates as Washington. Edward Braddock was born in Perthshire, Scotland, in 1695. Four days after the battle he died at Great Meadows, whither Washington had conducted the retreat. The Scotch surname Braddock means "the dweller at a gorge or gulley." The English family name Braddock signifies "the dweller by a broad oak." Braddock became a borough in 1867, and North Braddock was incorporated in 1897.

Canonsburg, in Washington County, was named for its founder, John Canon, who migrated to this region from Virginia and in 1788 laid out the town on his tract of 1,192 acres. Colonel John Canon was a militia officer, an Indian fighter, a member of the Pennsylvania Assembly, and the donor of the land on which Jefferson College stood before it became part of Washington and Jefferson College.[4] Canonsburg was incorporated in 1802. During the past decade it has grown rapidly into an important mining and industrial centre. The family name Canon is derived from the common noun *canon,* the name of a church dignitary connected with a cathedral.

The borough of **Carnegie,** in Allegheny County, was formed in 1894 by the consolidation of the two older boroughs of Chartiers and Mansfield, which lay on the north and the south sides of Chartiers Creek. The name of Carnegie was bestowed on the new municipality as a compliment to Andrew Carnegie, who, up to the time of its incorporation, had had no interest in the town. None

[4] Information furnished by Mr. David H. Fee of Canonsburg.

of his numerous works were located there. Since the naming and the incorporation of the town, however, Mr. Carnegie has given the borough an excellent library, which he has endowed with several hundred thousand dollars.[5] Carnegie lies in the heart of the fertile Chartiers Valley, which was settled shortly after the Revolutionary War. The family name Carnegie was originally a Celtic place name signifying "the fortress in the gap, or notch." Carnegie occurs as a family name as early as 1410.

The origin of the name of the city of **Clairton**, in Allegheny County, cannot be given with certainty and fulness. One can be fairly sure that the name Clairton has been made by adding the locative suffix *ton* ("town") to *Clair* ("clear, bright, or illustrious"), the second syllable of the surname St. Clair or its variant form, Sinclair. The current traditional explanation is that the name Clairton is derived from the name of Samuel Sinclair, who once owned a tract of 215 acres of land on which part of the present city is built, and not from General Arthur St. Clair, who was a prominent figure in the early history of western Pennsylvania, and for whom the old township of Saint Clair and the former borough of Saint Clair, in Allegheny County, were named. Clairton was incorporated as a borough in 1903 and received a city charter in 1922.

Coatesville, in Chester County, became a post-office in 1812; and its first postmaster was Moses Coates, who owned a large tract of land now occupied by the town. He planned the place and called it Coatesville,[6] but it is not known whether he named the town for himself or for his grandfather, Moses Coates, an Irish Quaker, who

---

[5] Data furnished by Mr. James H. Duff of Pittsburgh, solicitor for the borough of Carnegie.

[6] *A Genealogy of Moses and Susannah Coates* (compiled by Truman Coates), p. 91.

14

had emigrated to Pennsylvania in 1717. The family, as the name indicates, was of English origin. The word *coate*, in the north of England, is the equivalent of the Anglo-Saxon, *cot*, signifying "thatched cottage." Coates would naturally become first a village name, and then a family name.

Columbia, in Lancaster County, was laid out in 1788 by Samuel Wright, grandson of the Quaker, John Wright,[7] who was one of the first settlers in this region. For a long time the place had been known as Wright's Ferry. No record has been left to explain just why Samuel Wright called his town Columbia. This name was then comparatively new, having apparently been bestowed on the town before it had gained its great popularity from Joseph Hopkinson's famous song, *Hail Columbia,* first sung in Philadelphia in 1798.[8]

The first instance that the author has been able to find of the use of the name Columbia goes back to 1775, when Philip Freneau, the poet of the American Revolution, published "American Liberty, a Poem," in which he referred to America as Columbia, thus explaining the novel name in a footnote: "Columbia, America, sometimes so called from Columbus, the first discoverer." Nine years later the patriotic "regents of the State University" changed the name of King's College in New York to Columbia College. The Columbia River on the Pacific coast took its name from the Boston merchant ship *Columbia,* which entered that river in 1787. These are some of the earliest instances of the use of this name.

About 1789,[9] or a little later, the name Columbia was

---

[7] See Lancaster County, page 42.

[8] Opinion of Colonel Samuel Wright, a descendant of the founder of Columbia. See also Columbia County, page 162.

[9] In the same year the town of Columbia, in South Carolina, was laid out, named, and officially designated as the new capital of the State, the seat of government having previously been at Charleston.

bestowed on the new town recently laid out at Wright's Ferry; possibly the place was so named in hopeful anticipation of the establishment of the national capital here. During the sessions of 1789 and 1790 Congress spent a number of days in a bitter debate over the location of the permanent seat of government. The House voted in favor of Wright's Ferry "on the east bank of the River Susquehanna in the State of Pennsylvania"; but the Senate refused to concur, sending the bill back to the House with amendments favoring either Philadelphia or the present location on the Potomac. President Washington is said to have preferred Wright's Ferry, now Columbia. If the Pennsylvania representatives had been a little more energetic and diplomatic, Columbia might have been chosen as the capital of the United States. The debate ended, as we know, in an agreement that Philadelphia was to be the national capital for the next ten years, and that in 1800 the permanent seat of government was to be located on the Potomac River near Georgetown. Thus Columbia missed its opportunity to become a great city; and a decade later its name was assumed by the District of Columbia.

The city of **Connellsville**, the great coke town of Fayette County, was laid out in 1793 by Zachariah Connell, who called his village Connellsville. Connell had come into this region in 1770 and was entertained at the cabin of the ill-fated Captain William Crawford,[10] who had settled two years before on a plateau across the river from the site of Connellsville. The young pioneer was greatly smitten by the charms of his host's daughter, Ann Crawford, whom he married in 1773. Not until two years after he had plotted his proposed town did Zachariah Connell secure full title to the tract of land

---

[10] See Crawford County, pages 97-100.

on which Connellsville now stands. William McCormick, another son-in-law of William Crawford, was one of the first settlers of Connellsville. The township of Connellsville was named for the town. The name Connell means "conflict."

The site of **Coraopolis**, in Allegheny County, in 1769 came into possession of Andrew (sometimes called Henry) Montour, son of Madame Catherine Montour, for whom Montour County was named.[11] During the American Revolution Robert Vance settled near Montour's tract, and in his honor the post-office was long called Vance Fort. Before 1886 the little village at this point was commonly known as Middletown because it was situated midway between Pittsburgh and Beaver. Since there was an older place in Pennsylvania called Middletown, in 1886 the village was incorporated as Coraopolis, both the post-office and the borough receiving this name in honor of Cora Watson, the daughter of Thomas F. Watson, who had recently laid out an important addition to the town. Cora Watson, now the wife of an attorney, William T. Tredway, resides in Coraopolis.[12] The name is composed of the two Greek words, *Cora,* meaning "a girl," and *polis,* "a city."

Corry, in Erie County, owes its existence to the coming of the railroad into its neighborhood. In 1861 the Atlantic and Great Western Railroad bought the farm of Hiram Corry, and in recognition of his liberal dealing, Mr. Hill, the general superintendent of the railroad, substituted the name of Corry for the long, unwieldy appellation, Atlantic and Erie Junction. The little town at the junction grew so fast that within two years it was incorporated as a borough. The Scotch surname Corry

[11] See Montour County, pages 116, 117.
[12] Information given by Mr. J. T. Butler of Coraopolis.

originally meant "a dweller at the *corrie*," a word that Sir Walter Scott, in a footnote to *The Lady of the Lake*, explains as meaning "the hollow side of a hill where game usually lies." In the above-mentioned poem Scott uses the phrase, "fleet foot in the *corrie*."

Crafton, an attractive residential borough in Allegheny County, was laid out about 1870 by Charles C. Craft, and named in honor of his father, James S. Craft, a prominent Pittsburgh lawyer, from whom he inherited the land on which the town is built. The founder of Crafton sold lots on easy terms and materially aided many men of moderate means to build their own homes. He was justly esteemed for his generosity and public spirit. The town was incorporated in 1890. The name Craft is a variant of Croft, "the dweller at the croft or farm." [13]

Dickson City, in Lackawanna County, was named in honor of Thomas Dickson, president of the Delaware and Hudson Canal Company from 1869 until his death in 1884. At one time he was an extensive coal operator in the neighborhood of Dickson City. The son of a Scotch machinist, Thomas Dickson came to America in his boyhood with his father, who first settled in Canada, but later came to the region of Carbondale, where the lad had to go to work at the age of thirteen. Although he developed into a man of scholarly tastes and habits, he spent his youth in hard labor and was entirely self-taught. When thirty years old, he became interested in the manufacture of iron, and in 1856 he organized the Dickson Manufacturing Company, which soon became an important producer of locomotives and mining machinery. In 1860 he became identified with the Delaware and Hudson Company; four years later he was its general superintendent; and in 1867 he was made vice-president.

[13] Information furnished by Mr. George Hardy of Crafton.

As an officer or director in a score or more of industrial companies, he became a man of large wealth, influence, and usefulness in Scranton, where he lived, and in all the surrounding country. "Tom" Dickson was everywhere loved and respected. Dickson City was incorporated as a borough in 1875. Dickson, "the son of Dick," is a Scotch patronymic surname.

Donora, a large and important industrial town that has recently sprung up on the west bank of the Monongahela River, in Washington County, was laid out in 1900 by the Union Improvement Company, of which William H. Donner was president. Another prominent stockholder in this company was Andrew W. Mellon of Pittsburgh. The name Donora was devised for the new town by combining the first syllable of the family name Donner with Nora, the baptismal name of Mrs. Mellon.

The city of **DuBois,** in Clearfield County, was first called Rumberger for John Rumberger, who laid out a town and sold building lots in 1772. In the same year John DuBois, a famous lumberman, who owned large tracts of white pine timber in Clearfield County, and who had exhausted the supply that could conveniently be floated down the Susquehanna to his mills at Williamsport, came to the little cluster of three or four houses on the western slope of the Allegheny Mountains, and at the age of sixty-three began extensive lumbering operations on his Sandy Creek tract. In May, 1876, his great mills were completed. Owning land adjacent to the settlement already begun, he built a hundred or more houses for his employees after his business was well established, and he devoted his declining years to clearing and improving his great farm of twelve hundred acres.

Shortly after his arrival the post-office of DuBois was

established, and in 1880 the town was incorporated under the name of DuBois, given in honor of John DuBois, its most important citizen, to whose energy, integrity, and business ability the place owed its real beginning and most of its early prosperity. John DuBois was a New Yorker of Huguenot descent, his name being the French equivalent of the English surname Wood. The borough of DuBoistown, in Lycoming County, where he first began his lumbering operations in Pennsylvania, was also named in his honor.

The name of **Dunmore**, in Lackawanna County, was given on the strength of great expectations that were never realized. About 1838 Charles Augustus Murray, second son of George Murray, fifth Earl of Dunmore, and younger brother of Alexander Edward Murray, who had succeeded to the earldom in 1836, spent many delightful weeks in hunting and fishing in the Moosic Mountain and the Lackawanna valley. Three enterprising Pennsylvanians, Henry W. Drinker, William Henry, and Edward Armstrong, succeeded in interesting the wealthy young Englishman in their project of building a railroad to connect this region with the Morris Canal in New Jersey, so as to secure transportation facilities between the Lackawanna valley and New York.

The hopes of the three Pennsylvania promoters rested upon young Murray, who, on his return to England, was authorized and expected to raise $1,500,000 for the execution of the project. Meanwhile, about 1840, the little settlement ceased to be called Bucktown—a name bestowed upon it because of the number of deer—and was hopefully christened Dunmore as a compliment to the noble family to which Charles Augustus Murray belonged. After his return to England, however, he seems to have lost all interest in the enterprise, and disappointed his

American friends by his failure to raise any funds. Young Murray afterwards entered the diplomatic service and became British envoy to Persia.[14] The village of Dunmore made no real growth until 1847, when the Pennsylvania Coal Company located its machine-shops there. The Gaelic name Dunmore literally means "the great hill-fort."

The city of **Duquesne,** in Allegheny County, which was incorporated in 1891, was so called for old Fort Duquesne, which was built at the forks of the Ohio in 1754, and named in honor of the Marquis Duquesne de Menneville, then governor of New France.[15] The present town includes an earlier settlement long known as Germantown, which is supposed to have received its name from the first German colony in America, planted near Philadelphia in 1683.[16] The name Duquesne, always very popular in the region of Pittsburgh, has been applied to many institutions and business concerns. The town of Duquesne has grown up rapidly about the plant of the Duquesne Steel Company, which was later acquired by the Carnegie Steel Company. Probably the borough took its name directly from these steel works; but in the last analysis its origin must be traced to the historic old French fort.

Duryea, in Luzerne County, once called Babylon because it was a Babel of tongues and nationalities, was named for Abram Duryea of New York, who bought coal lands in this neighborhood in 1845, and opened mines round which the town of Duryea has grown up. He entered the Civil War as colonel of the Fifth New York

---

14 Burke's *Peerage,* and J. C. Platt's *Reminiscences of the Early History of Scranton,* p. 70.
15 See Pittsburgh, page 121.
16 See Germantown, page 34.

Infantry in May, 1861, and was brevetted major-general four years later for gallant and meritorious services.

East Pittsburgh, in Allegheny County, began its existence in 1888, when George Westinghouse bought about five hundred acres of land near the Brinton railroad station in the Turtle Creek valley, and organized the East Pittsburgh Improvement Company. The new town which this company laid out grew so fast that twelve years later the borough of East Pittsburgh had a population of nearly three thousand. In thus appropriating the name of the metropolis of Allegheny County, East Pittsburgh[17] was less fortunate at its christening than its sister town of Wilmerding,[18] which was laid out at the same time and by the same company.

In 1884 the borough of **Edwardsville,** in Luzerne County, was formed by the incorporation of parts of old Plymouth and Kingston Townships. The new borough was named in honor of Daniel Edwards, a Welshman, who was then superintendent of the Kingston Coal Company, whose mining operations were situated entirely within the limits of the new municipality. By naming their town for Mr. Edwards, the citizens of Edwardsville showed their appreciation of the valuable services he had rendered in the industrial development of this region. He had charge of the operations of the Kingston Coal Company from 1868 until his death in 1901.[19] The family name Edwards is derived from the baptismal name Edward, meaning "noble guardian."

Ellwood City, in Beaver County, was laid out in 1890 by the Pittsburgh Company, and was named in honor of Colonel I. L. Ellwood of DeKalb, Indiana, a pioneer in the manufacture of wire-fencing and one of the chief

---

[17] See Pittsburgh, page 122.
[18] See Wilmerding, page 237.
[19] Data furnished by the Reverend T. C. Edwards, D.D., of Kingston.

stockholders in the company that founded the town. Ellwood City was incorporated as a borough in 1892.[20] Ellwood is probably derived from the Anglo-Saxon *ealdwudu,* "the old forest."

In 1911, the large borough of South Sharon, in Mercer County, which had been incorporated ten years before, was renamed **Farrell** in honor of James A. Farrell, president of the United States Steel Corporation, which plays so important a part in the industrial life of the place. The name of the post-office was changed at the same time. James A. Farrell was born at New Haven, Connecticut, in 1863, and began active life at the age of fifteen as an unskilled laborer in the New Haven wiremills. When nineteen years old, he was a wire-drawer for the Oliver Wire Company in Pittsburgh. At the age of twenty-six he had become general manager of the Pittsburgh Wire Company. In 1901 he took charge of the export department of the United States Steel Corporation, of which he became president ten years later. The surname Farrell signifies "warrior, champion, man of valor."

Ford City, in Armstrong County, was named in honor of Captain John B. Ford, "the father of the plate-glass industry in America," who erected his plate-glass factory here in 1887. Ford City has become the largest manufacturing centre in the world for plate-glass.[21]

Frackville, an important anthracite coal town in Schuylkill County, was laid out in 1861, and named for its founder, Daniel Frack, Sr. Fifteen years later it was incorporated as a borough. Its recent rapid growth has been due to the fact that, unlike many other coal towns, it is a desirable residential centre.

---

[20] Information furnished by Mr. Warren Griffiths of Ellwood City.
[21] Information given by Mr. H. M. McCue of Ford City.

Greenville, in Mercer County, was laid out in 1819 by Thomas Bean and William Scott on the west bank of the Shenango, though the principal part of the village later grew up on the east side of the stream. The town, which was long called West Greenville, is generally believed to have been named for General Nathaniel Greene.[22] No other plausible or authoritative explanation has ever been given. The dropping of the final *e* in the spelling of the name was doubtless due to carelessness in orthography, so common in pioneer times. In 1844 Greene Township, which lies a little to the northwest of Greenville, was also named in honor of General Greene. In 1837 West Greenville was incorporated; and in 1865 its name was changed to Greenville.

Jeannette, in Westmoreland County, was named in honor of Jeannette McKee, wife of H. Sellers McKee, a glass manufacturer, who constructed his works here in 1889, and whose business enterprise and activity have been largely instrumental in quickly building up a great industrial town where nothing but an old farmhouse stood in 1888.[23]

Johnsonburg, in Elk County, is said to have received its name from John Johnson, the traditional pioneer settler in that region, who about fifty years before the town was laid out in 1888, occupied a small cabin at the junction of the east and west branches of the Clarion River, near the centre of the present town.[24] Johnsonburg is noted for its extensive paper mills. Johnson is a patronymic surname meaning "the son of John."

The city of **Johnstown,** in Cambria County, was named for Joseph Johns, Jahns, or Yahns (as the name was variously spelled), a native of Switzerland, who came to

---

[22] See Greene County, pages 89-91.
[23] Letter from Mr. J. C. Loughead of Jeannette.
[24] Information furnished by Mr. Alva H. Gregory of Johnsonburg.

America in 1769, at the age of nineteen. He first settled
in Berks County, whence he soon migrated to the neighborhood of Meyersdale in Somerset County. In 1793
Joseph Johns bought "the Campbell tract" of 249 acres,
on which a large part of Johnstown is now built. The
town that he laid out was christened by him Conemaugh,
for the Conemaugh River.[25] When he died in 1813, his
son, Joseph Johns, Jr., inherited his real estate. The
town was incorporated as the borough of Conemaugh in
1831, and three years later the Legislature formally
changed its name to Johnstown. The Johnstown flood,
which wrecked the city and killed more than two thousand inhabitants, occurred in May, 1889.

Kane, in McKean County, was named in honor of
Thomas Leiper Kane of Philadelphia, who led an exploring expedition into this locality in the summer of 1859.
He was the great-grandson of John O'Kane, an Irish immigrant who came to America in 1752. His maternal
grandfather was Thomas Leiper, the Revolutionary patriot and leader of the Democratic party in Philadelphia;
and his father was the well-known jurist, Judge John K.
Kane of Philadelphia. Thomas L. Kane was a brother
of Dr. Elisha Kent Kane, the naval officer and famous
arctic explorer. He was so much attracted by the natural
beauty and abundant promise of this region that he
bought an extensive tract of land where the town now
stands, and began to build his home here in 1860. Then
the war broke out, and he organized a famous regiment
composed mainly of hunters and woodsmen, and known
as "the Bucktails," celebrated throughout the war for
their bravery and endurance.

Kane made a brilliant military record in the Civil
War, having fought in thirty-five battles, in five of which

---

25 See East Conemaugh, page 189.

he was wounded. At the close of the war he was brevetted major-general for gallant services at the battle
of Gettysburg. After the war General Kane returned
to his project of founding a town, which began to grow
in earnest after the completion of the Philadelphia and
Erie Railroad. The Irish patronymic O'Kane—originally O'Cahan, a family name of great antiquity—signifies ''a descendant of the warrior.''

Knoxville, in Allegheny County, occupies the land
which was once the famous fruit farm of the Reverend
Jeremiah Knox, a Methodist minister, who came to this
locality from Cadiz, Ohio. For many years the straw-
berries, blackberries, and grapes from the Knox farm
were staple articles in the Pittsburgh market. In 1873
the heirs of Jeremiah Knox laid out a town and named
it Knoxville in his honor. The Knoxville Land Company,
which was organized at that time, is still in existence.[26]
Jeremiah Knox was the uncle of Philander C. Knox, who
served as United States Senator for Pennsylvania and as
Secretary of State and as Attorney-General of the United
States. The Scotch territorial surname Knox was originally Knocks, the plural of the Gaelic *knock,* ''a round-
topped hill.''

Lansford, the largest town in Carbon County, situated
on a plateau which forms the first terrace above the
Panther Creek valley, was originally composed of two
distinct settlements, one called Ashton for Mr. Ashton,
an early resident, and the other known as Storm Hill because on this hill a violent storm had overturned the
house of Peter Fisher. In 1877 Ashton and Storm Hill
were consolidated and incorporated under the name of
Lansford. Lansford was the middle name of Asa Lans-

[26] Information furnished by the late Senator Philander C. Knox.

ford Foster, a pioneer and a very influential citizen in this region, in whose honor the town was named.

Mr. Foster, a native of Rowe, Massachusetts, at the age of twenty migrated to Bloomsburg, Pennsylvania, where he kept store for eight years. After securing additional mercantile experience in a large Philadelphia store, he came, in 1827, to Mauch Chunk, where he served as the storekeeper of the Lehigh Coal and Navigation Company for about ten years, until the company store was discontinued. In 1837 he helped to organize the Buck Mountain Coal Company, of which he became superintendent. Until his death in 1868, he was widely known as coal operator, mining engineer, and progressive citizen. He was a staunch champion of the common school system at a time when it had few friends in this region. Foster Township, in Luzerne County, was also named for Asa Lansford Foster. Lansford is probably a corruption or modification of Langford, "the dweller at the long ford."

Larksville, in Luzerne County, was originally called Blindtown, probably from some blind person; but in 1895, when Mrs. Rachel Pace celebrated there her eighty-sixth birthday, the name was changed to Larksville in honor of her ancestress, Peggy Lark, who had lived there and died at the age of one hundred and six years.[27] The family name Lark belongs to a numerous class of surnames derived from common birds and beasts.

Latrobe, in Westmoreland County, was laid out in 1851 by Oliver J. Barnes, a civil engineer in the employ of the Pennsylvania Railroad. Mr. Barnes, however, bought the land himself, laid out the town, and sold building lots on his own account, and not as an agent of the railroad company. He named the town Latrobe in honor of

---

[27] Information furnished by the Reverend Horace Edwin Hayden, former secretary of the Wyoming Historical and Geological Society.

his friend, Benjamin Henry Latrobe, Jr., whose illustrious father has justly' been styled "the father of architecture in the United States," and who was himself a distinguished civil engineer. In this capacity he was employed by both the Baltimore and Ohio and the Pennsylvania Railroad. He was a resident of Baltimore, and was once elected mayor of that city. Latrobe was incorporated in 1854. The Latrobes were of Huguenot descent, the family name being derived from an old French place name.

The city of **McKeesport**, in Allegheny County, was named in honor of David McKee, a north-country Irishman, who, at the close of the French and Indian War, came to the Monongahela, where he was well received by Queen Aliquippa, who allowed him to settle at the mouth of the Youghiogheny River. In 1769 the colonial government confirmed to him the right of exclusive ferriage over the two rivers at their confluence. In the same year David McKee and his two sons, Robert and Thomas, secured title to a tract of 844 acres of land now occupied by the city of McKeesport. John McKee, son of David, inherited his father's property, and added much to it by numerous purchases. He possessed great energy and shrewd business ability, and soon became one of the largest individual landowners in Allegheny County. Judged by the standards of that day, he was a man of wealth. In 1793 he became surety for his brother-in-law, Judge John Redick, who was under contract to furnish supplies for the famous Indian expedition of General Wayne. John Redick failed to fulfill his contract, and his bondsman was required to meet obligations aggregating many thousands of dollars. John McKee's property was sold at a great sacrifice by the United States marshal for about $30,000.

After his financial reverses John McKee conceived the idea of retrieving his fortunes by laying out a town at the mouth of the Youghiogheny River. The site was not particularly inviting, much of the tract being either swamp or forest; but it presented unusual commercial possibilities because of its situation at the junction of the Monongahela and the Youghiogheny Rivers. Here, in 1795, John McKee laid out the town of McKeesport, which he is said to have named in honor of his father, David McKee. In 1830 McKeesport was still a mere country village. In that year, however, John Harrison opened coal mines; in a few years the mining and shipping of coal became an important industry; and McKeesport began its career as a great industrial town. It became a borough in 1842. The name McKee is a variant of McKay, which is said to mean "the son of fire."

McKees Rocks, in Allegheny County, once known as Chartiers, is situated on the Ohio River at the mouth of Chartiers Creek, which took its name from Peter Chartier, a famous half-breed Indian trader. Judge Hugh H. Brackenridge, in his description of Pittsburgh as it appeared in 1786, says: "There is a high rock known by the name of McKee's Rock, at a distance of about three miles below the head of the Ohio. It is the end of a promontory where the river bends to the northwest, and where, by the rushing of the floods, the earth has been cut away during several ages, so that now the huge overhanging rocks appear hollowed beneath so as to form a dome of majesty and grandeur nearly a hundred feet in height."

In 1770, Washington, in the journal of his visit to this region, mentions the fact that he "dined with Mr. Magee, two miles below the city." This Mr. Magee has been identified with Alexander McKee, who was a deputy

Indian agent at Pittsburgh until 1776. It was from this Alexander McKee and from the rocks described above that the town of McKees Rocks has taken its name. Because of his intimacy with the Tory, Dr. John Connolly, who was the active agent of Lord Dunmore of Virginia, Alexander McKee was suspected of treasonable designs, but before he could be brought to justice, he and the infamous Simon Girty made their escape from Pittsburgh, and by their influence with the Indians greatly aided the British in the barbarous warfare that they waged with their Indian allies against the exposed frontier settlements.

The origin of the name of the residential borough of **Mount Oliver,** adjoining the city of Pittsburgh in Allegheny County, is not definitely known. The fact that the town is built upon a hill sufficiently explains the prefix Mount. The name Mount Oliver, given to the post-office in 1872, was apparently not bestowed in honor of the Oliver family, now so prominently known in the Pittsburgh area. The traditional explanation, which is at least a very reasonable conjecture, is that Mount Oliver derived its name from Oliver Ormsby, who in 1840 owned several hundred acres of land situated in what is now the very heart of Mount Oliver. The next year this estate was apportioned among his eight children, one of whom was named Oliver and another Oliveretta. Before 1872 there was an old borough named Ormsby, which was later absorbed by the city of Pittsburgh. Mount Oliver became an incorporated borough in 1892.

The name of **Munhall,** in Allegheny County, was first used in 1872. In that year the Pittsburgh, Virginia, and Charleston Railroad was built through this region, and the late Captain John Munhall gave the railroad company a right-of-way through his land on condition that a

15

station be located at a point to be chosen by him. The company named the new station Munhall in his honor. A few years later the three Munhall brothers, John, Michael, and William, sold their land to the firm of Carnegie, Phipps, and Company, which later became the Carnegie Steel Company. The steel industry gave a great impetus to the growth of Munhall.[28]

Olyphant, in Lackawanna County, was named in honor of George Talbot Olyphant of New York, who became president of the Delaware and Hudson Canal Company in 1858. In that year the company extended its railroad six miles farther down the valley from Archbald in order to open up some of their undeveloped coal lands. Upon this tract the town of Olyphant was started. It was incorporated in 1876. The name is said to have been suggested by Thomas Dickson,[29] who succeeded Mr. Olyphant to the presidency of the Delaware and Hudson Company in 1869. George T. Olyphant was a man of culture, character, and influence, and a capable administrator of varied business interests, which have contributed largely to the development and prosperity of the Lackawanna region. Olyphant is usually explained as the Scotch and early English form of *elephant*. The name Olifant occurs in the Roll of Battle Abbey.

Palmerton, in Carbon County, was carefully planned and laid out in 1898 by the newly formed New Jersey Zinc Company on an extensive tract of farm land which that organization had recently bought up for the site of its great industrial town. Stephen Searles Palmer of New York, the first president of the New Jersey Zinc Company, was the moving spirit of this enterprise, and

---

[28] Information furnished by Mr. A. C. Munhall of Eustis, Florida, son of Captain John Munhall.
[29] See Dickson City, page 213.

the new town was named in his honor. When he died in
1913, one year after Palmerton became a borough, the
whole community felt as if they had lost a personal
friend. The great industrial concern that created
Palmerton has exerted a wise and beneficent influence
in fostering its growth and prosperity, and in promoting
the health, comfort, education, and material interests of
its people. In 1923 Palmerton showed its civic pride by
celebrating its twenty-fifth anniversary with appropriate
ceremonies. Palmer is a mediæval surname signifying
"palm-bearing pilgrim."

The first settlement at **Parsons**, in Luzerne County,
was called Laurel Run. When the Lehigh and Susquehanna Railroad was built, a station was established at
this point; but Charles Parrish, who represented the
railroad company, had to discard the name Laurel Run
because the railroad already had a station by that name.
So he christened the place Parsons in honor of Calvin
Parsons, who had inherited most of the town site from
his father, Hezekiah Parsons, and who was highly respected as a public-spirited citizen.[30] The settlement
flourished, and in 1876 Parsons was incorporated as a
borough. The town has grown rapidly during the past
decade. The name Parsons means "the parson's son."

Pitcairn, in Allegheny County, was laid out in 1892 by
the Pennsylvania Railroad Company as the site of its
extensive freight yards and car shops. Two years later
the new industrial town was incorporated under the name
of Pitcairn in honor of Robert Pitcairn, then superintendent of the Pittsburgh division of the Pennsylvania
Railroad.[31] Pitcairn means "cairn-croft."

Pittston, in Luzerne County, built up on the site of

---

[30] Information furnished by Mr. E. A. Evans of Parsons.
[31] Explanation given by Mr. William G. Irwin of Pitcairn.

old Fort Pittston, was one of the five original Connecticut townships. It was first settled in 1770, and was then called Pittstown in honor of the great English statesman, Sir William Pitt, who later became the Earl of Chatham.[32] In 1838 Pittston had only eight or ten houses. It was incorporated in 1855.

Four years later the borough of **West Pittston,** until then called Fort Jenkins, "an elegant suburb of Pittston," was also incorporated. Old Fort Jenkins, one of the most northern of the old pioneer stockade forts, named for Colonel John Jenkins, a capable officer in the Revolutionary War, was within the limits of the new borough of West Pittston, which lies just across the river from the city of Pittston. The two Luzerne County towns bearing the name of Sir William Pitt have now a combined population of more than 25,000.

Pottstown, in Montgomery County, was named for its founder, John Potts, one of the leading ironmasters of his time. He was a descendant of the Quaker, Thomas Potts, who settled in Burlington, New Jersey, in William Penn's time. In 1752, on the death of his father, who was also called Thomas Potts, and who succeeded Thomas Rutter as master of the old Colebrookdale Furnace, John Potts bought nearly a thousand acres of land in this region, and two years later he laid out a town, which was at first variously called Pottsylvania and Pottsgrove. When he died in 1768, the village contained only about a dozen houses. The name Pottstown occurs as early as 1770. His son Isaac was the owner of Valley Forge; and another son, Samuel, once held title to the land on which John Pott, a Pennsylvania-German, later laid out the town of Pottsville, the present county-seat of Schuylkill County.[33]   Dr. Jonathan Potts, the physician in charge of the military hospitals of the American army during the Revolutionary War, was also a son of John Potts, the founder of Pottstown.   In 1815 Pottstown became a borough.   Potts was ''originally a nickname for a maker or seller of pots.''

Rankin, in Allegheny County, lies just across the Monongahela River from Glassport and joins the borough of Braddock.   About 1870 a man named Thomas Rankin bought a farm, built a house, and lived where the town now stands.   At that time Rankin's house was the only one in sight, and the Baltimore and Ohio Railroad made it a stopping place, calling the station Rankin.[34]   The present town has grown up about the railway station.   The family name Rankin is a diminutive of Rann, or Rand, which has been shortened from Randolf or Randolph, ''the shield wolf.''

In 1904 the borough of **Saint Clair,** in Allegheny County, was separated from Lower Saint Clair Township, which once formed part of the original Saint Clair Township, organized in 1788 and named in honor of General Arthur St. Clair, a prominent Pennsylvania officer in the Revolutionary War.[35]   Arthur St. Clair, grandson of the Earl of Roslyn, was born in Scotland in 1734 and educated at the University of Edinburgh. In 1757 he entered the British army as ensign, and served under General Amherst at Louisburg and General Wolfe at Quebec.   In 1764 he resigned his lieutenancy and settled in the Ligonier valley in Pennsylvania, where he bought a tract of land, built a house, and became a pioneer miller and farmer.   During the next ten years

---

[33] See Pottsville, page 145.
[34] Information furnished by Mr. M. P. Schooley of Homestead.
[35] The borough of Saint Clair was annexed to the city of Pittsburgh in 1922.

he filled acceptably a number of civil offices, mainly in
Bedford and Westmoreland Counties, serving as surveyor, justice of the peace, clerk of the court, recorder,
prothonotary, and judge. In January, 1776, he entered
the Continental army as colonel, taking part in the unfortunate Canadian campaign. A year later he was appointed major-general, and rendered important services
throughout the war, figuring prominently at the battles
of Trenton, Princeton, and Brandywine. He was president of Congress in 1787, and governor of the Northwestern Territory from 1789 to 1802.

In March, 1791, he was made commander-in-chief of
an expedition against the hostile Indians in Ohio. On
November 4th, he was taken by surprise at the Miami
villages and utterly defeated. President Washington,
greatly incensed, refused a court of inquiry; but Congress later exonerated him from blame. In 1802 President Jefferson removed him from the governorship of
the Northwestern Territory. Feeling that he had been
publicly discredited and disgraced, Arthur St. Clair retired to a log cabin on the summit of Chestnut Ridge,
in Westmoreland County, where he spent the remaining
sixteen years of his life in poverty, in a vain attempt to
secure some settlement of his just claims against the
government, and in writing a vindication of his conduct
in the disastrous Indian campaign that ended his public
career.

Clair means "illustrious." The surname St. Clair is
derived from the name of a Norman village, St. Clere,
which, according to Dr. Isaac Taylor, "has bestowed its
name upon a Scottish family, an English town, an Irish
county, a Cambridge college, and a royal dukedom." In
the United States seven post-offices are called Saint
Clair, most of them having received their name from

General Arthur St. Clair. St. Clairsville, in Bedford County, was also named for him.

Saint Clair, in Schuylkill County, is generally, but erroneously, supposed to have been named for General Arthur St. Clair, who was once part owner of an extensive tract of land in this vicinity. This land was afterward sold to Samuel and Thomas Potts, who disposed of it to John Pott, the founder of Pottsville.[36] In point of fact, the town of Saint Clair took the Christian name of St. Clair Nichols, who owned the farm on which the town was built. In 1831 Messrs. Carey, Lee, and Hart bought the Nichols farm, laid out the town, and gave it the name of Saint Clair.[37]

Saint Marys, in Elk County, was founded in 1842 by the "German Catholic Brotherhood of Philadelphia and Baltimore," an organization that had bought a tract of 35,000 acres of forest land in what was then Jefferson and McKean Counties. On October 28, 1842, one party of colonists set out from Philadelphia and another from Baltimore; they met at Columbia, in Lancaster County, whence they traveled by canal as far as Freeport, in Armstrong County, from which point they completed their journey overland, reaching their destination on December 8th. As this date was the feast of the Immaculate Conception of the Virgin Mary, and as the name of the first white woman who set foot on the new town was also Mary, the settlers called the place Saint Mary's. Six years later Saint Mary's was incorporated as a borough. Elk County was formed the year after the founding of Saint Mary's.[38] The Hebrew word Mary means "bitter."

---

[36] See Pottsville, page 145.
[37] W. W. Munsell and Company's *History of Schuylkill County*, p. 207. Facts vouched for by Messrs. David Duffy and D. G. Lubold of Pottsville.
[38] The postal authorities now insist that the name be written Saint Marys.

In 1870 **Sayre**, in Bradford County, was a railroad station known as the "Ithaca and Athens and Southern Central Junction." Here the Lehigh Valley Railroad Company erected a roundhouse and began the construction of locomotive works. The location of the railroad shops at this point greatly stimulated building operations, and a town rapidly grew up at the junction. In 1873 the station and the new town received the name of Sayre in honor of Robert H. Sayre, then superintendent of the Lehigh Valley Railroad. Mr. Sayre, who was born in Mauch Chunk in 1824, became chief engineer of the Lehigh Valley Railroad in 1852 and for many years afterwards was actively engaged in constructing its main line and its numerous extensions. From 1885 to his retirement in 1898 he was second vice-president of the company.[39] His youngest son, Francis B. Sayre, married President Woodrow Wilson's daughter. The Welsh surname Sayer or Sayre means "carpenter."

Scottdale, in Westmoreland County, was laid out in 1872 by Julius Shipley, a civil engineer of Uniontown, on farms owned by Peter and Jacob Loucks, whose grandfather, Peter Loucks, had removed to this region from Bucks County in 1800. In 1873 the southwest branch of the Pennsylvania Railroad was completed as far as the Loucks farms, and at the suggestion of Congressman George F. Huff, the new town was called Scottdale in honor of Colonel Thomas Alexander Scott, then president of the Pennsylvania Railroad. The next year the borough of Scottdale was incorporated. Before the town was laid out, the place was known as Fountain Mills from an old mill that then stood on the present site of the Scottdale Furnace Company. In 1861 Thomas A. Scott

---

[39] Information furnished by Mr. D. G. Baird, secretary of the Lehigh Valley Railroad Company.

was appointed Assistant Secretary of War under President Lincoln, and by his skill in transportation rendered efficient service to his country, which honored him with the rank of colonel.[40]   The surname Scott was first used as an indication of the bearer's nationality.

Sharpsburg, in Allegheny County, was named in honor of James Sharp, the original owner of the land, who settled here in 1826.   Three years later, when the canal was opened, the town began to grow.   Sharpsburg was incorporated in 1841.   James Sharp kept a temperance hotel here, and was active in promoting the growth and welfare of his town until his death in 1861.   He was highly esteemed for his courtesy, friendliness, hospitality, and public spirit.   The surname Sharp was originally given to ''a keen, active, acute man.''

Swissvale, in Allegheny County, was built up on the farm of James Swisshelm, who inherited it from his father, John.   The name Swissvale is said to have been invented by Jane Gray Swisshelm, the wife of the proprietor.   When the Pennsylvania Railroad decided to establish a station at this point in 1854, James Swisshelm donated half an acre of land for the site, and the railroad company, in recognition of his generosity, adopted the name of Swissvale for the station, around which the present town has sprung up.[41]   The name Swisshelm refers to personal appearance or characteristic, and signifies ''Swiss helmet.''

Swoyersville, in Luzerne County, was named about 1888 in honor of the late John Henry Swoyer, who operated two large coal breakers here, and who was much respected for the fairness with which he treated his em-

---

[40] Information furnished by Mr. R. L. O'Donnel when he was general superintendent of the Western Division of the Pennsylvania Railroad.
[41] Information furnished by Mr. Ernest S. Craighead of Swissvale.

ployees. The town was laid out by P. M. Boyle, and the name Swoyersville was suggested by Anthony Callahan.[42] The name Swoyer is an Americanized form of the German surname of personal characteristic, Schweier or Schweyer, signifying "strong, vigorous, or powerful."

Taylor, in Lackawanna County, a borough which has grown to be a place of consequence within the past twenty years, was named for the late Moses Taylor, a prominent New York merchant and capitalist, who had extensive business interests in the place that now bears his name. Moses Taylor was born in New York in 1806, began his business career as a clerk at the age of fifteen, and when twenty-five years old went into business for himself. As merchant and ship-owner he built up an extensive trade with Cuba. As banker and as a member of the "Union Defense Committee" during the Civil War, he helped to get subscribers for more than $200,000,000 worth of government bonds. He was a wise and energetic promoter of railway construction in Pennsylvania. In 1882 he spent $250,000 in establishing at Scranton the Moses Taylor Hospital for miners, iron-workers, and employees of the Delaware, Lackawanna, and Western Railroad. The surname Taylor designated the occupation of the man who first bore it.

Throop, in Lackawanna County, was named in honor of Dr. Benjamin Henry Throop, the pioneer physician of Scranton. Doctor Throop built his modest cottage near Slocum Hollow in 1847, and for many years was the beloved physician of the valley, when Scranton was a mere hamlet and the surrounding country was thinly settled. Doctor Throop was fifth in line of descent from William

---

[42] Facts furnished by the Reverend Horace Edwin Hayden, former secretary of the Wyoming Historical and Geological Society, and by Mr. Henry E. Miller, secretary of the borough of Swoyersville.

Throope the Puritan, who settled at Barnstable, Massachusetts, in 1660. Doctor Throop was postmaster of Scranton in 1853. Being convinced that coal was destined to be the chief source of wealth in this region, he purchased extensive tracts of valuable coal land. He also added to his great wealth by buying up farms and dividing them into building lots, which he sold at a reasonable price, but always at a handsome profit. He was the founder not only of Throop, but also of Blakely, and was one of the prime movers in the formation of Lackawanna County. The family name Throop is a variant of Thorpe, and signifies a "dweller in the thorp, or village."

The city of **Titusville**, in Crawford County, was named in honor of Jonathan Titus, a pioneer surveyor, who obtained title to eight hundred acres of land, and built his cabin on the site of the town as early as 1796. He was the grandson of Peter Titus, a German immigrant who had settled on Staten Island about 1750. Jonathan Titus, a man of heroic mould, kept open house for all comers. His hospitable homestead became widely known as "Titus's," and in 1818, when he founded a town on his land, the settlement naturally took the name of Titusville. The place, however, did not really begin to grow until oil was discovered here in 1858. During the next year oil was struck in great abundance, and the future of Titusville was assured. The excitement became so intense, and speculation and expectations ran so high, that the village soon had 15,000 inhabitants,—nearly twice its present population. The family name Titus has its origin in the common Latin prænomen *Titus*, which is presumably a modification of *tutus*, "safe."

The important industrial town of **Vandergrift**, in Westmoreland County, was laid out in 1895 by Frederick L. Olmstead for theApollo Iron and Steel Company, and named in honor of J. J. Vandergrift of Pittsburgh, a large stockholder in this company.[43] Two years later the borough was incorporated. Its growth has been very rapid.

Waynesboro, in Franklin County, was laid out in 1797 by James Wallace, Jr., who named it Waynesboro in honor of General Anthony Wayne,[44] whose death in the previous year was a reminder of the heroic services he had rendered his state and country. During the first decade or two of its history many people persisted in calling the place Wallacetown for its founder. In 1818 the town was incorporated as Waynesborough, a name that is now generally written Waynesboro.

Wilkinsburg, one of the oldest towns in Allegheny County, once known as McNairsville, was named in honor of William Wilkins, for more than fifty years a prominent citizen of Pittsburgh, where he opened his law office in 1801. Fifteen years later he was president of the Common Council. During his long and useful career he filled with distinction many public offices, serving as member of the Legislature, president judge, Federal district court judge for western Pennsylvania, United States Senator, minister to Russia, and Secretary of War under President Tyler. William Wilkins was energetic in promoting every enterprise likely to benefit Pittsburgh and Allegheny County. He helped to organize the Bank of Pittsburgh and to build the bridge across the Monongahela, and he materially aided the Pennsylvania Railroad in reaching Pittsburgh. The borough of Wilkinsburg was incorporated in 1887 from Wilkins Township, which was formed in 1821. The family name of Wilkins is a diminutive of William, which means ''resolute helmet.''

---

[43] Facts furnished by Mr. C. H. Omo and Miss Pauline Freshwater of Vandergrift.

[44] See Wayne County, pages 91-93.

Wilmerding, in Allegheny County, was at first a mere railroad station, built about 1885, on land originally owned by Major William B. Negley. The name Wilmerding was suggested by Robert Pitcairn,[45] then superintendent of the Pittsburgh division of the Pennsylvania Railroad, out of compliment to Major Negley's wife, Joanna *Wilmerding* Negley, whose maiden name was Joanna *Wilmerding* Bruce. Wilmerding was the family name of her mother. Several years after the station was established, George Westinghouse bought about five hundred acres of land in the Turtle Creek valley and organized the East Pittsburgh Improvement Company, which later laid out the town of Wilmerding. When the Westinghouse Air Brake Company built its works here, a movement was started to call the place Westinghouse, but this suggestion, it seems, did not meet with the approval of Mr. Westinghouse; and when the town was incorporated in 1890, it borrowed the name of Wilmerding from the railway station.[46]

The name of **Windber,** in Somerset County, was selected by the Pennsylvania Railroad Company in 1897 for its new station at this point. This name, which was suggested by E. J. Berwind, the chief stockholder in the Berwind-White Coal Company, was formed by transposing the two syllables of the family name Berwind. Shortly after the station was established, the Wilmore Coal Company, which owned the land, planned and laid out a town under the supervision of their engineer, James C. Cunningham. The town and the post-office adopted the name of the railway station.[47]

[45] See Pitcairn, page 227.
[46] Information furnished by Mr. Christopher Horrocks of Wilmerding, and by Mr. John F. Miller, vice-president of the Westinghouse Air Brake Company.
[47] Data furnished by Mr. E. H. Delaney, chief engineer of the Berwind-White Coal Company.

Winton, in Lackawanna County, was named in honor of its founder, William W. Winton, who established the Winton coal breaker here in July, 1874, and later laid out the town on his land. His father, Andrew Winton, had migrated from Otsego County, New York, and settled near the present site of Scranton in 1833, where his son William, fresh from school, was first employed as the village schoolmaster. He later became a storekeeper, a banker, and a prosperous coal operator. In 1894 he died at the age of eighty, having spent nearly all his life at Scranton.[48] Winton was incorporated in 1877. The family name Winton was originally taken from an English place name, Wintonia being a Latinized form of Winchester.

---

[48] Information furnished by Mrs. Katherine Winton Murray of Scranton, granddaughter of William W. Winton.

III

VILLAGES AND TOWNSHIPS

CHAPTER XX

A GENERAL SURVEY OF THE VILLAGE NAMES

IN 1922 Pennsylvania had more than three thousand post-offices. Only a few years before, the number was close to four thousand, many of the smaller offices having disappeared with the extension of the rural delivery system. Most of those which now remain indicate the presence of a village or at least a hamlet. To attempt an explanation of the origin of all these village names[1] within the scope of this book would be impossible. Part III contains a commentary on the more notable names of the smaller Pennsylvania towns and villages, and on representative township names.

We have seen that our geographical names may be roughly divided into aboriginal names, borrowed place names, borrowed personal names, and "invented" names. Indian names, village names derived from family names, oddities in local nomenclature, place names possessing historical or other special interest, and township names will be discussed in separate chapters.

1. A multitude of village names have been borrowed from almost every part of the world. Nine *European capitals* are represented:

Athens	Dublin	New Paris
Berlin	Edinboro	Rome
Berne	New London	St. Petersburg

Athens, in Bradford County, took the name of old Athens Township, which was formed in 1786 by the Sus-

---

[1] The phrase *village names* is here used to refer to all towns having a population of less than five thousand, according to the census of 1920.

quehanna Company of Connecticut, and apparently
named for the capital of Greece.[2] The site of Athens
was famous as Tioga Point long before the first white
settler, John Secord, built his cabin here in 1778. This
settlement was made possible by Colonel Thomas Hart-
ley, who, in that year, with a force of four hundred armed
pioneers, came to old Tioga Point and burned the palace
and town of "that Indian fury," Queen Esther, who was
a granddaughter of Madame Montour.[3] In the following
year General John Sullivan erected Fort Sullivan at
Tioga Point and made it the base of his punitive expedition against the warlike Iroquois of New York.[4] In the
time of Conrad Weiser, Tioga Point was known as the
most extensive Indian settlement in Pennsylvania north
of the Indian town of Shamokin (now Sunbury). It was
here that Colonel John Butler and the half-breed, Joseph
Brant, had assembled their savage warriors before de-
scending upon Wyoming, and it was hither that they
returned after the massacre. Tioga Point began to be
called Athens about 1803, and the borough was incorporated under that name in 1831.

Berlin, one of the oldest villages in Somerset County,
was settled about 1769 by the German sect of Dunkard
Brethren. The town was accordingly called Berlin, and
the fertile region surrounding it named Brothers' Valley.

East Berlin, in Adams County, was laid out in 1764 by
John Frankenburger, a German settler, who christened
it Berlin.[5]

Berne and **Bernville,** in Berks County, were settled

---

[2] Bradford County is rich in ambitious names. Here are located Rome,
Troy, Athens, Cadis, and Canton. Perhaps the pseudo-classicism prevalent
a century or more ago sufficiently explains the borrowing of such names
as Athens, Rome, and Troy.

[3] See Montour County, pages 116-118.

[4] See Sullivan County, pages 108, 109.

[5] See also New Berlin, page 164.

early in the eighteenth century by religious refugees from the Swiss canton of Berne, who named their settlements for their ancestral home, now the capital of Switzerland.

New London and **London Grove**, in Chester County, were named directly for the London Company, which once owned about 17,000 acres of land in Chester County, out of which were formed the old townships of New London, London Grove, and London Britain.

Saint Petersburg, in Clarion County, was at first called Petersburg in honor of Judge Richard Peters [6] of Philadelphia, who once owned the town site. When the post-office was established here in 1862, the postal authorities, to avoid confusion with Petersburg in Huntingdon County, added the prefix "Saint" in imitation of the name of the former capital of Russia.

2. The following thirty-three names—about half the total number—have a distinctively *English* flavor:

Avon	Falmouth	Nottingham
Bath	Harrow	Oxford
Birmingham	Hellam	Rydal
Bridgewater	Hereford	Salisbury
Buckingham	Kennett Square	Sheffield
Cambridge	Lansdowne	Shrewsbury
Cheltenham	Liverpool	Southampton
Devon	Ludlow	Warminster
Dover	Malvern	Warwick
Durham	Manchester	Windsor
Exeter	Norwich	Worcester

Birmingham, in Huntingdon County, was laid out in 1797 by John Cadwallader, who was ambitious to start a manufacturing town at the head of navigation on the Juniata River. The village owed its early growth to the iron industry, and its founder, hopeful that it would be-

[6] See page 34.

come a great industrial centre, named it for the English city of Birmingham.

The borough of **Exeter,** in Luzerne County, derived its name from old Exeter Township, which was organized in 1790 by settlers from Exeter, Rhode Island. The Rhode Island town was named for Exeter in England.

The name of the borough and the township of **Hellam,** in York County, is a corrupt spelling of Hallam. Samuel Blunston, one of the founders of York County, named the place for his native town of Upper Hallam in Yorkshire.

Hereford, in Berks County, has taken its name from old Hereford Township, which was formed in 1753 and named for Herefordshire by the English ironmasters who prospected in this region.

The name of **Kennett Square,** in Chester County, was suggested by Francis Smith, who had come from near Kennet in Wiltshire, and who, in 1686, settled at the mouth of Pocopson Creek. "Kennet Township" is mentioned in court records as early as 1705.

Oxford, in Chester County, derived its name directly from old Oxford Township, which was formed in 1754 and named for the English university town. The borough of **New Oxford** and the township of Oxford, in Adams County, received their names from the same source.

The borough of **Shrewsbury,** in York County, has taken the name of Shrewsbury Township, which was organized in 1739 by settlers from Shrewsbury, England.

Warwick, in Warwick Township, Chester County, was first settled by the ironmaster, Samuel Nutt, who christened his place the Warwick Iron Works for his native Warwickshire.

Windsor, in York County, took its name from Windsor

Township, which was formed in 1758 and named for Windsor in England by Thomas Armor, an Englishman, who was then the presiding justice.

3. The following are a few of the names borrowed from *Scotland:*

Athol	Glasgow	Lanark
Clyde	Grampian	Paisley
Elgin	Greenock	Scotland

Grampian, in Clearfield County, was named in 1809 by Dr. Samuel Coleman from the striking resemblance that this region bore to the Grampian Hills of Scotland, whence he and his forbears had sprung.

Scotland, in Franklin County, was named by the first settler, Alexander Thompson, for his native land.

4. Here are a dozen Pennsylvania names borrowed from the *Welsh:*

Bryn Mawr	Haverford	Pen Argyl
Cynwyd	Lampeter	Radnor
Duffryn Mawr	Merion Station	Tredyffrin
Gwynedd	Nantmeal Village	Uwchland

Haverford, in Montgomery County, was so named by the early Welsh settlers, who had come from the neighborhood of Haverford-West in Pembrokeshire. Haverford Township, now in Delaware County, existed as early as 1722.

Merion Station, in Montgomery County, bears the name of old Merion Township (now divided into Upper and Lower Merion), which was formed before 1714 by settlers from the Welsh county of Merioneth.

Nantmeal Village, in Chester County, was named for old Nantmeal Township, now divided into East and West Nantmeal and Honey Brook Townships. **Honey Brook** is an English translation of the Welsh Nantmel, ''sweet water." The Welsh settlers in this region had migrated from Nantmel in Radnorshire.

Radnor, in Delaware County, took its name from Radnor Township, which was settled and named in 1683 by Welsh Friends from Radnorshire.

Tredyffrin, in Chester County, is a Welsh name signifying "the township in the valley." The name Valleytown, which occurs in some colonial documents, is an evident effort to Anglicise the name.

Uwchland, in Chester County, was originally Uwchlan, a Welsh word meaning "upland, or above the valley." The correct form of the word is preserved by Uwchlan Township.

5. *Ireland* has furnished the following names:

Antrim	Donegal	Queenstown
Armagh	Drumore	Sligo
Belfast	Greencastle	Ulster
Derry	Limerick	Waterford

Antrim, in Tioga County, was named by its founder, Duncan S. Magee, for his native County Antrim. A company of promoters, who came here from New York State in 1868, gathered around one of the springs, and "Duncan S. Magee, dipping a glassful of water from its crystal depths, formally christened the place Antrim."

Greencastle, in Franklin County, was laid out in 1782 by Colonel John Allison and named in honor of his native Green Castle, a fishing town and tiny seaport in County Donegal.

Waterford, in Erie County, occupies the site of the old French Fort Le Boeuf,[7] "the bull, or the buffalo," erected in 1753 on the Le Boeuf Creek, at the headwaters of the Allegheny River. Here, in the same year, George Washington received the guarded answer of the com-

---

[7] See page 127.

mandant, de St. Pierre: ''I shall transmit your letter to the Marquis Duquesne. His answer shall be a law to me; and if he shall order me to transmit it to you, sir, you may be assured I shall not fail to dispatch it to you forthwith.'' Waterford was laid out by Andrew Ellicott in 1795; and both the village and the township of Waterford were named in deference to the Irish settlers, some of whom had come from County Waterford. Le Boeuf Township, named for the creek and fort, lies south of Waterford Township.

6. *Germany* and *Austria* have furnished Pennsylvania with more than a score of names like these:

Baden	Germania	Manheim
Bingen	Hamburg	Saxonburg
Franconia	Lititz	Strasburg

Bingen, in Northampton County, was so called about 1850 by the Ueberoth family, because they had come from the region of Bingen on the Rhine.

Germania, in Potter County, began its existence about 1854 as a German colony in which the German language and all the customs of the Fatherland were to be perpetuated.

Lititz, in Lancaster County, was settled by the Moravians in 1754. The scattered English settlers had previously named the place Warwick after the English shire. In 1756 Count von Zinzendorf changed its name to Lititz after the barony of Lititz in Moravia, where the Moravian Church had been organized in 1456. In 1757 John Reuter and the Reverend Nathaniel Seidel formally laid out the town of Lititz. The property was owned entirely by the Moravian Brethren, and for a long time all its interests were controlled by them. The old name of Warwick was retained by the township in which Lititz is situated. For more than a century and a half, Lititz, one of the most interesting and attractive villages in Pennsylvania, has exercised a religious and educational influence that is out of all proportion to its size.

Manheim, in Lancaster County, was founded by "Baron" Heinrich Wilhelm von Stiegel, who came here from Philadelphia in 1761, bought two hundred acres of land, laid out a town, which he named Manheim after his native city in Germany, and erected a "grand castle, very singular in its structure," at which he entertained his friends with ostentatious hospitality. He started glass works at Manheim, where he made the famous "Stiegel glass," and he also began to manufacture iron. To the Lutheran church he presented a building lot on condition that the congregation pay an annual rental of one red rose. Once a year, to this day, a red rose is proffered, with much ceremony, to his descendants or representatives. His castle near Manheim had cannon mounted on the tower in order that a salute might be fired whenever he returned home.

Saxonburg, in Butler County, is all that now remains of an ambitious German colony, which, in 1831, under the leadership of Karl and Johann A. Roebling, of Mühlhausen, in Old Saxony, bought 16,000 acres of land in Jefferson Township. Early in 1832 three hundred families from Mühlhausen embarked at Bremen for their new home; but because of the pernicious activities of colonizing agents at Philadelphia and Baltimore, only a few families found their way to Saxonburg, which was named for their former home in Old Saxony. The founder of this colony, John A. Roebling, afterward attained eminence as a civil engineer and a builder of suspension bridges.

Strasburg, in Strasburg Township, Lancaster County, "the town by the road or street," dates back to 1733.

The LeFevres, Ferrees, and other early settlers gave it this name because they had come from the region of Strasbourg in Alsace.

7. A dozen or more Pennsylvania village names, such as Loretto, Milan, Pavia, Venetia, and Verona, have been borrowed from *Italy*.

Loretto, in Cambria County, was founded and named by the devoted priest, Prince Demetrius Augustine Gallitzin,[8] who lived and labored here many years. Father Gallitzin named the village Loretto for the Italian town of Loreto on the Adriatic, the seat of the famous shrine of "our Lady of Loreto."

The village of **Pavia,** in Bedford County, became a post-office in 1861. The Italian Pavia is the foremost town on the Ticino, which rises in the Swiss Alps; and the little Bedford County village is also situated on a stream that takes its rise in "the Schweitz," or Switzerland, the local name of a wild and beautiful region extending from the northwestern part of Union Township into Blair and Cambria Counties.

8. About a dozen *Spanish names*, like Arroya, Buena Vista, Gibraltar, and Valencia, adorn the map of Pennsylvania. Several of these, such as Matamoras, Monterey, and Vera Cruz, date from the Mexican War.

About seventy villages in Pennsylvania bear the names of rivers, cities, states, provinces, or countries in various parts of the world. The names in the following list have, for the most part, little or no significance except as a proof of the ingenuity of the postal authorities:

Albion	California	Degolia
Aleppo	Cornwall	East Texas
Andalusia	Corsica	Finland
Bermudian	Dalmatia	Helvetia

---

[8] See Gallitzin, page 263.

Holland	Mexico	Numidia
Jeddo	Moscow	Ottawa
Lima	Nebraska	Platea
Livonia	New Britain	Swedeland
Lorane	Newfoundland	Utahville
Luxor	New Grenada	Yukon

9. The influence of the *classical languages* is seen in the following names:

Alba	Delphi	Pardus
Amaranth	Eureka	Parnassus
Apollo	Expedit	Salix
Argentine	Hector	Seneca
Argus	Homer City	Troy
Atlas	Instanter	Ulysses
Castanea	Lycippus	Utica
Conifer	Mars	Venus

10. The pious character of the early settlers of Pennsylvania is attested by their fondness for *Biblical names:*

Ararat	Ephrata	New Salem
Bethel	Galilee	Nineveh
Damascus	Goshen	Olivet
Egypt	Mount Nebo	Tyre
Emaus	Nazareth	Zion

Perhaps the most noteworthy of these Biblical names are Emaus, Ephrata, and Nazareth.

Emaus, in Lehigh County, first settled by Moravians about 1745, was named for Emmaus in Palestine. Emaus remained a "close denominational town" until 1835.

The borough and the township of **Ephrata**, in Lancaster County, are worthy of note because it was here that the little German sect of Seventh-Day Baptist Brethren established their monastic community in 1735. The old convent or *Kloster* and the *Gebrüderhaus* each contained about thirty-five devotees. Johann Conrad Beissel was the founder and prior of this strange Protestant monastery.

The town of **Nazareth**, in Upper Nazareth Township, Northampton County, was begun in 1740, when Peter Boehler, afterwards a Moravian bishop, worked as a mason on a large house that the Wesleyan missionary, George Whitefield, had planned as a school and orphanage for negroes. The next year, as a result of a disagreement between Whitefield and his Moravian brethren, the latter bought the tract and started a settlement, which they called Nazareth after the home of Christ in Galilee.

11. The following places were *named for churches:*

Belfry	Churchville	Kellers Church
Brickchurch	Derry Church	Spring Church
Chapel	Huffs Church	Stone Church

Derry Church, in Dauphin County, has taken the name of one of the oldest Presbyterian churches in Pennsylvania. The Scotch-Irish, who came here in 1720, called their settlement Derry for their native Londonderry, whose ancient Celtic name was Derry. The Derry congregation was organized in 1725 by the Reverend Robert Evans, who died two years later in Virginia. The old weather-beaten log church was built in 1729,—the same year in which Derry Township was organized. The new industrial town of Hershey [9] has grown up on the site of Derry Church.

Stone Church in Northampton County, was the name originally given to the old union church built about 1790 by the Lerches and the Kreiders for the joint use of the Lutheran and the Reformed congregations.

12. The following post-offices were named for *institutions of learning:*

Academy Corners	George School	Ogontz School
Collegeville	Normalville	State College

---

[9] See Hershey, page 276.

Academy Corners, in Tioga County, derived its name from the old Union Academy, which for many years shed the light of learning over this region.

Collegeville, in Montgomery County, was formerly known as Perkiomen Bridge and later as Freeland. In 1869 the Reformed Church established Ursinus College here, and in the same year the name of the village was changed to Collegeville.

Normalville, in Fayette County, once called Springfield, changed its name in deference to a local normal school.

State College, in Centre County, was so named because it is the seat of the Pennsylvania State College. The thriving borough owes its existence wholly to the college, which has had a phenomenal growth during the past decade. College Township received its name from the same source.

13. The following places bear the *baptismal names of men:*

Aaronsburg	Frank	Jamestown
Clarence	Fredericksburg	Jerome
Conrad	Fredericktown	Jonas
Davidsville	Georgetown	Petersburg
Elmer	Hiram	Ralphton

Aaronsburg, in Centre County, was named for Aaron Levy, who came from Northumberland and laid out the town in 1786. In 1804 he sold all his land to two other Jews, Simon and Hyman Gratz.

Fredericksburg, in Lebanon County, was laid out about 1755 by Frederick Stump and named for him. The founder of Fredericksburg, who was a peace-loving, God-fearing citizen, should not be confused with the notorious Indian-killer, Frederick Stump, who, shortly after the

French and Indian War, murdered ten inoffensive Indians near the site of Selinsgrove, in Snyder County.

Fredericktown, in Washington County, was christened in honor of Frederick Wise, who laid it out in 1790.

Georgetown, one of the oldest settlements in Beaver County, was started in 1793 by Benoni Dawson, who named it for his son George.

Jamestown, in Mercer County, which was formally laid out by John Keck in 1832, was named for James Campbell, the first white settler in this region.

Petersburg, in Huntingdon County, was laid out in 1795 by Peter Shoenberger, from whom it took its name.

14. A still larger number of places have been christened with the *baptismal names of women:*

Adelaide	Eleanor	Joanna
Adelia	Elizabeth	Josephine
Alice	Elizabethtown	Leola
Alinda	Elizabethville	Lucinda
Amyville	Ellentown	Marianna
Anita	Emmaville	Marysville
Annville	Enid	Mildred
Avis	Henrietta	Natalie
Barbara	Herminie	Port Matilda
Charmian	Idaville	Rowenna
Dora	Isabella	Victoria

Annville, in Lebanon County, was laid out about 1762 by Abraham Miller, who named the place in honor of his wife Ann. In its early days, however, the village was popularly known as Millerstown. Old Annville Township—now divided into Annville and North and South Annville Townships—was formed in 1799, and the Annville post-office was established in 1811.

Avis, a town that has recently sprung up in Clinton County, was named for Miss Avis Cochran of Williamsport, whose father was one of the chief promoters of the village.

Elizabeth, in Allegheny County, was laid out in 1787 by Stephen Bayard and named in honor of his bride, Elizabeth Mackay Bayard, daughter of Colonel Æneas Mackay, once commandant at Fort Pitt.

Elizabethtown, in Lancaster County, was in all likelihood named for Elizabeth Reeby, wife of Michael Reeby, who sold the first building lots about 1795.

Elizabethville, in Dauphin County, was laid out in 1817 by John Bender, who named the village in honor of his wife Elizabeth.

15. The presence of coal, iron, petroleum, and other *mineral products* has resulted in the following names:

Alum Bank	Derrick City	Ore Hill
Bitumen	Freestone	Oreland
Calcium	Ganister	Outcrop
Cannelton	Glen Carbon	Petrolia
Cementon	Gleniron	Port Carbon
Chalkhill	Ironore	Quarryville
Coal Bluff	Kaolin	Shaft
Coal Centre	Limekiln	Slatedale
Coal Glen	Limeport	Slateford
Coalmont	Limestone	Slate Hill
Coalport	Natrona	Slate Run
Cokeburg	Nickel Mines	Slatington

Alum Bank, in Bedford County, was so called because natural deposits of pure alum were found here.

Ganister, in Blair County, was named for the vast deposits of ganister—a siliceous, clayey rock—found in this vicinity.

Kaolin, in Chester County, was so named because of the large quantities of kaolin, or porcelain clay, found in this region.

Natrona, in Allegheny County, derived its name from

natron, "native carbonate of soda." Here, as early as 1853, was begun the manufacture of salt. Now various other chemicals are produced by the Pennsylvania Salt Manufacturing Company, one of the largest chemical concerns in the country.

Nickel Mines, in Lancaster County, began to grow into a little village in 1852, when Charles Doble discovered nickel in the abandoned workings of an old copper mine, which had been opened here as early as 1744.

Outcrop, in Fayette County, received its name from a prominent vein of bituminous coal that crops out at this point.

Petrolia, in Butler County, took its name from the oil industry. In February, 1872, the town site was a part of the Bear Creek wilderness. Two months later the "Fannie Jane" well was drilled into the oil land. Soon "the wilderness was filled with an army of excited oil men, and before the close of the year a town, said to contain about two thousand inhabitants, came into existence." Three years later its population was five thousand. Now it is less than four hundred.

16. About forty Pennsylvania villages and hamlets are *named for animals,* a fact that indicates the abundance of game in the early days:

Bear Lake	Buffalo	Elkland
Beaver Meadows	Coon Island	Pigeon
Buck Valley	Eaglerock	Raccoon

Beaver Meadows, in Carbon County, got its name from Beaver Creek, which flows by it, and on which many beaver dams were found when the region was first settled.

Elkland, in Tioga County, was named for old Elkland Township, organized in 1814, but now no longer in existence. At this point the valley of the Cowanesque River is only half a mile wide. Into this narrow valley the elks once trooped down to drink, and here great droves of them crossed over from one range of hills to the other.

Pigeon, formerly Pigeon City, in Forest County, was so called because it was the site of "the great pigeon roost" of 1868-71, when millions of passenger pigeons, a species of bird now believed to be extinct, flocked to this densely timbered region.

17. *Rural names* like these need no extended comment:

Blooming Glen	Farmersville	Haycock Run
Cereal	Gardenville	Rural Valley
Creamery	Grange	Spring House
Croft	Grapeville	Vinemont

18. More than a hundred names have been derived from *forests, trees, shrubs, or plants.* The following are typical:

Beech Creek	Greenbrier	Pine Grove
Briar Creek	Hazel Hurst	Plum Run
Brush Valley	Hickory	Spruce Creek
Bushkill	Ivyland	Sycamore
Buttonwood	Laurel	Tamarack
Cedars	Locust Gap	Walnutport
Chestnut Level	Maplewood	Willow Street
Cranberry	Oaks	Woodbine

Grove City, a thriving borough in Mercer County, offers a typical example of the way in which a name borrowed from the vegetable kingdom comes to be applied to a town. This place was at first called Pine Grove from a clump of pines that stood on a hill in the western part of the village. Since there was another Pine Grove in the State when the town was incorporated in 1883, the citizens voted to change the name to Grove City.

19. Fully a hundred names have been formed by the addition of some such industrial suffix as Mill, Furnace,

Mine, or Store; and more than five hundred place names are made by the wearisome addition of some descriptive word or family name to such geographical terms as Heights, Lock, Ferry, Falls, Rock, Summit, Point, Gap, Ridge, Ford, Brook, Creek, Lake, Port, Spring, Run, Grove, Glen, Hill, Valley, Dale, and Mount.

CHAPTER XXI

VILLAGES NAMED FOR NOTED MEN

OF the large number of places that have derived their names from surnames, those which perpetuate the family names of distinguished men are likely to be the most interesting. No apology is therefore needed for the following commentary on nearly all the villages named in honor of noted men.

Albany and Albany Township, in Berks County, were named in honor of James Stuart, Duke of York, afterward James II, whose Scottish title was the Duke of Albany.

Audubon, in Montgomery County, commemorates the fact that during his young manhood the celebrated ornithologist, John James Audubon, lived for some years on the Perkiomen Creek, where his father had purchased a tract of 285 acres. In the preface to his *Birds of America* Audubon gives the following account of his Millgrove estate: "In Pennsylvania my father, in his desire of proving my friend through life, gave me what Americans call a beautiful plantation, refreshed during the summer heats by the waters of the Schuylkill River and traversed by a creek called Perkioming. Its fine woodlands, its extensive fields, its hills crowned with evergreens, offered so many subjects to agreeable studies, with so little concern about the future as if the world had been made by me. My rambles invariably commenced at break of day; and to return wet with dew and bearing a feathered prize was, and ever will be, the highest enjoyment for which I have been fitted." Audubon's house on his Perkiomen estate became a veritable museum, filled with stuffed birds, festooned with strings of birds' eggs, and adorned with his matchless drawings and paintings of birds.   Audubon married an English girl, Lucy Bakewell, whose father occupied an adjoining estate.

Bainbridge, in Lancaster County, was named in honor of Commodore William Bainbridge, who won distinction in the war of 1812.

Bart and Bart Township, in Lancaster County, got their name from the abbreviated titular appendage of Sir William Keith, *Bart.* (i. e., Baronet), provincial governor of Pennsylvania in 1717-26, during which time the township was settled.

The village and the township of **Beccaria,** in Clearfield County, were apparently named for the celebrated Italian publicist and philosopher, Cesare, Marquis of Beccaria (1735-1794).

The borough and the township of **Benton,** in Columbia County, were christened in honor of the statesman, Colonel Thomas Hart Benton, United States Senator from Missouri.   Benton Township was organized in 1850, when Senator Benton was at the zenith of his power and popularity.

Bessemer, in Lawrence County, was named for the English inventor, Sir Henry Bessemer, whose discoveries in the metallurgy of iron have greatly reduced the cost and extended the use of steel.

The village and the township of **Bigler,** in Clearfield County, were named for William Bigler, a citizen of this county, who served as governor of Pennsylvania from 1852 to 1855.

Carrollton, in Carroll Township, Cambria County, was named by Father Gallitzin [1] in honor of his friend, the

---

[1] See Loretto, page 249, and Gallitzin, page 263.

distinguished prelate, John Carroll, who in 1788 became the first Roman Catholic bishop in the United States, and twenty years later was made Archbishop of Baltimore. He was a cousin of "Charles Carroll of Carrollton," who signed the Declaration of Independence.

Cassville, in Huntingdon County, took its name from Cass Township, which was named in 1843 for the statesman, Lewis Cass, shortly after the public welcome he had received in Philadelphia upon his return from France, where he had served as United States minister.

Chatham, in Chester County, was named in honor of the great English statesman, William Pitt, Earl of Chatham.

Claysville, in Washington County, was appropriately named by its founder, John Purviance, in honor of Henry Clay, the ardent champion and promoter of the great national highway, which at first extended from Wheeling to Cumberland, Maryland. "John Purviance had been keeping tavern in his large log house a number of years when the preliminary surveys were made for the great national road, and when it became certain that the road would pass through his place, he promptly surveyed and laid out a prospective town upon his land." Five townships in Pennsylvania have been named for Henry Clay.

Clymer, in Indiana County, was laid out in 1905 by the Dixon Run Land Company, which chose this name in honor of George Clymer,[2] a Pennsylvania signer of the Declaration of Independence and one of the framers of the Constitution of the United States.

The borough and the township of **Columbus**, in Warren County, were named for the discoverer of America.

Cornplanter, in Warren County, the site of the Corn-

---

[2] For George Clymer's connection with the founding of Indiana, see page 160.

planter Indian Reservation, bears the nickname of Gar-gan-wah-gah, "the Cornplanter," a half-breed Seneca Indian chief and noted warrior, son of John O'Bail, an Indian trader. In 1866 the Legislature of Pennsylvania honored Cornplanter by erecting here a marble shaft eighteen feet high, with this tribute: "Distinguished for talent, courage, eloquence, sobriety, and love for tribe and race, to whose welfare he devoted his time, his energies, and his means during a long and eventful life." Cornplanter Township, in Venango County, was also named for "the Cornplanter."

Covington, in Tioga County, first settled by Aaron Bloss in 1801, was formally laid out by William Patten in 1822. Both the village and the township of Coving-ton were named in honor of the great Indian fighter and comrade of Anthony Wayne, General Leonard Coving-ton, for whom Covington in Kentucky was also chris-tened.

Covode, in Indiana County, bears the name of a dis-tinguished Pennsylvanian, John Covode, who represented Indiana County in Congress from 1854 to 1870. "Honest John Covode," as he was commonly called, was the grandson of Garret Covode, a native of Holland, who had been kidnaped in childhood from the streets of Amsterdam by a sea captain, who brought him to Phila-delphia and sold him as a bond-servant or "redemp-tioner." Garret Covode is said to have been a domestic servant in the household of Washington. The name Covode was not the real name of the Dutch lad, but is supposed to have been originated by the wicked sea cap-tain.

Cresson, in Cambria County, once a famous health resort, was named in honor of Elliott Cresson, the well-known Philadelphia merchant and philanthropist. The name was suggested by Dr. Robert Montgomery Smith Jackson, a physician who once practised medicine at this place.

Cressona, in Schuylkill County, was named for John Chapman Cresson, who laid out the town. He was a noted civil engineer of Philadelphia, manager of the Schuylkill Navigation Company, president of the Mine Hill and Schuylkill Haven Railroad Company, and chief engineer of Fairmount Park in Philadelphia.

The village and the township of **Curtin,** in Centre County, were named for the Curtin family, to which belonged Andrew Gregg Curtin, governor of Pennsylvania from 1861 to 1867, who was distinguished for his earnest and able support of the national government during the Civil War, and was affectionately known as "the soldiers' friend."

Custer City, in McKean County, was christened in honor of General George Armstrong Custer, who had served with distinction throughout the Civil War, and who perished in June, 1876, in the battle of the Little Big Horn, in which his forces were greatly outnumbered by the confederated Sioux.

The borough and the township of **Dallas,** in Luzerne County, took their name from the Philadelphia author, lawyer, statesman, and financier, Alexander James Dallas, who won fame by his efficient administration as Secretary of the Treasury in 1814-17.

Dallastown, in York County, which was begun in 1842, was named two years later in honor of George Mifflin Dallas of Philadelphia, who served as United States Senator from Pennsylvania in 1831, as Vice-President of the United States during Polk's administration, and as minister to Great Britain from 1856 to 1861. George M. Dallas was the son of Alexander J. Dallas.

East Brady, situated just east of Brady's Bend on the Allegheny River in Clarion County, was named for the noted Indian fighter, Captain Samuel Brady, who "hunted and killed Indians like game in the forest." Brady's Bend was the scene of one of his famous exploits.

The town of **Fort Loudon,** in Franklin County, has taken the name of old Fort Loudoun, which was erected by Colonel John Armstrong in 1756 about a mile east of the present village. Fort Loudoun was named in honor of John Campbell, Earl of Loudoun, who, in July, 1756, arrived in America and succeeded William Shirley as commander-in-chief of the British forces. The Earl of Loudoun was irresolute, incompetent, and deservedly unpopular in America.

Fulton House, in Lancaster County, was named for the little house in which the great inventor, Robert Fulton, first saw the light of day in 1765. In 1844 Fulton Township was formed and named for Robert Fulton. The Fulton House post-office was established in 1853, and was long kept in the very house in which Fulton was born. The house is still standing in an excellent state of preservation.

Gallatin, a coal town in Allegheny County, received its name from Albert Gallatin, who was born at Geneva, Switzerland, in 1761, and who became famous as an American financier, statesman, and diplomat. He performed his greatest public service as Secretary of the Treasury from 1801 to 1814.[3]

Gallitzin, in Gallitzin Township, Cambria County, bears the honored name of the devoted priest, Prince Demetrius Augustine Gallitzin, one of the pioneers of Cambria County. Prince Gallitzin, the son of a Russian

---

[3] See New Geneva, page 315.

diplomat and the scion of an ancient and noble family, came to Baltimore on his *wanderjahr* in 1792 at the age of twenty-two. Shortly after his arrival he decided to study for the Roman Catholic priesthood. He was ordained in 1795. Five years later the Russian prince was hard at work as the leader and the parish priest of the Roman Catholic colony that had bought 20,000 acres of land in the wilds of Cambria County. The settlement prospered, and the work of the Church grew apace. For forty years the princely priest labored with ceaseless zeal, energy, and self-sacrifice.

Girard and Girard Township, in Erie County, and **Girardville,** in Schuylkill County, were named in honor of the great Philadelphia merchant and philanthropist, Stephen Girard, founder of Girard College and at one time the richest man in the United States. In both these localities Girard owned large tracts of land, upon which at the time of his death he was planning to make extensive improvements.

The village and the township of **Granville**, in Mifflin County, took their name from old Fort Granville, built about 1756 near the site of Lewistown and named for the English statesman, John Carteret, the Earl of Granville, then a member of the English Cabinet and president of the Council.

The borough and the township of **Halifax,** in Dauphin County, got their name from Fort Halifax, which was built in 1756 by Colonel William Clapham about half a mile north of the present town, and which, at the suggestion of Deputy Governor Robert H. Morris, was named in honor of George Montagu, second Earl of Halifax, who was once styled "father of the colonies" because as head of the Board of Trade he greatly increased British commerce in America. Halifax in Nova

Scotia was also named for him. The Pennsylvania town was laid out in 1784.

Harrisonville, in Fulton County, was named for William Henry Harrison during his presidential campaign of 1840.

Hastings, in Cambria County, was christened for Daniel Hartman Hastings of Bellefonte, who was interested in coal mines at this place, and who happened to be at Hastings at the time of the memorable Johnstown flood. Being then Adjutant-General of Pennsylvania, he at once assumed the arduous duty of directing the work of relief, and won general approval by his energy and efficiency. Thus he became available as a candidate for the governorship, to which he was elected five years later, serving from 1895 to 1899. The borough of Hastings was incorporated in 1894.

Herndon, in Northumberland County, was named at the suggestion of the postal authorities in honor of Commander William Lewis Herndon of the United States navy, who lost his life in the Gulf of Mexico on September 12, 1857, while heroically rescuing as many passengers as possible from his sinking steamer, the *Central America.* A daughter of Commander Herndon became the wife of Chester A. Arthur, who was afterward President of the United States.

The borough and the township of **Howard,** in Centre County, received their name in honor of the great English philanthropist, John Howard (1726-1790), who devoted his life to the betterment of the condition of all prisoners and captives.

Kossuth, in Clarion County, received its name from the Hungarian patriot and revolutionary leader, Louis Kossuth, who was a political exile in the United States in 1852. He was everywhere received in this country with great public demonstrations.

Langhorne, in Bucks County, preserves the memory of an early settler, Jeremiah Langhorne, chief justice of the province in 1739-43.

The borough and the township of **Ligonier,** in Westmoreland County, perpetuate the name of Fort Ligonier, built in 1758 by Colonel Henry Bouquet and named for a noted English soldier of French extraction, Field-Marshal Sir John Louis Ligonier, who was raised to an earldom in 1766. In the woods surrounding Fort Ligonier, on October 12, 1758, the French and their Indian allies met defeat in their last battle with the English in the hard-fought contest for the headwaters of the Ohio. The present town of Ligonier was laid out by James Ramsey in 1817.

Lincoln, in Lancaster County, which was laid out by John Reist in 1813 and called New Ephrata, was renamed Lincoln during President Lincoln's administration.

McClure, in Snyder County, once called Stucktown for a noted Indian fighter, now bears the name of Alexander Kelly McClure, well known as a Pennsylvania journalist and political leader, and as one of the founders of the Republican party.

Madisonville, in Lackawanna County, took its name from Madison Township, which was christened in honor of President James Madison.

Milesburg, in Centre County, brings to mind two noteworthy men. One of these was the Delaware chieftain, Wapalanné, or Bald Eagle,[4] whose town, known in colonial records as "the Bald Eagle's Nest," stood on the right bank of Bald Eagle Creek about a mile below the spot where Spring Creek empties into it. Here, be-

---

4 See page 166.

tween two white oaks, Bald Eagle built his wigwam. Not a trace of the once famous Indian village now remains. Bald Eagle was murdered on one of his visits to the Monongahela country, and his body was placed in the stern of his canoe, with a piece of johnny-cake in his mouth. The canoe floated down stream to the Province farm near New Geneva, where the body of the friendly old chief was buried.[5]

Milesburg was laid out in 1793 by Colonel Samuel Miles of Philadelphia, from whom it received its name. Samuel Miles, noted as an Indian fighter and Revolutionary patriot, was born in 1739; became an ensign in the Indian war of 1756, receiving a commission as captain in 1760; was a member of the Pennsylvania Assembly in 1772; was commissioned colonel in 1776; was taken prisoner in the same year at the battle of Long Island; and after his release served as deputy Quartermaster General of Pennsylvania until 1782. The next year he was appointed one of the judges of the High Court of Appeals of Pennsylvania, and in 1790 he was elected mayor of Philadelphia. He became a large landowner in Centre County, where he was associated with Colonel John Patton as one of the pioneers in the manufacture of iron. Miles Township was also named for him.

Milroy, in Mifflin County, was known as Perryville until about 1847, when it was renamed for Captain—afterward General—Robert Huston Milroy, who had become prominent in the war with Mexico.

Morrisville, in Bucks County, received its name from the patriot and financier, Robert Morris, one of the signers of the Declaration of Independence, who "resided here in a splendid mansion." Robert Morris, who

---

[5] Wither's *Border Warfare* and Linn's *History of Centre County*.

financed the American Revolution, was the second United States Senator from Pennsylvania.

Morton, in Delaware County, was named for John Morton, who is said to have cast the deciding vote of Pennsylvania in favor of the Declaration of Independence, and who afterward signed the momentous document.

Nicholson and Nicholson Township, in Wyoming County, were named for John Nicholson, comptroller of Pennsylvania from 1782 to 1794. He speculated extensively in wild lands in Pennsylvania, at one time holding title to 3,700,000 acres in thirty-nine counties. In 1797 Pennsylvania held an immense claim against him for unsettled land-warrants and accounts, and his vast holdings reverted to the State. He died in prison in 1800.

Oberlin, in Dauphin County, bears the honored name of the Alsatian preacher, teacher, and philanthropist, Jean F. Oberlin, for sixty years the self-sacrificing pastor at Steinthal on the borders of Alsace and Lorraine.

Packerton and Packer Township, in Carbon County, were named in honor of the capitalist, Asa Packer, projector and president of the Lehigh Valley Railroad, member of Congress, and founder of Lehigh University.

Paoli, in Chester County, took its name from the old Paoli Tavern, which bore the portrait of the Corsican general, Pasquale Paoli, who led a successful revolt against the Genoese between 1755 and 1768. Paoli's patriotic struggle for independence made him popular in the American colonies. On the night of September 20, 1777, General Wayne's little army was taken by surprise and cut to pieces near Paoli in a sudden night attack by a greatly superior force of British and Hessians.

Portersville, in Butler County, originally called Stewartsville for its founder, Robert Stewart, was, at the time of its incorporation in 1844, renamed in honor of David Rittenhouse Porter, then governor of the Commonwealth. Seven Porter Townships—in Clarion, Clinton, Huntingdon, Jefferson, Lycoming, Pike, and Schuylkill Counties—have been named for Governor Porter.

Quincy, in Franklin County, is situated in Quincy Township, which was formed in 1838 and named for John Quincy Adams, sixth President of the United States.

Ringgold, in Ringgold Township, Jefferson County, became a post-office in 1847, receiving its name from Major Samuel Ringgold, who was killed at Palo Alto in 1846,—the first American officer to fall in the Mexican War. **New Ringgold,** in Schuylkill County, was also christened in his honor.

Shirleysburg and Shirley Township, in Huntingdon County, preserve the name of old Fort Shirley, which was built in 1755 and stood within the present borough limits of Shirleysburg. On February 9, 1756, Deputy Governor Robert H. Morris wrote to the commander-in-chief of the British forces, General William Shirley: ''About twenty miles northward of Fort Lyttleton, another fort is erected, which I have taken the liberty to honor with the name of Fort Shirley.'' Shirleysburg occupies the site of the old Indian town of Aughwick.

The little village of **Shunk,** in Sullivan County, was christened for Francis Rawn Shunk, governor of Pennsylvania from 1845 to 1848.

Tylersville, in Clinton County, was named, during a presidential campaign, in honor of John Tyler, who was elected to the Vice-Presidency and afterward became President of the United States.

Vanport, in Beaver County, was named, during the presidential campaign of 1836, in honor of Martin Van

Buren, or "Matty Van," as he was familiarly called by his admirers.

Webster, in Westmoreland County, was laid out in 1833 and named in honor of the great orator and statesman, Daniel Webster, then at the height of his political power.

Wesleyville, in Erie County, was laid out in 1828 by John Shadduck, who built a Methodist church here and named the town in honor of John Wesley, the founder of Methodism.

Wynnewood, in Montgomery County, preserves the name of the Welshman, Thomas Wynne, president of the first colonial Assembly of Pennsylvania.

CHAPTER XXII

VILLAGES NAMED FOR LOCAL CELEBRITIES

ABOUT one-third of all the villages in Pennsylvania bear the family names of their founders or of local celebrities. English and German surnames predominate, with a considerable admixture of Scotch and Irish, and a sprinkling of Welsh, Dutch, and French. These names possess less general interest than any other group, and only those which designate places of some size or importance have been selected for brief comment.

Ambler, in Montgomery County, was named for a prominent family of early settlers. Joseph Ambler came to this locality in 1723.

Austin, in Potter County, was started as a lumber town in 1886, and in less than six months had seven hundred inhabitants. It was named for F. P. Austin, a local historian, a prominent citizen, and a member of the first borough council in 1888. In 1911 the bursting of a concrete dam and reservoir caused a disastrous flood at Austin.

Barnesboro, in Cambria County, was named for Thomas Barnes, a coal operator.

Bellwood, in Blair County, bears the name of a prominent family of pioneers named Bell. Until 1828 Edward Bell, who had settled in Antis Township in 1800 and had started a grist-mill, a saw-mill, and a store, was the only merchant in this region. The place was then called Bell's Mills. The present town was laid out in 1877 by Dr. A.

K. Bell, assignee of B. F. Bell; and the name was later changed to Bellwood.

Bentleyville, in Washington County, was named for Sheshbazzar Bentley, Jr., who in 1816 laid out the town on land that he had inherited from his father.

Birdsboro, in Berks County, was started in 1740 by the noted ironmaster, William Bird, for whom it was named. About Bird's furnace grew up a considerable settlement on both sides of Hay Creek.

Blossburg, in Tioga County, was named for Aaron Bloss, who removed here from Covington in 1802 and bought Gaylord's tavern at what was then known as "Peters' Camp."

Boalsburg, an unusually neat and attractive village in Centre County, was settled by Scotch-Irish in 1799, and was named in honor of Captain David Boal, a native of County Antrim in Ireland, who came to this region in 1798. In 1810 a German named Andrew Stroup bought some land, laid out an addition to the town, and made an unsuccessful attempt to change its name to Springfield, from several large springs in this locality. The Boalsburg post-office was established in 1820.

Boyertown, in Berks County, stands near the site of the old Colebrookdale Furnace, erected in 1720 by Thomas Rutter, the pioneer ironmaster. This was the first iron furnace in Pennsylvania. Boyertown was named for Henry Boyer, one of its earliest settlers, whose tavern and store formed the nucleus of the village. His descendants have always been prominent citizens of the town.

Brackenridge, in Allegheny County, was incorporated in 1900 and named for Henry Morgan Brackenridge, who has been largely instrumental in the great industrial development of the community. Both Brackenridge and

Natrona have been built up on the estate of two thousand acres left by Mr. Brackenridge's grandfather, the eminent judge, Henry Marie Brackenridge, son of Hugh Henry Brackenridge, whose name is intimately associated with the early history of Pittsburgh.[1]

Brockwayville, in Jefferson County, was named for two pioneers, Alonzo and Chauncey Brockway, who built their log cabins here in 1822 and laid out the town fourteen years later.

Brownsville, in Fayette County, occupies the site of Fort Burd, which was erected in 1759 and was widely known in colonial history as "Redstone Old Fort," because it was built at the mouth of Redstone Creek. Brownsville was formally laid out in 1785 by Thomas Brown, who died twelve years later, and whose body reposes in the old Brownsville graveyard with this choice inscription on his tombstone:

"Here lies the body of Thomas Brown,
Who was once the owner of this town."

West Brownsville, which lies just across the Monongahela River in Washington County, also took its name from Thomas Brown. West Brownsville is noted as the birthplace of James Gillespie Blaine, whose father, Ephraim L. Blaine, laid out the town in 1831 on land that originally belonged to Neal Gillespie, the great-grandfather of James G. Blaine.

Burgettstown, in Washington County, took its name from Fort Burgett, which was erected here during the Revolutionary War by Sebastian Burgett, a native of Germany. His son, George Burgett, laid out the town in 1795.

---

[1] See Tarentum, page 186.
18

Clarendon, in Warren County, which was laid out about 1872, was named for Thomas Clarendon, one of the owners of a tannery and a large saw-mill located here.

Curwensville, situated on the old Bellefonte and Meadville turnpike, in Clearfield County, was named for John Curwen of Montgomery County, who in 1798 obtained title to the land on which the town was laid out in 1812. He never resided at Curwensville.

Dawson, in Fayette County, has taken the name of George Dawson, who owned the town site.

Dorranceton, in Luzerne County, received its name from Dorrance Township, which was formed in 1840 and christened in honor of the patriot, Colonel George Dorrance, who fell in the Wyoming massacre. A few years ago Dorranceton surrendered its borough charter and became part of Kingston.

Downingtown, in Chester County, took its name from Thomas Downing, who, in 1739, bought Thomas Moore's mill and farm of 561 acres. For forty years thereafter the place was commonly known as Milltown. Downingtown stoutly resisted the project of making it the county-seat of Chester County in 1786: "not a lot could be obtained on which to erect the county buildings."

The borough and the township of **Dunbar,** in Fayette County, were named for Colonel Thomas Dunbar, who was here defeated by the French and Indians in 1755.

The name of **Duncansville,** in Blair County, is said to have been decided by lot. "In 1831 Samuel Duncan, as proprietor, laid out the village plot of Duncansville, and Jacob Walter laid out the plot to the eastward of Duncan's and named his town Walterstown. Soon afterward the two proprietors agreed to toss up a penny and let chance decide whether both plots should go under the name of Duncansville or Walterstown.   Mr. Duncan won; hence the name of Duncansville.'' [2]

The name of **Emlenton**, in Venango County, was derived from that of Hannah Emlen, the maiden name of the wife of Joseph M. Fox, who once owned most of the present town site.

Evans City, in Butler County, is the new name of an old settlement.   In 1796 George Boggs exchanged a mare for four hundred acres of land, built his cabin here, and started a mill.   Forty years later Boggs sold half of his land and the mill to Thomas B. Evans, who laid out a village, which he called Evansburg.   Since 1882 Evansburg has been the corporate name of the borough; the post-office is called Evans City.

Fleetwood, in Berks County, bore the name of Coxtown —after a pioneer settler—for sixty years or more, "until the establishment of the railroad in 1859, when the increasing settlement took the name of Fleetwood after a prominent English capitalist, who encouraged the construction of the railroad."

Flemington, in Clinton County, was named in honor of John Fleming, an associate judge of Lycoming County in 1798, who once owned the town site.

Freemansburg, in Northampton County, was named for the first settler, Richard Freeman.

Gilberton, in Schuylkill County, was originally made up of a number of smaller settlements, which were consolidated and incorporated as a borough in 1873.   The place was named in honor of John Gilbert, a wealthy coal operator.

Gordon, in Schuylkill County, stands on a tract of land that originally belonged to David and James McKnight, whose descendants laid out the town and named it in

---

[2] Africa's *History of Blair County*, p. 33.

honor of Judge David F. Gordon of Reading, to whom
they donated a building lot.

Hellertown, in Northampton County, was christened
for two brothers, Christopher and Simon Heller, who arrived from Germany in 1738 and settled here several
years later.

Hershey, a comparatively new industrial town in
Dauphin County, was laid out at Derry Church in 1903
by Milton S. Hershey, the chocolate manufacturer, who
gave his name to the beautiful town that he had founded.[3]

Houtzdale, an important coal town in Clearfield
County, was named for Dr. Daniel Houtz, who owned the
land on which the town was laid out about 1870.

The site of **Hughesville,** in Lycoming County, was
bought in 1816 by Jephtha Hughes, who laid out a town
which he called Hughesburg. In 1827, when the post-
office was established, the name was changed to Hughesville.

Hummelstown, in Dauphin County, laid out about 1762
by Frederick Hummel, was at first called Fredericks-
town. About 1780 its name was changed to Hummelstown. Both names were derived from that of its founder.
During the Revolution Hummelstown was an important
depot of arms and munitions for garrisons and forts
situated to the west and the north.

Hyndman, in Bedford County, was first called Bridge-
port, for which, at the time of its incorporation in 1877,
the name Hyndman was substituted, in honor of E. K.
Hyndman, president of the Pittsburgh and Western
Railroad.

Irvona, in Clearfield County, was named for its
founder, Colonel E. A. Irvin of Curwensville.

Irwin, in Westmoreland County, bears the name of its

---

[3] See Derry's Church, page 251.

founder, John Irwin, who laid it out in 1853. The forest of white oaks quickly became a bustling coal town.

Jenkintown, in Montgomery County, was named for the Welsh pioneer, William Jenkins, who settled here before 1697. The place was called Jenkins'-town as early as 1759.

Jermyn, in Lackawanna County, was at first called Gibsonburg in honor of John Gibson of Philadelphia, the original proprietor, who sold his land to the Delaware and Hudson Canal Company in 1874, when the railway station, post-office, and borough were renamed Jermyn in honor of John Jermyn, a wealthy English settler, to whom the town owed much of its material prosperity.

Karns City, once an important town in Butler County, was named for S. D. Karns, who, shortly after the discovery of oil in 1871, leased more than four hundred acres of land here. Five years later Karns City had a population of over two thousand. Now the village has less than three hundred inhabitants.

Kutztown, in Berks County, was laid out and named in 1779 by George Kutz. In 1866 the Manxatawny Seminary at Kutztown became the Keystone State Normal School.

Lamar and Lamar Township, in Clinton County, were christened for Major Marion Lamar, of the Fourth Pennsylvania Line, who was killed at the battle of Paoli in 1777.

Leechburg, in Armstrong County, was laid out about 1828 by David Leech, a native of Mercer County, for whom it was named.

LeRaysville, in Bradford County, was named for Vincent le Ray de Chaumont, son of James le Ray de Chaumont, who bought 7,600 acres of wilderness land in this region from Robert Morris, the Revolutionary patriot.

Linesville, in Crawford County, received its name from Amos Line, who was employed as a surveyor by the Pennsylvania Population Company, and who laid out the town about 1825.

Littlestown, in Adams County, owes its origin and name to its German founder, Peter Klein, who began the settlement in 1765. During its early years the village was indifferently called Petersburg and Kleine-staedtel. Finally the latter name was translated into Littlestown.

Luthersburg, in Clearfield County, was not named for the great reformer, Martin Luther, but for W. L. Luther, an early resident of this region.

The name of the borough and the township of **Lykens**, in Dauphin County, is a corruption of the surname of Andrew Lycan, the first settler in the Lykens valley.

McDonald, in Washington County, laid out in 1781, took its name from old Fort McDonald, which was built during the Revolutionary War on the land of John McDonald, who settled here in 1775. The western part of the town has grown up on the old McDonald farm.

McSherrystown, in Adams County, was named for an Irish settler, Patrick McSherry, who came here in 1765.

Mansfield, in Tioga County, took its name from the fact that the town plot was laid out in 1824 on the field of Asa Mann.

Masontown, in Fayette County, was laid out in 1798 by John Mason and subsequently named for him.

Meyersdale, in Somerset County, received its name from Peter Meyers, who, about 1844, converted sixty acres of his farm into building lots.

Millersburg, in Dauphin County, took its name from

Daniel Miller, who came here from Lancaster County in 1790 and plotted the town in 1807.

Mohnton, in Berks County, occupies the farm bought by Benjamin Mohn in 1846. Here he erected a mill, in which a store was opened by his cousin, Samuel Mohn. In 1857 Mohn's Store post-office was established. Fifty years later, when the village was incorporated, it was renamed Mohnton.

Montgomery, in Lycoming County, was at first called Montgomery Station in honor of Robert Montgomery, who, about 1850, donated land for the railway station and yards. Nearly forty years later, at the time of its incorporation, the village shortened its name to Montgomery.

Parkesburg, in Chester County, received its name from the Parkes, an old and influential family in this locality.

Patton, in Cambria County, was named for Colonel John Patton of Curwensville.

Philipsburg, in Centre County, was christened for its founders, Henry and James Philips, two Englishmen, who laid it out in 1797.

Reynoldsville, in Jefferson County, was begun by Woodward Reynolds, who settled here with his bride in 1838. The present town, which was named for him, was laid out about 1861 by his sons, David and Albert Reynolds.

Riegelsville, in Bucks County, was named for one of its prominent citizens, John C. Riegel.

Rimersburg, in Clarion County, was christened for its first settler, John Rimer.

Schaefferstown, in Lebanon County, once called Heidelberg, was named for its founder, Alexander Schaeffer, a German refugee, who fled from the Palatinate in 1744. On a high hill about two miles east of the village stand the ruins of "Baron" von Stiegel's celebrated "castle." [4] Over two hundred years ago the town contained a considerable settlement of German Jews, who were numerous enough to have a synagogue and a rabbi.

Sellersville, in Bucks County, received its name from Samuel Sellers, who kept a tavern and a store here about a hundred years ago. Sellers' Tavern, which was the name of the post-office until 1866, was once an important hostelry for wagons and coaches on the old Allentown road.

Sharpsville, in Mercer County, was named for James Sharp, one of the original owners of the town site.

Shillington, in Berks County, owes its name to Samuel Shilling, who, in 1860, laid out the town plot on his farm of 128 acres.

Spangler, in Cambria County, at the time of its incorporation in 1893, took its name from Colonel J. L. Spangler of Bellefonte.

Watsontown, originally Watsonburg, "the brick city" of Northumberland County, received its name from the original proprietor, John Watson, who in 1792 bought a tract of 609 acres, and two years later laid out the town.

Weatherly, in Carbon County, was started about 1840, and was named in honor of an early resident, David Weatherly, a clockmaker by trade.

White Haven, in Luzerne County, was begun in 1824 and incorporated in 1842 under the name of White Haven in honor of Josiah White of Philadelphia, one of the stockholders in the Lehigh Coal and Navigation Company.

Womelsdorf, in Berks County, was named for its founder, John Wommelsdorf, who laid it out in 1762.

---

[4] See Manheim, page 248.

Youngsville, in Warren County, owes its name to the devoted and eccentric bachelor schoolmaster, Matthew Young, who first pitched his tent here in 1796, and who was greatly beloved and honored by the whole community.

CHAPTER XXIII

VILLAGES BEARING INDIAN NAMES

MOST of the Indian names of Pennsylvania villages have been appropriated from the aboriginal names of neighboring streams. The general interest in the origin and meaning of these Indian names justifies the effort here made to explain the majority of them.

Aliquippa, in Beaver County, bears the name of the celebrated "Indian queen," who lived on the site of McKeesport about 1755. The name is said to signify "hat." She was frequently referred to as "Queen of the Delawares," though she was probably a Mohawk. Queen Aliquippa—sometimes called Allegrippus in the early days—took offense at Washington for not paying his respects to her when he traversed her domain in 1753. On his return he propitiated her with a bottle of rum. In his *Journal* he says: "I went up about three miles to the mouth of the Youghiogany to visit Queen Aliquippa, who had expressed great concern that we passed her in going to the fort. I made her a present of a watch-coat [1] and a bottle of rum, which latter was thought much the better present of the two."

Aquashicola, in Carbon County: "where we fish with the bush net."

Catasauqua, the Lehigh County iron town, derived its name from the Catasauqua Creek, which empties into the Lehigh River a little south of the town. Like Scranton, Catasauqua "owes its origin to the successful solution

---
[1] A waterproof cloak.

of the long-vexed problem of how to make iron by the use of anthracite coal as a fuel.''² The first settlement was called Cranesville, for the ironmaster, George Crane, of the Lehigh Crane Iron Company, which began operations here in 1839. About five years later the name was changed to Sideropolis, which is the Greek for ''iron city.'' This ponderous appellation was dropped after a few years, and in 1853 the growing town was incorporated as Catasauqua, a name corrupted from the Delaware Indian phrase *gotto-shacki,* ''burnt ground,'' ''parched land,'' or ''the earth thirsts.'' We can only guess why the Indians should have given so odd a name to this stream. Perhaps they wished to designate a spot or region which they had burnt over in successive years to destroy the undergrowth, in order that they might more freely follow the chase. The Indians were in the habit of clearing ground in this way.

Catawissa, creek, township, and borough in Columbia County, is a corruption of *gattawisi,* ''growing fat.'' The Indian hunters may have killed a deer along the stream in the season when deer fatten. Catawissa was laid out in 1787 by William Hughes, a Berks County Quaker.

Codorus, creek, township, and village in York County: ''rapid water.''

Conneaut Lake, Conneautville, and Conneaut Township, in Crawford County: according to Heckewelder Conneaut means ''it is a long time since they went''; according to Boyd it signifies ''snow place,'' so called because the snow remained frozen on the ice of the lake long after it had melted from the land.

Conoquenessing, creek, township, and borough in Butler County: ''for a long time straight.''

² See page 137.

Coplay, creek and borough in Lehigh County: "smooth-running stream."

Cowanesque, stream and village in Tioga County: "overrun with briers."

Cowanshannoc, creek, township, and village in Armstrong County: "greenbrier stream."

Daguscahonda, a hamlet in Elk County: "pure water."

Equinunk, in Wayne County: "where clothing was distributed."

Genesse, village and township in Potter County: "beautiful valley."

Hokendauqua, in Lehigh County: "searching for land." Probably the Indians noticed some surveyors at work along the stream.

Kinzua, stream, township, and village in Warren County: variously explained as "fish" and "they gobble"—in evident reference to wild turkeys.

Kishacoquillas, in Mifflin County: originally the name of a Shawnee Indian chief, signifying "the snakes have gone into their dens."

Lackawaxen, stream, township, and village in Pike County: "where the way forks,"—at the confluence of the Lackawaxen with the Delaware. Horace Greeley's famous Sylvania Association made its settlement in Lackawaxen Township. The little German community named Greeley, in Pike County, was started about thirty years ago.

Lenape, in Chester County: the Lenni-Lennape, or Delaware Indians, were "the native, genuine men," or "the first, or original people." Zeisberger says that the name means "Indians of the same nation."

Loyalhanna, stream, township, and village in Westmoreland County: "middle river."

Loyalsock, creek, township, and village in Lycoming County: "middle creek"; that is, a creek flowing between two others.

Macungie, in Lower Macungie Township, Lehigh County: "the feeding place of bears."

Mahoning, creek, village, and township in Armstrong County: "where there is a lick." The name *Mahonink* was applied by the Delaware Indians to many places containing saline deposits.

Manatawny, in Berks County: "here we drank."

Masthope, in Pike County: "beads of glass."

Mattawana, in Mifflin County: probably the same word as Matteawan, which means "river of shallows."

Maxatawny, creek, township, and post-office in Berks County: "bears'-path stream"; that is, the stream along which the bears have beaten a path.

Meshoppen, creek, township, and borough in Wyoming County: "glass beads." Masthope is a variant of the same name.

Monocacy and **Monocacy Station,** in Berks County: "a stream with several big bends."

Moosic, in Lackawanna County, took its name from the great herds of moose that once roamed the Lackawanna valley.

Moshannon, creek and village in Centre County: from *moos-hanne,* "moose stream."

Muncy, creek, township, and borough in Lycoming County: from *Minsi,* the name of the "Wolf Tribe." *Minsi* does not mean "wolf," as many people suppose, but "the great stone." The Minsis or Monseys were "people of the stony country." In 1826 Muncy was incorporated as Pennsborough because it was built on John Penn's Manor of Muncy; but the next year the corporate name was changed to Muncy by act of Legislature.

Nescopeck, creek, township, and borough in Luzerne County: "black, deep, and still water."

Neshaminy, creek and village in Bucks County: "double stream"; that is, a stream formed by the confluence of two others. The famous "Log College" was located on the Neshaminy Creek.

Neshannock, creek and township, and **Neshannock Falls,** in Lawrence County: from *nisham-hanne,* "double stream." Neshaminy is a corruption of this word.

Nesquehoning, in Carbon County: "at the black lick." The name and the locality suggest coal.

Ogontz, in Montgomery County: the name of an Indian chief who became a missionary among his own people.

Ohiopyle, in Fayette County: corrupted from *ohio-pehelle,* "water whitened by froth,"—by its rapid descent over rocks and stones.[3]

Oley, township and village in Berks County: said to be corrupted from *olink,* "a hollow."

Oswayo, creek, township, and borough in Potter County: "the place of flies."

Paupack, hamlet in Pike County, situated near the Wallenpaupack Creek, which forms part of the boundary between Pike and Wayne Counties. Wallenpaupack means "deep, stagnant water."

Paxinos, in Northumberland County: the name of a Shawnee Indian chief who showed marked friendliness toward the white settlers in the French and Indian War.

Pequea, creek, township, and village in Lancaster County: "from Piqua," according to Gannett, "the

[3] An engraving of the "Ohiopyle Falls" appears in Turbout and O'Brien's *History of North America,* published in New York in 1796.

name of a band of Shawnee Indians who once inhabited the valley of the Pequea.''

Perkiomenville and Perkiomen Township, in Montgomery County, took their names from the Perkiomen Creek, a tributary of the Schuylkill. The name Perkiomen is a corruption of *pakihmomink,* "where there are cranberries.''

Pocono, Pocono Lake, Pocono Manor, Pocono Pines, and Pocono Township, in Monroe County: the name Pocono is said to be a corruption of *pocohanne,* "a stream between two mountains." It is probably a modification of *Pahackqualong* or *Pahaqualing,* the Indian name for the Delaware Water Gap, signifying "a mountain with a hole (or gap) in it.''

Quakake, in Schuylkill County, is a corruption of *cuwenkeek,* "pine lands.''

Salunga, in Lancaster County: part of the Indian word *chickiswalunga,* "place of crawfish." The first half of the word has given a name to **Chickies,** a small place in Lancaster County.

The name of **Sewickley,** township, borough, and creek in Allegheny County, is derived from that of an Indian tribe.

Sheshequin, township and village in Bradford County: "the place of a rattle," according to Zeisberger.

Shickshinny, in Luzerne County: said to mean "five mountains.''

Shohola, township and village, and **Shohola Falls,** in Pike County: a corruption of *schauwihilla,* "weak, faint, or depressed.''

Skippack, stream, township, and village in Montgomery County: "a pool of stagnant water.''

Tamanend, in Schuylkill County, bears the name of Tamanend, Tamanee, or Tammany, a great and good chief of the Delawares, with whom William Penn made a treaty in July, 1694. Tammany and his tribe dwelt and hunted along the Neshaminy Creek, in what is now Bucks County. His people revered him as a man of almost divine wisdom and goodness. In the Revolutionary period an effort was made to canonize him as the patron saint of America, and his name was actually inserted in some calendars, his festival being held on May first. The Tammany Society of Philadelphia, organized at the close of the Revolution, always celebrated St. Tammany's Day with great pomp, "parading the streets with bucktails in their hats," and holding a great conclave, at which the calumet was solemnly smoked. The Tammany Society of New York, which was named for the great chief, was organized in 1789.

Tatamy, in Northampton County: the name of a Delaware chief prominent in colonial history.

Tidioute, in Warren County: variously interpreted as "seeing far," "straight water," and "cluster of islands."

Tobyhanna, township and village in Monroe County: "alder stream."

Tohickon, in Bucks County: "driftwood stream."

Tulpehocken, stream, township, and village in Berks County: "the land of turtles." The stream is historic on account of the transplanted German colony which, in 1723, came from the Schoharie and the Mohawk valleys down the Susquehanna and up the Tulpehocken.

Wapwallopen, stream and village in Luzerne County: "where the white hemp grows."

Wiconisco, creek, township, and village in Dauphin County: "wet and muddy camp."

Wyalusing, stream, township, and borough in Bradford County: "home of the old warrior."

Wyomissing, in Berks County: said to mean "place of flats."

Wysox, stream, township, and village in Bradford County: "place of grapes."

Yohoghany, in Westmoreland County: "a stream flowing in a roundabout course."

CHAPTER XXIV

ODDITIES IN NOMENCLATURE

A GOOD many Pennsylvania villages are named for abstractions, concrete objects, adjectives, verbs, old tavern signs, and peculiar personal names; and a few defy any classification except as oddities.

1. The following places bear the name of some *abstract idea:*

Amity	Effort	Intercourse
Climax	Endeavor	Liberty
Concord	Enterprise	Mount Hope
Decorum	Freedom	Progress
Defiance	Harmony	Prosperity
Desire	Independence	Time
Economy	Industry	Unityville

Amity, in Washington County, was laid out in 1797. The settlement grew up about the old Amity Presbyterian Church, a name significant of "the religious and social amity which the people desired to foster." Here, shortly before his death in 1816, the Reverend Solomon Spaulding of Connecticut, who had been graduated from Dartmouth College in 1785, and who had served as a Revolutionary soldier, is said to have written the first draft of the famous *Book of Mormon.* He was an antiquary, much interested in Indian relics. He wrote a romance which purported to be translated from curious inscriptions on certain tablets found in one of the Indian mounds in this vicinity.

A Mr. Patterson of Pittsburgh undertook to publish the romance under the title *The Manuscript Found,* but failed to fulfill his contract. For two or three years the manuscript remained in the hands of the would-be publisher, and one of his printers, Sidney Rigdon by name, copied it. "Hearing of Joseph Smith's digging operations for money through the instrumentality of necromancy, Rigdon resolved that he would turn this wonderful manuscript to good account and make it profitable to himself. An interview took place between Rigdon and Smith, terms were agreed upon, the whole manuscript underwent a partial revision, and in process of time, instead of finding money, they found curious plates, which, when translated, turned out to be the 'Golden Bible, or Book of Mormon,' which was found under the prediction of Mormon in these words: 'Go to the land Antun, unto a hill, which shall be called Shin, and there have I deposited unto the Lord all the sacred engravings concerning this people.'"[1] After reading all the contemporary evidence given by persons who knew Spaulding and had heard him read parts of his manuscript, one must at least admit the probability that the wandering evangelist and antiquary, Solomon Spaulding, may have written the first draft of the *Book of Mormon* at the little village of Amity.

Defiance, in Bedford County, probably derived its name from the frontier defense known as Fort Defiance, erected in this region during the Indian wars. Its exact location has not been determined.

Endeavor, in Forest County, took its name from the fact that about thirty-five years ago the Reverend J. V. McAnich organized here a Christian Endeavor Society, which ripened into a Presbyterian church and gave its name to the village.

Harmony, in Butler County, owes its existence and its

---

[1] Alfred Creigh's *History of Washington County*, p. 89 *et seq.*

name to a remarkable German colony widely known as the Harmony Society. The history of this strange community can here be sketched only in the barest outline. George Rapp, for more than forty years the religious and industrial leader of the Harmony Society, was born in Würtemberg in 1757. Although he came from peasant stock and had but a meager education, he was a man of extraordinary energy and great natural ability. When about thirty years old he began to advocate certain religious ideas more or less at variance with the established faith. A few years later he and his followers became obsessed with a burning desire to return to what they conceived to be primitive Christianity. In 1803, because of bitter persecution, Rapp came to Pennsylvania and bought of the eccentric Dettmar W. F. Basse[2] about five thousand acres of land in the fertile valley of the Conoquenessing. Hither, in 1804, he brought from Germany about six hundred of his adherents, and in the ensuing year they organized the Harmony Society. They laid out a town, which they called Harmony to indicate one of the principles of their organization.

Though the community was without a definite creed and never became a distinct sect, its members were deeply religious. Three main facts distinguished them from other Christians: they held all property in common; they adopted a distinctive and uniform dress; and most of them practised celibacy in the hope of attaining greater sanctity. The Harmony Society was noted for sincere piety, extraordinary industry, practical efficiency, and common sense. Within five years they had cleared half their land and were producing annually about 20,000 bushels of grain, 10,000 bushels of potatoes, and several tons of flax. They started breweries, distilleries, fur-

---

[2] See Zelienople, page 322.

naces, foundries, and brick-kilns. In fact, they practised almost every craft and occupation necessary to a self-sustaining community. And they did all these things in the fear of the Lord while they were hourly awaiting His second coming.

In 1815, lured by rumors of more fertile lands in the valley of the Wabash, the Society made the mistake of selling all its property in Butler County for $100,000 and of migrating to Posey County, Indiana, where they bought 25,000 acres and started the town of New Harmony. Here they remained nine years. Scourged by malaria, they sold their Indiana property for $150,000 to the English socialist, Robert Owen, who was eager to make a communistic experiment of his own.

In 1825 the Harmony Society moved once more into Pennsylvania, bought about three thousand acres of land, and founded the town and the township of **Economy** in Beaver County, on the east bank of the Ohio, seventeen miles northeast of Pittsburgh. Here, by industry, thrift, and capable business administration, they again grew rich and prosperous.[3] Economy was no misnomer: for the society exercised an economy which supervised with the closest scrutiny all the operations of dwelling-house, farm, and workshop. Their business enterprises extended over most of western Pennsylvania. They opened coal mines and started salt works. They engaged in extensive lumbering operations. They established cotton, woolen, and silk mills. Finally, the discovery of oil on their lands made them immensely wealthy.

Meanwhile the community suffered greatly from frequent and prolonged litigation, from bitter internal dissensions, and from the unnatural state of celibacy. In 1903 Susie C. Duss became sole trustee of the society;

[3] See Beaver Falls, page 196.

and a few years ago, in default of heirs or successors, the property of the Harmony Society, which once numbered eight hundred members, reverted to the State. The village of Economy has become part of the borough of Ambridge.[4]

Prosperity, in Washington County, was so named by the postal authorities from the glowing account of the prosperity of the village, furnished by those who wished to see a post-office established here.

2. A number of *concrete objects* have furnished names to villages:

Arrow	Monument	Slippery Rock
Buckhorn	Obelisk	Snow Shoe
Cottage	Picture Rocks	Three Springs
Driftwood	Rock	Torpedo
Grindstone	Shinglehouse	Wall

The explanation of the name of **Buckhorn**, in Columbia County, is purely traditional. Perhaps it is only a bit of folk etymology. "It is said that before any settlement had been made in this region the antlers of a deer, fastened between the forked branches of a white-oak sapling, marked the course of an old Indian trail. The tree stood on the edge of a swamp within three miles of Catawissa. The sight of this tree to the weary traveler from the distant settlement was an assurance of his nearness to friends and safety. Other way-marks disappeared, but the sapling grew apace and gradually locked the antlers in a vice-like embrace."[5]

Driftwood, the oldest settlement in Cameron County, was so called from Driftwood Creek, which received this name because of its constant accumulation of driftwood.

[4] See Ambridge, page 194.
[5] Battle's *History of Columbia County*, p. 257.

Driftwood Creek empties into the Sinnemahoning at Driftwood.

Shinglehouse, in Potter County, derived its curious name from an old pioneer house clapboarded with shingles, which a Frenchman named Jaundrie built in 1806.

Slippery Rock, situated in Slippery Rock Township, Butler County, and originally called Centreville, was recently renamed from Slippery Rock Creek, a designation that goes back to the aborigines, whose name for the stream was translated and appropriated by the white settlers. The creek, which is wide and deep, has places where one can cross on large rocks, which were often slimy and slippery.

Snow Shoe, in Snow Shoe Township, Centre County, was formerly known as Snow Shoe Camp. The traditional explanation is that it took its name from the adventure of a party of white hunters, who were overtaken by a snowstorm on the old Chinklacamoose trail leading to Clearfield, and who finally made snow-shoes on which they walked into the Bald Eagle settlement. Where Snow Shoe now stands there was once an old Indian village. The most plausible explanation of the name, which first appears in the old surveys of this region, is that white hunters or explorers, wandering into this locality, may have found some discarded snow-shoes here at the old Indian camp.

Three Springs, in Huntingdon County, was named for the three springs that form the creek of the same name. The name is very old: the "Three Springs Tract" was purchased by Colonel George Ashman in 1779.

The village of **Torpedo,** in Warren County, is said to owe its name to a curious accident. In the winter of 1883 the horses hitched to a wagon bound for the oil-fields and loaded with nitroglycerine—colloquially known as a "torpedo"—slipped and fell while crossing the railroad. A train at full speed struck the wagon, which was partly embedded in deep mud,—a circumstance which is supposed to have broken the terrific shock of the explosion that ensued, for the train was not greatly injured. The place was called Torpedo in commemoration of the event. The author has not been able to verify the foregoing explanation, which does not seem very convincing. It may be only another example of folk etymology.

3. The following dozen *adjectives* form an interesting group of place names:

Brave	Imperial	Rough and Ready
Crisp	Large	Straight
Drab	Lofty	Superior
Federal	Mammoth	Universal

The village of **Imperial,** in Allegheny County, was laid out in 1879 by the Imperial Coal Company and named for their Imperial Mine.

The name of **Rough and Ready,** in Schuylkill County, was apparently borrowed from that of the mining town in Nevada County, California, which was so named by the gold hunters of 1849.

4. Several verbs have been boldly transformed into names for places in Pennsylvania. One of these, Nolo, "I will not," seems to strike a note of defiance. The others are more hopeful,—Fearnot, Seek, and Cresco, "I am growing." [6]

5. More than a dozen *old tavern signs* have given names to Pennsylvania villages and hamlets. Most of these are interesting enough to receive comment.

Bird-in-Hand, in Lancaster County, received its name from an old hotel sign bearing an appropriate picture

---

[6] See also Renovo, page 203.

with the legend, "A bird in the hand is worth two in the bush." It is not definitely known when this tavern was started. In 1734 the first surveyors in this region made it their headquarters. The Bird-in-Hand hotel building is still standing. Four hotel buildings in succession have been erected upon the same foundation walls.

Blue Ball, in Lancaster County, was begun in 1766 by Robert Wallace, who built a store here and opened a hotel at the sign of "the Blue Ball." In colonial days the Blue Ball tavern was a noted stopping place on the old Paxtang road.

Broad Axe, in Montgomery County, took its name from the Broad Axe inn, which certainly dated back as far as 1792, and perhaps much earlier. The hotel sign originally contained a broad axe, a square, and a compass.

Compass, in Chester County, got its name from an old tavern on the Lancaster road, at the sign of "the Mariner's Compass."

King of Prussia, a post-office and village in Montgomery County, was named for an old colonial inn, the sign of which bore a portrait of the King of Prussia.

Lionville, in Chester County, received its name from the old Red Lion tavern, around which the hamlet has grown up.

Red Lion, in York County, was named for another old Red Lion tavern, which had the picture of a lion painted red on a swinging sign in front of the house.

The name of **Temple,** in Berks County, has nothing to do with religion, but comes from an old hotel sign which bore the invitation, "Stop at Solomon's Temple." Solomon was the baptismal name of the innkeeper. The place, once known as Solomon's Temple, is now called simply Temple.

White Horse, in Chester County, was named for a wayside tavern at the sign of "the White Horse."

Yellow House, a hamlet in Berks County, received its name from a country tavern which was always painted yellow, and which was widely known as "the Yellow House." The house is still standing and is still painted yellow.

6. A score or more of rather unusual village names have been derived from *peculiar personal names.*

Cessna, in Bedford County, bears the name of John A. Cessna, who was instrumental in extending the railroad to this point.

Dravosburg, in Allegheny County, was named in honor of John F. Dravo, a pioneer coal operator.

Drums, in Luzerne County, was christened for a tavern kept here nearly a hundred years ago by Abram Drum.

Dryville, a hamlet in Berks County, was named in 1852 for its first postmaster, Benjamin Dry.

Enola, in Cumberland County, has of late years become important because here the Pennsylvania Railroad has built its large freight-classification yards. The erroneous popular explanation of this peculiar name is that the call for the lonely telegraph tower which once stood across the river from Harrisburg was the word *alone,* and that the name Enola was suggested by spelling this word backward.

In point of fact, the name Enola has been traced to Mrs. Amanda Gingrich Underwood of Mechanicsburg, Pennsylvania. In 1861 Mrs. Underwood read a novel entitled *The Dangers of Darkness.* Both she and her husband were so much attracted by the name of Enola, one of the characters in the story, that they christened their baby girl Enola Underwood. Wesley G. Miller, living near Harrisburg, married a cousin of Mrs. Underwood, Miss Fannie Longsdorf, and they named their first daughter Enola Miller. Mr. Miller purchased the Longsdorf place, the homestead of his wife's parents. When the residents of this region petitioned the Pennsylvania Railroad Company for a station, a site was purchased from Mr. Miller, who proposed the name of Longsdorf for the new station. But the Pennsylvania Railroad already had a station with this name, and at the suggestion of Mr. Miller the new station was called Enola in honor of his four-year-old daughter, Enola Miller.[7] How Enola originated as a baptismal name is not known.

Fagundus, in Warren County, derived its name from Charles Fagundus, the first settler on the site of the town.

Hauto, in Carbon County, bears the name of George F. D. Hauto, one of the organizers of the Lehigh Coal and Navigation Company.

Hites, in Allegheny County, was named for P. Y. Hite, who settled here in 1857, opened coal mines, and started salt works.

Hollsopple, in Somerset County, derived its peculiar name from the surname of the man who owned the farm on which the town is built.

Jollytown, in Greene County, was named for Titus Jolly, who once owned the tract where the village stands.

Karthaus and Karthaus Township, in Clearfield County, derived their name from Peter A. Karthaus of Baltimore, who built an iron furnace here about 1820. Karthaus is the German equivalent of Carthusian, the name of a monastic order.

Mausdale, a hamlet in Montour County, owes its name to a numerous family of German settlers called Mau.

The village and the township of **Roulette,** in Potter

---

[7] Information furnished by Enola Miller Snyder of Camp Hill.

County, were named for the Frenchman, Jean Roulette, who was interested in the Ceres Land Company, of which John Keating was manager.[8]

Salladasburg, in Lycoming County, bears the name of its founder, Captain Jacob P. Sallada.

The name of **Saulsburg,** in Huntingdon County, seems to have had no connection with that of the great king of Israel. The hamlet was founded by Henry Widersall, who was familiarly called "Sall." This nickname was eventually changed to Saul, to which *burg* was added.

Tower City, a populous borough in Schuylkill County, was named in 1868 for its founder, Charlemagne Tower, Sr., whose son Charlemagne later served as American ambassador to Germany.

The name of **Townville,** in Crawford County, which seems to be a curious specimen of tautology, is explained by the fact that it was derived from the name of the founder of the village, Noah Town, who laid it out in 1824.

Wescosville, in Lehigh County, took the name of Philip Wesco, who kept a wayside inn here in 1828.

Wilgus, in Indiana County, was christened for a coal operator named Wilgus.

Wilpen, in Westmoreland County, which is an undignified abbreviation of William Penn, was named in honor of William Penn Snyder, the promoter and chief owner of the Shenango Furnace Company, which operates the mines north of Ligonier.

7. The following group of *oddities* in local names may be found interesting:

Bruin, in Butler County, received its name from Bear Creek, which runs through the village, and which was so called because bears were once numerous here.

---

[8] See pages 82, 83, and 104.

Burnt Cabins, in Fulton County, obtained its curious name from the fact that the first settlement, consisting of squatters' cabins, was burnt by order of the colonial government. "The adventurous pioneers of Cumberland County, disregarding the limits of purchases from the Indians, had penetrated to a number of places on the Juniata, beyond the Kittatinny mountain. But by order of the provincial government, and in consequence of complaints from the Indians, Richard Peters and others, in May, 1750, routed these intruders and burnt their cabins. Hence the name of Burnt Cabins, still given to that place." [9]

Cheat Haven, in Fayette County, is situated on the Cheat River, the name of which is based upon the tradition that in colonial times the river was likely to rise suddenly, so that crossing was extremely dangerous and those who attempted to ford it in the belief that the passage was safe were often deceived, or *cheated*. The little village of Cheat Haven was begun in 1905, when a branch of the Baltimore and Ohio Railroad was built here.

Doublinggap, in Cumberland County, received its odd name from two mountain gaps that meet and double upon each other at this point, forming two great loops in the northern boundary of Cumberland County.

Echo, in Armstrong County, took its name from three ravines that center here, causing almost any sound to produce an echo.

Eighty-four, in Washington County, was so named because the post-office at this point was established in the year 1884.

Exchange, in Montour County, is situated on an old mail route at a point where it was necessary to exchange horses in the old stage-coaching days.

---

[9] Day's *Historical Collections,* page 363.

Fallentimber, in Cambria County, is said to have taken its name from a remarkable windfall, caused by a terrific storm that here cut a great swath or path through the primeval forest.

Hop Bottom, in Susquehanna County, was christened for Hop Bottom Creek, which derived its name from the abundance of wild hops that grew here.

Indian Head, in Fayette County, was so named by the postal authorities simply because it was near the head of Indian Creek.

Notch, in Pike County, was named for a notch or gap in the ridge of mountains at this point.

Panther, in Pike County, marks a locality in which many panthers were found in the early days.

Pen Mar, in Franklin County, lies on the boundary between Pennsylvania and Maryland, its name being composed of the first syllables of the names of these two states. A number of strange names, somewhat similarly fashioned, occur throughout the United States, such as Calexico, Kanorado, Kenova, Kensee, Marydel, Texarkana, Texhoma, and Texla.

Surveyor, in Clearfield County, was named for Surveyor Run. About 1805 Samuel Fulton, a surveyor, with a party of men, got lost here in the wilderness, and the stream since then has been called Surveyor Run. Samuel Fulton became the first prothonotary of Clearfield County.

Tenmile, in Washington County, took its name from Ten Mile Creek, which was so called because it empties into the Monongahela River just ten miles southwest of Brownsville, the site of the historic "Redstone Old Fort," a very important place in pioneer days.

CHAPTER XXV

NINETY NOTABLE NAMES

ANTES FORT, in Lycoming County, took its name from the famous stockade fort that Colonel John Henry Antes built in 1776 "on the point of a high bluff, just below the mouth of Antes Creek." This fort soon became an important place, to which the scattered settlers from all the surrounding country frequently resorted for safety. John Henry Antes was born in 1736 near Pottstown in Montgomery County, whence he migrated in his youth to the region of Antes Fort. He was a famous frontiersman and held a commission as lieutenant-colonel in the Revolutionary army. His father, Heinrich Antes, born in Germany in 1701, was a man of sincere piety and attained fame as a lay preacher.

> "He stood by the side of Whitefield,
>   And prayed in the German tongue,
>   While the clarion voice of the preacher
>   Over the hills of Frederick rung.
>   They knew not each other's language,
>   Nor did they need it then;
>   For the one cried Hallelujah,
>   And the other said, Amen."

The name Antes is a Greek paraphrase of the German *Blume,* "flower," adopted as a disguise during the religious persecutions of 1620.

Apollo, in Armstrong County, laid out in 1815 by William Johnston and J. R. Speer, was at first called Warren because it occupied a site then known as "Warren's Sleeping Place." Edward Warren was an Indian trader, who was in the habit of camping here when the region was still in the possession of the Indians. In 1827, when the community was in need of a post-office, Dr. Robert McKisson, who was the first physician in that vicinity, and who was also a student of the classical languages and ancient mythology, and had published his poems in two volumes, is said to have suggested the name of Apollo in honor of the Greek god, the name of Warren having already been preëmpted for a Pennsylvania post-office. Doctor McKisson afterwards edited the first newspaper and became the first burgess of Apollo.

The hamlet and the township of **Asylum,** in Bradford County, are all that now remain of an ambitious and visionary French colony established in Pennsylvania in 1794 as an asylum for refugees at the time of the French Revolution. Robert Morris[1] and John Nicholson[2] were the chief American promoters of this scheme, which was partly philanthropic and partly speculative. Two noblemen, Louis Marie, Viscount de Noailles, a French officer in the American Revolution and a brother-in-law of the Marquis de la Fayette, and Antoine Omer, Marquis de Talon, were the French leaders in this enterprise.

By 1801 the Asylum Company had purchased about 400,000 acres of land and had its settlement well under way. Some of the exiled Frenchmen were nobles, many were soldiers, a few were clergymen, but all had been reared in the city, where they had become accustomed to a life of luxurious ease. Their settlement was doomed to utter failure because they did not know how to clear and till the land, to endure toil and hardship, or to adapt themselves to their new surroundings and their backwoods American neighbors. In its early days Louis

[1] See Morrisville, page 267.
[2] See Nicholson, page 268.

Philippe, Duke of Orleans and afterward King of France, spent some time at Asylum.

The name of **Axemann**, in Centre County, commemorates a remarkable family and a notable industry. Thomas Mann came to America from Ireland in 1750, and made axes and other edged tools at Braintree, Massachusetts, and later in the province of New York. His son William followed the same business at Johnstown, New York; and his grandsons, William Mann, Jr., and Harvey Mann, migrated to Centre County, Pennsylvania, in 1828 and started the Mann Axe Factory two miles southeast of Bellefonte. The descendants of these two pioneer axe-makers later established large factories at Mill Hall, Tyrone, and Yeagertown, Pennsylvania. These works were wisely located, because ''from the beginning of the nineteenth century down to 1842 more iron was produced in Huntingdon and Centre Counties than anywhere else in the country.''[3]

Since practically all this iron was smelted in charcoal furnaces, it was properly carbonized, was free from impurities, and was particularly well suited to the manufacture of steel for edged tools. For a hundred and fifty years the Mann axes have sung their own praises in every wilderness of America. In 1880 the Mann factory at Tyrone was turning out four hundred axes a day; and in 1886 the daily output of the Yeagertown works was fourteen hundred axes. These axes were shipped to every state in the Union, to all parts of western Europe, and even to South America, Australia, New Zealand, China, and Capetown. For five generations the Mann family have been famous axe-makers. The Manns were perhaps the greatest makers of axes in the history of the world.

---

[3] Pennypacker's *Pennsylvania—The Keystone,* p. 237.

20

The origin of the name **Brandywine,** still retained in Brandywine Creek and Brandywine Summit, cannot be given with certainty. One tradition tells how a vessel laden with *branntwein,* or brandy, was once lost in its waters. Another explanation identifies the name with that of Andrew Braindwine, who once owned land near its mouth. A third theory explains that this name was given because "the slough near Downingtown discharged its muddy waters into the creek, tingeing it the color of brandy." **Brandywine Summit** lies several miles east of Chadds Ford.

California, in Washington County, was laid out in 1849, shortly after the discovery of gold in California, when this alluring and sonorous name was in every one's mouth.

Centre Hall, in Centre County, was first settled by John Lyon, an ironmaster of Scotch-Irish descent, who married Jane, daughter of William Maclay, a prominent political leader and the first United States Senator from Pennsylvania.[4] The town was built on John Lyon's farm. Henry Whitmer, in 1847, named the place Centre Hall because it was midway between the eastern and western ends of Penn's Valley. No very satisfactory explanation of the "Hall" has ever been given; it is supposed to have originated in imitation of the British practice of using Hall as the name of a manor-house with an adjoining hamlet.

Chadds Ford, in Delaware County, made famous by the battle of Brandywine, which took place there on September 11, 1777, was named for John Chadds, son of Francis Chadds, or Chadsey, who emigrated from Wiltshire in 1689, and settled on a tract that included all the present village of Chadds Ford. "As the tide of emigra-

---

[4] See page 66.

tion moved westward, public travel increased, and as the Brandywine in rainy weather and in springtime was so swollen that it was almost impossible to cross it, John Chadds was solicited to establish a ferry at this place; and to aid him in that public work, the county of Chester lent him thirty pounds to meet the expense he was put to in building a 'flatt or schowe.' '' He entered upon his duties as ferryman at Chadds' Ford in 1737. He was also allowed to open an inn on the road from Philadelphia to Nottingham. John Chadds kept ''the Chadds' Ford tavern'' for ten years, but he was apparently in charge of the ferry until his death in 1760. Joseph Davis was the innkeeper at the time of the battle of Brandywine.

Chalfont, in Bucks County, was originally the name of a station on the Doylestown branch of the Philadelphia and Reading Railroad. The name was later adopted by the town. No doubt some railway official of Quaker ancestry named the station for Chalfont St. Giles in Buckinghamshire, where William Penn was buried, and where Milton wrote the latter part of *Paradise Lost*.

Christiana, in Lancaster County, was not named, as has often been asserted, for King Christian and Queen Christiana of Sweden, but for Christiana, the first wife of William Noble, who built the first house and started a machine-shop here in 1833.

Cogan House, in Lycoming County, was named for the first settler, David Cogan, who came here about 1825, built a log house, and cleared the land. His place gradually fell into decay, and came to be known among hunters as Cogan's House. The post-office takes its name directly from Cogan House Township, which was formed in 1843.

Confluence, in old Turkeyfoot Township, Somerset

County, derived its name from the confluence of three streams at this point. The "turkey-foot" is formed by the junction of Laurel and Casselman Creeks with the Youghiogheny River.

Delaware Water Gap, in Monroe County, has taken its name from the famous "water gap" in the Blue Mountains.

Dunkard, in Greene County, as well as Dunkard Creek and Dunkard Township, was named for a large colony of Dunkards, or German Baptists, who came hither from eastern Pennsylvania.

Dushore, in Sullivan County, is the corrupted surname of its founder, Aristide Aubert Dupetit-Thouars, a captain in the French navy and a member of the unfortunate Asylum Company.[5] Here the genial, high-spirited French exile, affectionately nicknamed "the Admiral," bravely tried to hew out a new home in his wilderness tract of four hundred acres.

Eagles Mere, or "the eagle's lake," a popular summer resort in the mountains of Sullivan County, is the poetic designation given about fifty years ago to what had long been known as Lewis's Lake, which took its name from a wealthy Englishman named Lewis, who came thither about 1810 and started extensive glass works. The isolated location and the lack of facilities for transportation rendered the enterprise unprofitable.

Eidenau, in Butler County, which is the German for "the vale of Eden," was so named by George Rapp, founder of the famous Harmony Society.[6] Eidenau was a part of the tract that Rapp bought of Dettmar Basse.

Euclid, in Butler County, was named about 1880 by Thomas McCall, the first postmaster, not for the famous

[5] See Asylum, page 304.
[6] See Harmony and the Harmony Society, pages 291-294.

Alexandrian mathematician, but for Euclid Avenue in Cleveland.

Factoryville, in Wyoming County, was the site of an old woolen mill about a hundred years ago. Hither the New England settlers came from miles around to have their homespun wool woven into cloth. The old woolen factory gave its name to the town.

Fannettsburg, in Franklin County, took its name from old Fannett Township, formed a century and a half ago by Scotch-Irish settlers, who named it after Fannett Point, a promontory and lighthouse in County Donegal, Ireland.

Fort Hunter, in Dauphin County, received its name from a very important pioneer fort built about 1755 "where the Blue Hills cross the Susquehanna," six miles north of Fort Harris (now Harrisburg), on the land of a miller named Hunter, a son-in-law of Thomas Chambers, whose brother Benjamin built Fort Chambers and founded Chambersburg.

The borough of **Forty Fort,** in Luzerne County, bears the name of old Forty Fort, a pioneer stockade enclosing about an acre of land, built here in 1770 and named for the first forty Connecticut settlers who came into the Wyoming valley early in 1769. This fort figures prominently both in the "Pennamite war" and in the Revolutionary struggle.

Frankstown and Frankstown Township, in Blair County, were named for Frank Stevens, who is generally but erroneously called Stephen Franks, an important Indian trader operating in central and western Pennsylvania as early as 1734. Frank's Town was the name that the Indian traders gave to the old Delaware and Shawnee Indian town at this place. Frank Stevens may have set up a trading cabin at this point. When Conrad Weiser traversed the famous "Frank's Town Path" in 1748, he "came to Frank's Town, but saw no houses or cabins."[7]

Freeport, in Armstrong County, was laid out in 1796 by William and David Todd, and was long called Toddstown in spite of its founders' desire that it should be named Freeport. They intended that it should always be a *free port* for all river craft. The old Pennsylvania Canal, crossing the Allegheny about a mile above Freeport, passed through the town. The name Freeport became fixed in 1833, when the town was incorporated.

Frenchville, in Clearfield County, was so called because it was settled mainly by French pioneers from Normandy and Picardy.

Friedensville, in Lehigh County, derived its name from the old German *Friedenskirche,* "the church of peace."

Friendsville, in Susquehanna County, was laid out in 1819 by Dr. R. H. Rose, the Quaker physician for whom the town of Montrose was named.[8] He named this village Friendsville because he had induced a colony of Friends to settle here.

Gap, in Lancaster County, popularly known for two hundred years as "the Gap," is a notch or opening in the hills, the highest point on the old road leading from Philadelphia to the Susquehanna. This locality was once a favorite resort of the notorious "Gap gang," a body of thieves and kidnapers of free and escaped negroes.

The borough and the township of **Great Bend,** in Sus-

---

[7] See Hanna's *Wilderness Trail,* vol. I, pp. 259, 260, and numerous other passages. Mr. Charles A. Hanna has satisfactorily cleared up the whole matter. The following quotations are pertinent: "Ever since Jones's fabulous and harmful *History of the Juniata Valley* appeared in 1856, all writers on the early history of this district have followed his false stories about an imaginary 'old German trader named Stephen Frank.'" "Owing to the misplacing of an apostrophe in the printed account of John Harris's description of the road to Allegheny, Jones assumed that 'Frank's (Stephens') Town,' as written by Harris, meant Stephen Frank's Town."

[8] See Montrose, page 131.

quehanna County, derived their name from the fact that the Susquehanna River here makes a great bend or loop by taking a northerly course into New York.

Hatboro, situated on the old York Road in Montgomery County, took its name from the labors of John Dawson, a hatter, who plied his trade here two hundred years ago in an old stone house, which later became the "Crooked Billet Tavern," a name borrowed from the famous old Philadelphia inn on Water Street, at which Benjamin Franklin breakfasted on his first arrival in the Quaker city. The name Hatborough occurs as early as 1749.

Helen Furnace, in Clarion County, contrary to the common custom, did not receive its name from the wife or the daughter of its owner, but seems to be a corruption of Hieland (i. e., Highland) Furnace, so named in honor of Alexander McNaughton, an early settler at this place, who boasted of his being a Hielander. Highland Township, in Clarion County, also took its name from this settler.

Hosensack, the name of a creek and a village in Lehigh County, is the German for "breeches pocket," a designation said to have been bestowed by a German hunter who once lost his way in this valley.

Julian, in Centre County, received its name from the old Julia Ann Furnace. Julia Ann was the wife of General James Irvin, one of the owners of the furnace.

The name of **Kerrmoor,** in Clearfield County, was made by combining two surnames, after the manner of Wilkes-Barre. It perpetuates the family names of its founders, James Kerr and Milton and Robert Moore.

Light Street, in Columbia County, was so named by the Reverend Marmaduke Pearce, who had once lived on Light Street in Baltimore.

Loop, in Indiana County, was named for the extraordinary bend or loop in the big Mahoning Creek at this point. "A person can stand on the bluff and throw stones into the creek in two directions, and yet the water has flowed a distance of nearly two miles between the two points."

The village of **McAlevys Fort**, in Huntingdon County, took its name from the pioneer fort built here in 1778 by Captain William McAlevy, the first settler in this locality.

McKees Half Falls, in Snyder County, was named for Thomas McKee, an Indian trader, who settled at this point on the Susquehanna River in 1752, on a large tract of land extending above and below "the half falls."

Mapleton Depot, in Huntingdon County, was originally the name of a "depot" established here when the Pennsylvania Railroad was completed. The presence of maple trees gave the station its name. The village, which took the name of the station, did not begin to grow until about 1860.

Marietta, in Lancaster County, was originally two distinct settlements,—New Haven, laid out by David Cook in 1803, and Waterford, laid out at "Anderson's Ferry," by James Anderson in 1804. In 1812 the two villages were incorporated under one charter as Marietta, a name said to have been compounded of Mary and Etta, the Christian names of Mrs. Cook and Mrs. Anderson, the wives of the two founders.

Martha Furnace, in Centre County, was named for Martha, daughter of Roland Curtin, one of the owners of the furnace which was started here about 1830, and which formed the nucleus of the village.

Mason and Dixon, in Franklin County, is situated, as its name indicates, near the famous boundary line between Pennsylvania and Maryland, which was run in 1763-7 by Charles Mason and Jeremiah Dixon, two noted

English mathematicians and surveyors. To mark the boundary, they set up, at five-mile intervals, large stones bearing William Penn's coat of arms on one side and Lord Baltimore's on the other. At every mile between these large stones smaller markers were erected with P on one face and M on the other. Thus the line was run westward from the Delaware, and marked for nearly 250 miles; and thus was settled a bitter boundary dispute that had lasted nearly a century. In 1784 David Rittenhouse continued and completed the Mason and Dixon line after the settlement of a similar territorial controversy between Pennsylvania and Virginia.

Maytown, in Lancaster County, was so named because it was laid out on the first day of May, 1762. ''To celebrate the day of laying out Maytown, a fair, or 'gathering of loose heels,' was held, and dancing performed in its best style in the middle of the main street of the houseless town.''

Mechanicsburg, in Cumberland County, received its name from the number of mechanics who lived here and worked in the foundry and machine-shops.

Millheim, in Centre County, was laid out by Philip Gunkel in 1797 and received its name from the fact that there were several mills here, but little else; hence Millheim, ''the home of mills,'' suggested itself as an appropriate name. Perhaps the German settlers may have wished to perpetuate the name of the ancient town of Mühlheim in Würtemberg.

Modena, in Chester County, was named for the Mode family. Alexander Mode, who settled in East Fallowfield about 1739, used the waters of the Brandywine to run a saw-mill. About 1850, W. A. Mode started a paper-mill here and called the place Modeville, a name that the village retained until about 1873, when the Wilmington and Reading Railroad was built. The railway officials chose the more euphonious name of Modena for their station, and a little later the post-office received the same name. They may have had the Italian city of Modena in mind.

Moravia, in Lawrence County, marks an old settlement begun by the devoted Moravian missionary, David Zeisberger. "All that remains of this once pleasant Christian town is the name Moravia, applied to a hamlet and a railway station."

Morganza, in Washington County, was named for the famous Morganza Farm of Colonel George Morgan, who was Indian agent in this region from 1776 to 1779. After the Revolutionary War he retired to the Morganza Farm. In 1786 Colonel Morgan received, from the Philadelphia Society for Promoting Agriculture, which is still a flourishing organization, a gold medal for writing the best essay on "The Farmyard." Thomas Pickering, in the letter transmitting the medal, said, "This is the first premium ever given in America in agriculture." The medal, still cherished by Colonel Morgan's descendants, bears the motto, "Venerate the Plow."

Mount Union, in Huntingdon County, was laid out in 1849 by the firm of Dougherty and Speer, who here owned a large tract of land. The town was named Mount Union by its first postmaster, Colonel William Pollock, "in consequence of such a number of mountains coming together at or near this place." East of the town Jack's Mountain and Stone Mountain are united.

New Freedom, in York County, was first named Freedom for the Free family, who were among the earliest settlers of the town. E. K. Free was a member of the first borough council in 1879. The name was changed to New Freedom because there was an older town and post-office called Freedom in Beaver County.

The hamlet and the township of **New Garden,** in Chester County, were settled about 1720 by Friends from Ireland, who named the place for their former home, New Garden in County Carlow.

New Geneva, in Fayette County, derived its name from the native city of the Switzer, Albert Gallatin,[9] who purchased his plantation in this locality in 1785. Here, in partnership with his brother-in-law, James W. Nicholson, and the two Kramer brothers, Albert Gallatin became a pioneer in the manufacture of glass. After Gallatin attained national distinction in public life, he erected a pretentious mansion about two miles from New Geneva. New Geneva is in Nicholson Township, which was named for James W. Nicholson.

Newport, in Perry County, was at first called Reidersville in honor of its founder, Daniel Reider, who laid it out in 1814. Six years later, ambitious to become the county-seat of Perry County, it changed its name to Newport because it had become a *new port* for shipping on the Pennsylvania Canal.

New Tripoli, in Lehigh County, was named in 1816 to mark the success of the United States navy in the war against the pirates of Tripoli.

Newry, in Blair County, was founded about 1793 by Patrick Cassidy, an Irishman, who had come to America as a servant for a British officer, bought three hundred acres of land here at the close of the Revolution, and laid out a town, which he named for his native town of Newry in County Down.

Nicktown, in Cambria County, received its name from

9 See Gallatin, page 263.

the old Roman Catholic church of St. Nicholas, about which the village has grown up.

The borough of **North East,** in Erie County, took its name from North East Township, which was formed in 1800 and named for its location in the northeastern part of the county.

Orangeville and Orange Township, in Columbia County, were not named in honor of the house of Orange, but in deference to the wishes of the early settlers, some of whom had come from Orange County in New York.

Palmyra, in Lebanon County, was laid out during the Revolutionary period by John Palm, a native of Germany, who came to America in 1749. Palm called his settlement Palmstown. Much later the name of the Syrian city was imposed upon this modest and well-kept village.

Paradise, in Paradise Township, Lancaster County, was first settled by Abraham Witmer,[10] who built a mill there. In 1804, when a name was needed for the post-office, he remarked that to him the place was Paradise, and it has been so called to this day.

Parnassus, in Westmoreland County, was so named for the old Parnassus Church, which in turn took its name from the surveyor's poetic designation of the original tract on which the church was erected.

Peach Bottom, in Lancaster County, and Peach Bottom Township, in York County, trace their name to John Kirk's peach orchard, which was a well-known landmark when the township was organized more than a hundred years ago.

Pit Hole City, once a large and thriving city in Venango County, is now a mere hamlet not large enough to require a post-office. The town derived its name from

---

[10] See Clearfield, pages 144, 145.

Pit Hole Creek. No other city in the United States has ever sprung up so rapidly, or flourished for so brief a time amid so much excitement, or declined so quickly and completely. What was a farm in May, 1865, became, within five months after the discovery of oil, a bustling city of 15,000 inhabitants, with streets, hotels, churches, theaters, and public buildings. At the height of the excitement some building lots sold for $15,000 each. But the small basin amid the rocks was soon drained of its oil; business declined when the bubble had burst; and the once proud and populous city at Pit Hole Creek has vanished from the map of Pennsylvania.

The borough and the township of **Portage**, in Cambria County, preserve the name of the old Portage Railroad, which once extended from Hollidaysburg to Johnstown. This unique railroad, completed in 1832 under the patronage of the State, carried the canal boats across the Allegheny Mountains. Thus continuous communication was established between Philadelphia and Pittsburgh. The boats were loaded upon cars, and ''drawn up and let down inclined planes by means of stationary engines and endless wire ropes.'' The portage—or land passage between waters—consisted of five of these inclines on each side of the mountains. Thus an elevation of more than a thousand feet was successfully surmounted. The extension of the Pennsylvania Railroad to Pittsburgh in 1852 put an end to the portage system.

Quakertown, in Bucks County, derived its name from the Quakers who came hither from Gwynedd about 1700. The town, which was built on a fertile meadow, was at first called Flatland and later Richland. The latter name has been retained by Richland Township.

Raymilton, in Venango County, was so named by its founder, A. W. Raymond, who in 1844 built here a furnace and a grist-mill. To the first syllable of his family name he added *milton* (i. e., mill-town), thus forming a rather fanciful name to commemorate both himself and his mill.

Sadsburyville, in Sadsbury Township, Chester County, derived its name from Sudbury in the English county of Suffolk. In old records the name of Sadsbury Township is sometimes written Sudbury.

Saint Thomas, in Franklin County, was originally called Campbellstown in honor of Thomas Campbell, who laid it out in 1790. Some years later the town adopted the baptismal name of its founder and added the pious prefix. Saint Thomas Township was organized in 1818.

The name of the pleasant village of **Salona,** in Clinton County, was—curiously enough—derived from that of ancient Thessalonica. About 1840 the citizens met to choose a more acceptable name than that of Mudtown, McGheestown, or Mechanicsburg, as the place was then variously called. Mrs. Samuel Wilson, better known as Aunt Betsy Wilson, a devout Methodist, had recently been greatly impressed by an article in the *Christian Advocate* on the Methodist mission at Salonica in Turkey. She suggested this name for the village, and her townsmen shortened it to Salona.

Saltsburg, in Indiana County, which was laid out in 1817, took its name from the many salt wells and works that once flourished here. For more than fifty years this part of Indiana County was one of the chief inland centres for the manufacture of salt. In the early days of this town the name was often spelled Saltzburg, a fact which suggests that the early German settlers may have had the ancient Austrian city in mind.

The name of **Scenery Hill,** in Washington County, was given about thirty years ago to the ancient village of

Hillsborough by Dr. Byron Clark, a resident physician. Hillsborough was laid out and named by Stephen Hill in 1819, shortly after the completion of the old National Road, which ran through the village. Scenery Hill, which occupies a considerable elevation, received its name from its magnificent view of the surrounding country. The "Hill" may be a punning reference to the name of its founder.

Shawnee-on-Delaware, in Monroe County, was named for the Shawnee Indian tribe. The name Shawnee, which signifies "the southerners," was given to this tribe because they had migrated thither from the south, their original home being in the valley of the Savannah River.

Sinking Spring, in Berks County, derived its name from "a singular spring, which here rises out of the ground with a considerable volume of water, and almost immediately sinks again. Its flow is periodic, being much greater at some seasons than at others." The region is underlaid with limestone.

Spring City, in Chester County, was at first called Springville from a large spring situated where the pump now stands, at the corner of Yost and Main Streets. About 1872, when the post-office was established and the town incorporated, the name was changed to Spring City because there was already one Springville in Pennsylvania.

The village and the township of **Sugarloaf**, in Luzerne County, derived their name from an isolated conical hill, or "monadnock," which rises about five hundred feet above the surrounding country.

Sugar Notch, in Luzerne County, was so named by the New England settlers because many of their favorite sugar-maple trees were found growing here in the notch or gap in Little Mountain.

Summerhill, in Cambria County, took its name from old Summerhill Township, which was organized in 1810, and then called Somerhill for Joseph and David Somers, two important landowners in this locality.

Swarthmore, in Delaware County, has been built up about Swarthmore College, from which it received its name. The college was established by Friends in 1864, and named for Swarthmore Hall, the home of George Fox, the founder of the Society of Friends.

Trappe, in Montgomery County, according to Governor Francis R. Shunk, received its name from an old tavern, one of the first houses built here, the approach to which was made by a high flight of steps, or *treppe,* to use the German word. Hence the inn was called the Trappe Tavern.

Union Deposit, in Dauphin County, was in 1845 christened Union or Unionville by its founder, Philip Wolfersberger. After it became a place of deposit for the shipment of grain and produce by canal, the name was gradually changed to Union Deposit.

Ursina, in Somerset County, which was laid out in 1868 by Judge William J. Bear, exhibits one of the humors of local nomenclature. The Latin adjective *ursina* means "belonging to a bear."

Valley Forge, in Chester County, is known to every schoolboy as the place where Washington encamped with the Revolutionary army during the winter of 1777-8. Here, in a deep, rugged hollow at the mouth of Valley Creek, stood an old forge erected before 1759, belonging to Isaac Potts, son of John Potts, the founder of Pottstown. The old forge at the mouth of Valley Creek has given Valley Forge its name. On the steep sides of the valley or hollow stood Washington's camp. In 1893 the state of Pennsylvania established a park at Valley

Forge, containing 472 acres, in order that the site and the fortifications "may be maintained as nearly as possible in their original condition." Every year more than 300,000 pilgrims visit Valley Forge.

The borough of **Versailles,** in Allegheny County, has taken its official designation from old Versailles Township, which was named for the palace of the French kings. The name is a perpetual reminder of the valiant but vain struggle that the French made for the possession of western Pennsylvania.

Virginville, in Berks County, is situated on Maiden Creek. Both the village and the stream derived their names from a translation of the Indian name Ontelaunee, which means "virgin, or maiden." The name Ontelaunee has been given to one of the townships of Berks County.

Warriors Mark, situated in the township of Warriors Mark, Huntingdon County, received its name from certain strange marks which, according to the early settlers, had been carved on the trees by the Indians.

Water Street, in Huntingdon County, an important place in the days of the old Pennsylvania Canal, takes its name from the Water Street branch of the Juniata, which lies in the gap through Tussey Mountain, several miles east of Water Street village. It was so named because in the early days the road in the narrow ravine or gap, traveled by pioneers and traders, occupied the bed of the shallow mountain stream. The first road was literally a *water* street.

The borough and the township of **Westfield,** in Tioga County, derived their name from Westfield, Massachusetts, the native town of Henry B. Trowbridge, in whose woolen mill the Westfield post-office was established in 1821.

Wheatland, in Mercer County, was laid out about 1865

21

by James Wood of Pittsburgh, who was a staunch Democrat, and who named his town Wheatland after President James Buchanan's estate near Lancaster.

Windgap, in Northampton County, took its name from the famous "wind gap" in the Blue Mountains, the first notch to the south of the Delaware Water Gap. "The Wind Gap is a depression or opening in the Blue Mountain, which is very abrupt, and extends from the top nearly to the bottom of the mountain." It resembles the famous Cumberland Gap of Kentucky in the fact that no stream passes through it.

Zelienople, in Butler County, derived its name, which means "Zelie's city," from Zelie Basse, the daughter of its scholarly and romantic-minded founder, Baron Dettmar W. F. Basse, "whose ample means, when he came here from Frankfort in Germany, in 1802, enabled him to purchase 10,000 acres of land, lay out a village, and erect a three-story wooden castle, which he called Bassenheim. It seems to have been Basse's ambition to establish a sort of baronial estate in the wilderness." In 1803 he sold half of his tract to his visionary countryman, George Rapp, on which the latter founded the village of Harmony.[11] Baron Basse, after spending about ten years at Bessenheim, met with financial reverses and returned to Germany. His daughter Zelie remained, becoming the wife of Philippe Passavant. Basse usually signed his name Dettmar Basse Müller (i. e., Dettmar Basse, the miller), from which circumstance he came to be known as D. B. Müller.

---

[11] See pages 291-294.

CHAPTER XXVI

THE TOWNSHIP NAMES

ACCORDING to the census of 1920 Pennsylvania has 1,556 townships. By the repetition of the same name for townships in different counties and by the addition of the prefixes East, West, North, South, Lower, Middle, and Upper, and of such appendages as Creek, Lake, -field, or -hill, 780 different names are made to suffice for these 1,556 townships.

Of these 780 different township names, 346—a little more than two-fifths—are derived from the names of persons; 142—nearly one-fifth—are borrowed place names; 139—another fifth—have been appropriated from geographical location, natural features, plants, and animals; seventy-eight—exactly one-tenth—are Indian names; and the remaining seventy-five come from various miscellaneous sources.

The following fifty-one names, each of which has been given to five or more townships in different counties, furnish an official designation to more than four hundred townships:[1]

Union 25	Greene 9	Liberty 7
Washington 22	Springfield 9	Milford 7
Franklin 22	Wayne 9	Monroe 7
Penn 20	Hopewell 8	Porter 7
Jackson 18	Mahoning 8	Taylor 7
Beaver 11	Pine 8	Brady 6
Hanover 10	Allegheny 7	Eldred 6
Jefferson 10	Bethel 7	Heidelberg 6
Perry 10	Centre 7	Mifflin 6

[1] In the list that follows, the numeral after a name indicates the number of Pennsylvania townships bearing this name.

Providence 6	Fallowfield 5	Morris 5
Salem 6	Greenwood 5	Mount Pleasant 5
Allen 5	Hamilton 5	Richland 5
Buffalo 5	Limestone 5	Rush 5
Clay 5	Londonderry 5	Saint Clair 5
Clinton 5	Madison 5	Southampton 5
Donegal 5	Mahanoy 5	Spring 5
Fairview 5	Manheim 5	Tyrone 5

In seventeen counties there are townships bearing the same name as the county; and forty-four county names have been applied to townships outside the counties whose names have thus been borrowed. The names of many towns and villages, as is evident from the preceding chapters, have been borrowed from township names; and occasionally the name of a township has been taken from that of a town whose settlement antedates the formation of the township. Nearly two-fifths of the different township names have already been explained, being identical in form and origin with the names of counties, large towns, and villages which have received special comment.

1. Townships Named for Persons.—Over five hundred townships have been named for noted men and for local celebrities, the former being slightly in the majority.

Besides the four Presidents whose names are borne by counties, the following nine others have also furnished names for townships: Madison, John Quincy Adams, Jackson, William Henry Harrison, Polk, Taylor, Lincoln, Grant, and Cleveland.

Naturally many townships have taken the names of prominent Pennsylvanians. The following is a partial list of those named for Pennsylvania worthies not already referred to:

Black Township, in Somerset County, was named in honor of the eminent judge, Jeremiah Sullivan Black, a native of this county, who became chief justice of Pennsylvania in 1851, and resigned the position a few years later to become attorney-general of the United States under President Buchanan.

Dickinson Township, in Cumberland County, was named in 1785 for John Dickinson, then governor of Pennsylvania under the title of "President of the Supreme Executive Council."

The two Gibson Townships, one in Clearfield and the other in Susquehanna County, were named for John Bannister Gibson, one of the ablest of Pennsylvania jurists, who became chief justice of the State in 1827.

Gregg Township, in Centre County, received its name from Andrew Gregg, a citizen of this county, who represented it in Congress from 1791 to 1807, and served as United States Senator from 1807 to 1813.

Hamilton Township, in Franklin County, was named in 1752 in honor of James Hamilton, then colonial governor of Pennsylvania.

Rush Township, in Centre County, was formed and named in 1814, one year after the death of the illustrious patriot, Dr. Benjamin Rush of Philadelphia, a signer of the Declaration of Independence, and an eminent physician and teacher of medicine.

Wilmot Township, in Bradford County, was named for David Wilmot, a citizen of this county, who was a member of Congress from 1845 to 1851.[2]

About a dozen other townships christened in honor of *famous men* not already mentioned are worthy of special comment:

Decatur Township, in Clearfield County, bears the name of the popular naval hero, Commodore Stephen

---

[2] See page 94.

Decatur, who won undying fame in our second war with England and in the war against the pirates of the Barbary states, and who was killed in a duel in 1820 by Commodore James Barron. Commodore Decatur was born in Maryland, whither his parents had gone during the British occupation of Philadelphia. Three months after his birth the family returned to their Pennsylvania home.

Huntington Township, in Luzerne County, was formed in 1793 and named by the Connecticut settlers in honor of the patriot, Samuel Huntington, then governor of their native State. He was one of the signers of the Declaration of Independence, and served as president of the Continental Congress from 1779 to 1781.

The four Marion Townships, in Beaver, Berks, Butler, and Centre Counties, have all been named for the popular Revolutionary hero, General Francis Marion of South Carolina, appreciatively known as the "Swamp Fox" because of his shrewdness and the swiftness of his movements. Seventeen counties in the United States bear the name of this favorite Southern hero of the Revolution.

Napier Township, in Bedford County, was formed about 1812 and may have been named for the great English general, Sir William Francis Patrick Napier, who had but recently distinguished himself in the famous "Peninsular Campaign" against Napoleon. General Napier, who afterward wrote a *History of the War in the Peninsula,* is one of the great English military historians.

Steuben Township, in Crawford County, bears the name of the Prussian soldier, Friedrich Wilhelm Augustus, Baron von Steuben, an aide of Frederick the Great in the Seven Years' War and a major-general and drillmaster in our Continental army during the Revolution. Counties in New York and Indiana have been named for Baron von Steuben.

Tilden Township, in Berks County, was christened in honor of Samuel Jones Tilden, governor of New York in 1875, long the leader of the Democratic party, and in 1876 the unsuccessful Democratic candidate for the Presidency. In that year the election was bitterly contested, and many citizens of the new township firmly believed that Tilden should have been seated as President of the United States.

The three Worth Townships, in Butler, Centre, and Mercer Counties, were formed between 1848 and 1854, and named in honor of Major-General William Jenkins Worth, one of the popular heroes of the Mexican War, second in command to General Zachary Taylor.

Of the *local celebrities* whose family names have been perpetuated in the names of townships, four groups seem to be noteworthy,—early settlers, large landholders or their agents, judges, and leading citizens.

(*a*) Many of the counties of Pennsylvania have honored some pioneer settler by giving his name to a township. The following are noteworthy examples of this commendable custom:

Barnett Township, in Jefferson County, was named for the patriarch, Joseph Barnett, the first white settler who, in 1800, came into this wilderness region over "Mead's Trail." [3]

Bloomfield Township, in Crawford County, was formed in 1811 and christened in honor of Thomas Bloomfield, one of the earliest permanent settlers.

Buck Township, in Luzerne County, was named for George Buck, an early settler, who kept the first tavern in this locality.

[3] See page 100.

328 PENNSYLVANIA PLACE NAMES

Cromwell Township, in Huntingdon County, was named for the pioneer, Colonel Thomas Cromwell, who, in 1785, helped to build the first iron furnace west of the Susquehanna near the present borough of Orbisonia.

The name of East and West Fallowfield Townships, in Chester County, was not, as one might guess, derived from the untilled soil at the time of the first settlement, but from Launcelot Fallowfield, a native of Great Strickland, in Westmoreland County, England, one of the first settlers to buy land of William Penn.

Parker Township, in Butler County, took its name from John Parker, a pioneer surveyor who came to this region in 1794.

Price Township, in Monroe County, was formed in 1830 and named for John Price, the first settler in this township.

Robeson Township, in Berks County, was organized in 1729 and named for the Swedish pioneer, Andrew Robeson, who later became a man of large wealth and influence in his community. The borough of Robesonia was also named for him.

Terry Township, in Bradford County, was named in honor of the pioneer settler, Captain Jonathan Terry.

(b) The following five names exemplify the practice of naming townships for great landowners or their agents:

Benzinger Township, in Elk County, was christened in honor of Colonel Mathias Benzinger, who, as the agent of the German Catholic settlers from Baltimore, bought about 60,000 acres of land in what is now Elk County.

Gaskill Township, in Jefferson County, was named for Charles C. Gaskill, agent of the Holland Land Company, which owned and colonized large tracts of land in Jefferson and adjoining counties.

Newlin Township, in Chester County, received its name from Nathaniel Newlin, who, in 1724, bought from the Free Society of Traders a tract of 7,700 acres, which was later organized as Newlin Township.

East and West Pikeland Townships, in Chester County, were originally "Pike's land," a name designating the tract that William Penn granted in 1705 to Joseph Pike, an Irish merchant from Cork.

Smithfield Township, in Bradford County, took its name from David Smith, who claimed the township under the Connecticut title.

(c) About fifty townships are known to have taken the family names of presiding or associate judges of counties or districts, who, because of their prominence in the county and of the official part that they played in the organization of new townships, were likely candidates for such distinction. The following half-dozen township names, chosen almost at random, are typical of this group:

Barrett Township, in Monroe County, was formed in 1859 and named for George R. Barrett, then presiding judge of the county courts.

The two Burrell Townships, one organized in 1853 in Indiana County, and the other two years later in Armstrong County, were named in honor of Jeremiah Murray Burrell, presiding judge of this judicial district.

Herrick Township, organized as a part of Susquehanna County in 1825, and Herrick Township, formed twelve years later in Bradford County, received their name from Edward Herrick, then presiding judge of this district.

Kline Township, in Schuylkill County, was formed in 1873 and christened in honor of Jacob Kline, then associate judge of the county.

Ross Township, in Luzerne County, was formed in

1842 and named for William G. Ross, then associate county judge.

Old Taylor Township, in Cambria County, formed in 1857, took its name from Judge George Taylor. In 1884 this township was divided into East and West Taylor Townships.

(d) Many townships have been named for influential citizens. The following are notable examples:

Benner Township, in Centre County, was christened in 1853 in honor of General Philip Benner, a prominent politician, who had founded the *Centre Democrat* in 1827.

Clover Township, in Jefferson County, formed in 1841, received its name from Levi G. Clover, then prothonotary of the county.

Graham Township, in Clearfield County, is notable as being one of the few townships named for the persons who were chiefly instrumental in their formation. Graham Township was named for James B. Graham, an enterprising citizen of the new township.

Gulich Township, in Clearfield County, was named for Gerhard Philip Gulich, "well-known in all that vicinity for his thrift and stability of character."

Larimer Township, in Somerset County, was christened in 1854 in honor of General William Larimer, Jr., then president of the Pittsburgh and Connellsville Railroad.

The name of Moore Township, in Northampton County, was given in 1765 in honor of John Moore, who represented his county in the provincial Assembly in 1761-2.

Noyes Township, in Clinton County, formed in 1875, was named for Colonel A. C. Noyes, then the most prominent citizen within its limits.

2. **Townships with Borrowed Place Names.**—Many of

the place names appropriated from various parts of the world and given to townships have already been mentioned in the preceding chapters. The following townships bear borrowed place names not previously mentioned: [4]

Germany is represented by the townships of Alsace (Berks), East and West Brunswick (Schuylkill), Franconia (Montgomery), Hanover (Beaver, Lehigh, Luzerne, Northampton, Washington), Heidelberg (Berks, Lebanon, Lehigh), and Weisenberg (Lehigh).

English place names have been given to the townships of Aston (Delaware), Bedminster (Bucks), Caln (Chester), Lower and Upper Chichester (Delaware), East, North, and South Coventry (Chester), Edgemont (Delaware), Marlboro (Montgomery), Middlesex (Butler, Cumberland), Salford (Montgomery), Solebury (Bucks), and Thornbury (Chester).

Ireland has contributed names to the townships of Fermanagh (Juniata), Letterkenny and Lurgan (Franklin), Munster (Cambria), Rostraver (Westmoreland), and Straban (Adams).

The Yankee settlers in the northern and northeastern counties have named a number of townships for their native New England towns. Thus the township and the village of Brooklyn (Susquehanna), the township and the borough of Canton (Bradford), and the township of Farmington (Tioga) have all borrowed their names from Connecticut towns. Newport Township, organized in 1790 as one of the original townships of Luzerne County, was so named by Rhode Island settlers from the neighborhood of Newport. Springfield Township (Bradford) is said to have received its name from Springfield

---

[4] In the list that follows, and on page 332, after each township name, the county in which it is situated is given in parentheses.

in Massachusetts. In 1802 Mt. Zion Township (Bradford), which had been formed the year before, was renamed Orwell on petition of Ebenezer Coburn and other settlers, who had come from the town of Orwell in Vermont.

Several states of the Union have given names to townships. It is but natural that both Allegheny and Beaver Counties should have an Ohio Township lying close to the Ohio River. Wayne County has a township named Oregon and another called Texas.

The Bible furnishes names for Eden Township (Lancaster) and Hebron Township (Potter).

The following half-dozen township names have been appropriated from as many different countries: Armenia (Bradford), Ayr (Fulton), Lausanne (Carbon), Sparta (Crawford), Sweden (Potter), and Warsaw (Jefferson).

3. **Township Names Derived from Location, Natural Features, Plants, and Animals.**—The following list, from which have been excluded all names already mentioned, comprises more than one-third of the total number of township names derived from this source:

Bear Creek (Luzerne)	Forest Lake (Susquehanna)
Beaver (Snyder)	Forks (Northampton)
Black Creek (Luzerne)	Glade (Warren)
Blooming Grove (Pike)	Greenfield (Blair)
Branch (Schuylkill)	Greenwood (Juniata)
Broad Top (Bedford)	Hemlock (Columbia)
Brush Creek (Fulton)	Hempfield (Lancaster)
Buffalo (Union)	Hickory (Forest)
Cherry (Sullivan)	Lake (Luzerne)
Chestnuthill (Monroe)	Limestone (Montour)
Deer Creek (Mercer)	Locust (Columbia)
Fairfield (Lycoming)	Longswamp (Berks)
Falls (Bucks)	Muddycreek (Butler)
Fawn (York)	Oakland (Susquehanna)
Fishing Creek (Columbia)	Oil Creek (Crawford)

Otter Creek (Mercer)
Pine (Indiana)
Plainfield (Northampton)
Plum (Allegheny)
Point (Northumberland)
Redbank (Armstrong)
Redstone (Fayette)
Richhill (Greene)
Richland (Bucks)
Roaring Brook (Lackawanna)
Rockland (Berks)

Sandy (Clearfield)
Scrubgrass (Venango)
Snake Spring (Bedford)
South Bend (Armstrong)
Southwest (Warren)
Spring (Centre)
Stonycreek (Somerset)
Summit (Potter)
Valley (Chester)
Wheatfield (Perry)
White Deer (Union)

The reason for most of the foregoing names is evident without much comment. A few of them, however, are deserving of special notice.

Broad Top Township, in Bedford County, and the borough of Broad Top City, in Huntingdon County, have derived their names from Broad Top Mountain, situated in these two counties.

Fishing Creek Township, in Columbia County, took its name from the little stream that has been made famous by the so-called Fishing Creek Confederacy. A small company of men who had been drafted into military service during the Civil War, refusing to obey the summons that called them to serve their country, retreated into the wilds of Fishing Creek valley in the hope that they might thus escape being forced into the army. In spite of a good deal of sensational fiction that has been written about the "confederacy," the plain truth is that the little band of malcontents formed no organization against the government and offered no open resistance to the Federal authorities.

Forks Township, in Northampton County, lying north of the confluence of the Lehigh River with the Delaware, took its name in 1754 from the "forks of the Delaware."

Old Hempfield Township, in Lancaster County, now divided into East and West Hempfield, was so styled because in the early days a good deal of hemp was grown there. Hempfield Township, in Westmoreland County, was settled and named by pioneers from Lancaster County; and Hempfield Township, in Mercer County, was so named by settlers who had moved thither from the Westmoreland township of Hempfield.

Longswamp Township, in Berks County, formed in 1761, received its name from the swampy condition of its soil.

Plainfield Township, in Northampton County, derived its name from the fact that when organized into a township in 1762 this region, unlike the surrounding country, was an open plain or field, almost devoid of timber except on the margins of its watercourses.

Richhill Township, in Greene County, took its name from the nature of its soil and surface, "for it is one stretch of hills throughout its broad domain, and the soil is everywhere deep and rich."

Rockland Township, in Berks County, was named in 1758 for the many large rocks found there. These great natural monuments are still standing undisturbed.

Scrubgrass Township, in Venango County, was named more than a century ago for Scrubgrass Creek, which was so styled because of the peculiar vegetation that bordered its banks.

Spring Township, which contains the county-seat of Centre County, was christened for the beautiful and copious spring that gave Bellefonte its name.

4. Townships Bearing Indian Names.—To the numerous aboriginal names already explained, many of which have been applied to townships, may be added the following as representative of the township names:

East and West Chillisquaque Townships, in Northumberland County: "the resort of snow birds."

East and West Cocalico Townships, in Lancaster County: "where snakes gather in holes."

Conewago Township, in Dauphin County: "at the rapids."

Conewango Township, in Warren County: Conewango is a variant of Conewago, "at the rapids."

Conoy Township, in Lancaster County: the Conoys or Gawanese, signifying "cornshellers," were an Indian tribe.

Kiskiminetas Township, in Armstrong County: "plenty of walnuts."

Upper Mahantango Township, in Schuylkill County: Mahantango means "where we had plenty of meat."

Nippenose Township in Lycoming County: "like the summer."

Nockamixon Township, in Bucks County: "at the three houses."

Pymatuning Township, in Mercer County: "the home of the man with the crooked nose."

Quemahoning Township, in Somerset County: "pine-tree lick."

Upper Saucon Township in Lehigh County and Lower Saucon Township in Northampton County: Saucon is a corruption of *sakunk,* "at the mouth of the river."

Towamensing Township, in Carbon County: "uninhabited country."

5. **Township Names Derived from Miscellaneous Sources.**—To this group belong names that do not readily or obviously fall within the four preceding classes. A number of townships have been named for abstractions, such as Triumph Township, in Warren County. One might readily guess that this unusual name was born of the jubilant feelings of men who had "struck oil." The

following names may be taken as fairly representative of this miscellaneous group:

Amity Township, in Berks County, formed in 1719, received its name from the friendly relations that existed between the Indians and the Swedes whom William Penn induced to settle here.

The name of Brokenstraw Township, in Warren County, is a translation of Cushandauga, the Indian name of the Irvine Flats, which once bore a crop of tall, stiff prairie grass, which in autumn would become brittle, break off, and fall over.

Charlestown Township, in Chester County, bears the baptismal name of Charles Pickering, an early settler, whose surname was given to Pickering Creek, which flows through the township. In 1683 Charles Pickering was convicted of setting up a private mint for "the quoining of Spanish bitts and Boston money."

Concord Township, in Delaware County, was so called because of "the harmonious feelings which in early times prevailed among the settlers there." Concordville was named for the township.

The name of Delmar Township, in Tioga County, is composed of the first syllables of Delaware and Maryland, whence the first settlers came more than a century ago.

The townships of Earl, East Earl, and West Earl, in Lancaster County, owe their name to Hans Graaf, a Swiss refugee who settled in this locality in 1717. Earl is the English equivalent of the German *Graf*.

Halfmoon Township, in Centre County, received its name from Half-Moon Creek, which was so called by the early settlers because of the rude representations of half-moons that they found carved on trees, apparently marking the course of an Indian trail through the valley.

Mount Joy Township, formed in 1759 from old Donegal Township, in Lancaster County, received its curious name from the title of General Sir William Stewart, who owned large estates in County Donegal, who was raised to the peerage of Ireland in 1683 as Baron Stewart and Viscount Mountjoy, and who later deserted the cause of James II for that of William III and was killed at Steinkirk in 1692. The borough of Mount Joy was named for the township.

Manor Township, in Lancaster County, was christened for the old Conestoga Manor, laid out by the Penns two centuries ago, and situated mainly in this township. Manor Township, in Armstrong County, was in like manner named for the Kittanning or Appleby Manor, one of the two score manors in Pennsylvania belonging to the Penns. Manorville, in the same county, also received its name from this manor.

Oliver Township, in Perry County, received the baptismal name of Commodore Oliver Hazard Perry, for whom the county was named. Oliver Township, in Jefferson County, was so christened because it was formed from Perry Township.

Pine Creek Township, in Jefferson County, did not receive its name from any stream in that region, but from Pine Creek in Lycoming County, from whose banks the hardy pioneer, Joseph Barnett, had emigrated.

The name of Standing Stone Township, in Bradford County, had an origin quite different from that of the Indian village of Standing Stone, which was situated on the site of Huntingdon.[5] This township was named for an important natural landmark mentioned in many early surveys,—a huge upright rock about sixteen feet wide,

---

[5] See page 114.

22

338 PENNSYLVANIA PLACE NAMES

four feet thick, and fully twenty feet above the surface of the Susquehanna River.

Toby Township, in Clarion County, was not named for a person, but for Toby's Creek, a pioneer name for the stream now called the Clarion River.[6]

---

[6] See Clarion County, page 146.

APPENDICES

APPENDIX A

LIST OF BOOKS CONSULTED [1]

General

Appleton's Cyclopedia of American Biography. New York, 1898.
The National Cyclopedia of American Biography.
Dictionary of National Biography.
The Encyclopedia Britannica.
The International Encyclopedia.
Harper's Encyclopedia of United States History. New York, 1902.
The Historians' History of the World. New York and London, 1904.
Lippincott's New Gazetteer of the World.
Lippincott's Pronouncing Biographical Dictionary.
The Pennsylvania Magazine of History and Biography. Published by the Historical Society of Pennsylvania.
Smull's Legislative Handbook of the State of Pennsylvania. Published annually. Harrisburg.
The United States Official Postal Guide.
Bulletins of the Thirteenth and the Fourteenth Census of the United States.

Histories

The Wilderness Trail. By Charles A. Hanna. New York, 1911.
The History of Pennsylvania in North America. By Robert Proud. Philadelphia, 1797.
Historical Collections of the State of Pennsylvania. By Sherman Day. Philadelphia, 1843.
The History of Pennsylvania. By William Mason Cornell. Philadelphia, 1876.
History of the Commonwealth of Pennsylvania. By William H. Egle. Harrisburg, 1876.
History of Pennsylvania. By Thomas S. March. New York, 1915.
Pennsylvania—The Keystone. By Samuel W. Pennypacker. Philadelphia, 1914.
A Short History of Pennsylvania. By L. S. Shimmell. New York, 1910.
History of Pennsylvania. By Allen C. Thomas. Boston and New York, 1913.
Stories of Pennsylvania. By Joseph S. Walton and Martin G. Brumbaugh. New York, 1897.

---

[1] This is only a partial list of the books consulted. For lack of space most histories of single towns or communities have been omitted.

The German and Swiss Settlements of Colonial Pennsylvania. By Oscar Kuhns. New Edition. New York, 1914.

A Gazetteer of the State of Pennsylvania. By Thomas F. Gordon. Philadelphia, 1832.

Report of the Commission to Locate the Pioneer Forts of Pennsylvania. Second Edition. Harrisburg, 1916.

History of Lancaster and York Counties. By I. D. Rupp. Lancaster, 1844.

History of the Counties of Lebanon and Berks. By I. D. Rupp. Lancaster, 1844.

History of Northampton, Lehigh, Monroe, Carbon, and Schuylkill Counties. By I. D. Rupp. Harrisburg, 1845.

History and Topography of Dauphin, Cumberland, Franklin, Bedford, Adams, and Perry Counties. By I. D. Rupp. Lancaster, 1846.

History and Topography of Northumberland, Huntingdon, Mifflin, Centre, Union, Columbia, Juniata, and Clinton Counties. By I. D. Rupp. Lancaster, 1847.

History of Allegheny County. Philadelphia, 1876.

History of Allegheny County. Chicago, 1889.

Centennial History of Allegheny County. By A. E. Lambring and J. W. F. White. Pittsburgh, 1888.

History of Armstrong County. By Robert W. Smith. Chicago, 1883.

History of Beaver County. Philadelphia and Chicago, 1888.

History of Beaver County. By Joseph H. Bausman. New York, 1904.

History of Bedford, Somerset, and Fulton Counties. Chicago, 1884.

History of Bedford and Somerset Counties. By William H. Koontz. New York and Chicago, 1906.

The Annals of Bedford County. By William P. Schell. Bedford, Pa., 1907.

History of Berks County. By Morton L. Montgomery. Philadelphia, 1886.

Historical and Biographical Annals of Berks County. By Morton L. Montgomery. Chicago, 1909.

History of Bradford County. By H. C. Bradsby. Chicago, 1891.

History of Old Tioga Point and Early Athens. By Louise Welles Murray. Athens, Pa., 1908.

History of Bucks County. New York and Chicago, 1905.

History of Butler County. Published by R. C. Brown & Co., 1895.

History of Cambria County. By H. W. Storey. New York, 1907.

History of Carbon County. By Fred Brenckman. Harrisburg, 1913.

History of Centre and Clinton Counties. By John Blair Linn. Philadelphia, 1883.

History of Chester County. By J. Smith Futhey and Gilbert Cope. Philadelphia, 1881.

History of Clarion County. By A. J. Davis. Syracuse, 1887.

History of Clearfield County. By Lewis C. Aldrich. Syracuse, 1887.

Past and Present of Clinton County. By J. Milton Furey. Williamsport, Pa., 1892.

History of Columbia County. By John G. Freeze. Bloomsburg, Pa., 1883.

History of Columbia and Montour Counties. By J. H. Battle. Chicago, 1887.

History of the Founding of Meadville and Settlement of Crawford County. Meadville, Pa., 1888.

History of Cumberland and Adams Counties. Chicago, 1886.

History of the Counties of Dauphin and Lebanon. By William H. Egle. Philadelphia, 1883.

History of Dauphin County. New York, 1902.

History of Delaware County. By Henry G. Ashmead. Philadelphia, 1884.

Biographical and Historical Cyclopedia of Delaware County. New York, 1894.

History of Erie County. By Laura G. Sanford. Philadelphia, 1862.

History of Erie County. Chicago, 1884.

History of Fayette County. By Franklin Ellis. Philadelphia, 1882.

Biographical Dictionary and Historical Reference Book of Fayette County. Uniontown, Pa., 1900.

Historical Sketch of Franklin County. By I. H. McCauley. Harrisburg, 1878.

History of Franklin County. Chicago, 1887.

History of Greene County. By Samuel P. Bates. Chicago, 1888.

History of Hanover Township and the Wyoming Valley. By Henry B. Plumb. Wilkes-Barre, 1885.

History of Huntingdon County. By Milton S. Lytle. Lancaster, 1876.

History of Huntingdon and Blair Counties. By J. Simpson Africa. Philadelphia, 1883.

Biographical and Historical Cyclopedia of Indiana and Armstrong Counties. Philadelphia, 1891.

History of Jefferson County. By Kate M. Scott. Syracuse, 1888.

A Pioneer History of Jefferson County. By W. J. McKnight. Philadelphia, 1898.

History of the Early Settlement of the Juniata Valley. By U. J. Jones. Harrisburg, 1889.

History of the Lackawanna Valley. By H. Hollister. Third Edition. Scranton, 1875.

History of Lancaster County. By Franklin Ellis and Samuel Evans. Philadelphia, 1883.

Brief History of Lancaster County. By Israel S. Clare. Lancaster, 1892.

Historical Review of the Towns and Business Houses of Lawrence County. By Wick W. Wood. New Castle, Pa., 1887.

History of Lehigh County. Allentown, 1914.

History of the Counties of Lehigh and Carbon. By Alfred Mathews and A. N. Hungerford. Philadelphia, 1884.

Annals of Luzerne County. By Stewart Pearce. Philadelphia, 1860.

History of Luzerne County. Chicago, 1893.

History of Luzerne, Lackawanna, and Wyoming Counties. New York, 1880.

History of Lycoming County. By John F. Meginness. Chicago, 1892.

APPENDIX A

History of the Counties of McKean, Elk, and Forest. Chicago, 1890.

History of the Counties of McKean, Elk, Cameron, and Potter. Chicago, 1890.

History of Mercer County. Chicago, 1888.

History of Mifflin County. By Joseph Cochran. Harrisburg, 1879.

History of the Susquehanna and Juniata Valleys, Embracing the Counties of Mifflin, Juniata, Perry, Union, and Snyder. Philadelphia, 1886.

History of Montgomery County. By Theodore W. Bean. Philadelphia, 1884.

The Monongahela of Old. By James Veech. Pittsburgh, 1892.

History of Northampton County. Philadelphia and Reading, 1877.

History of Northumberland County. By Herbert C. Bell. Chicago, 1891.

A Pioneer History of Northwestern Pennsylvania. By W. J. McKnight. Philadelphia, 1905.

Annals of Philadelphia and Pennsylvania. By John F. Watson. Revised Edition. Philadelphia, 1905.

History of Philadelphia. By J. T. Scharf and Thomas Westcott. Philadelphia, 1884.

A History of Philadelphia and Its People. By Ellis P. Oberholtzer. Philadelphia, 1912.

The Lives of Eminent Philadelphians. By Henry Simpson. Philadelphia, 1859.

History of Schuylkill County. New York, 1881.

History of Scranton and Its People. By Frederick L. Hitchcock. New York, 1914.

Journal of the Military Expedition of Major-General Sullivan against the Six Nations of New York in 1779. By George S. Conover. Auburn, 1887.

Centennial History of Susquehanna County. By R. M. Stocker. Philadelphia, 1887.

History of Tioga County. By J. W. Powell. Harrisburg, 1897.

History of Venango County. Chicago, 1890.

History of Warren County. By J. S. Schenck. Syracuse, 1887.

History of Washington County. By Alfred Creigh. 1870.

History of Washington County. By Boyd Crumrine. Philadelphia, 1882.

History of Wayne County. By Phineas G. Goodrich. Honesdale, Pa., 1880.

History of Wayne, Pike, and Monroe Counties. By Alfred Mathews. Philadelphia, 1886.

History of the County of Westmoreland. By George D. Albert. Philadelphia, 1882.

History of Wilkes-Barre. By Oscar J. Harvey. Wilkes-Barre, 1909.

History of York County. By John Gibson. Chicago, 1886.

Virginia Counties: Those Resulting from Virginia Legislation. By Morgan Poitiaux Robinson. Bulletin of Virginia State Library. Richmond, 1916.

Names

The Origin of Certain Place Names in the United States. By Henry Gannett. Second Edition. Washington, 1905.

Virginia County Names. By Charles M. Long. New York and Washington, 1908.

British Family Names. By Henry Barber. Second Edition. London, 1903.

Dictionary of English and Welsh Surnames. By C. W. Bardsley. London and New York, 1901.

Family Names and Their Story. By S. Baring-Gould. London, 1910.

Surnames of the United Kingdom. By Henry Harrison. London, 1912.

Words and Places. By Isaac Taylor. In Everyman's Library. London, 1915.

Names and Their Histories. By Isaac Taylor. Second Edition. London, 1898.

History of Christian Names. By Charlotte M. Yonge. Revised Edition. London, 1884.

Place Names and Altitudes of Pennsylvania Mountains. By Henry W. Shoemaker. Altoona, 1923.

Changing Historic Place Names in Pennsylvania. By George P. Donehoo and Henry W. Shoemaker. Altoona, 1921.

Indian Local Names with Their Interpretation. By Stephen G. Boyd. York, Pa., 1888.

Aboriginal Place Names of New York. By William M. Beauchamp. Albany, 1907.

Names which the Lenni-Lennape or Delaware Indians Gave to Rivers, Streams, and Localities within the States of Pennsylvania, New Jersey, Maryland and Virginia, with Their Signification. By John G. E. Heckewelder. 1822.

APPENDIX B

THE FORMATION AND THE NAMING OF COUNTIES

COUNTY	WHEN FORMED	TAKEN FROM	SOURCE OF NAME
1. Philadelphia	Nov., 1682	One of the original counties	City in Asia Minor
2. Chester	Nov., 1682	One of the original counties	English County of Chester
3. Bucks	Nov., 1682	One of the original counties	English County of Buckingham
4. Lancaster	May 10, 1729	Chester	English County of Lancaster
5. York	Aug. 19, 1749	Lancaster	James, Duke of York
6. Cumberland	Jan. 27, 1750	Lancaster	English County of Cumberland
7. Berks	March 11, 1752	Philadelphia, Chester, Lancaster	English County of Berks
8. Northampton	March 11, 1752	Bucks	English County of Northampton
9. Bedford	March 9, 1771	Cumberland	The Duke of Bedford
10. Northumberland	March 21, 1772	Cumberland, Berks, Bedford, Northampton	English County of Northumberland
11. Westmoreland	Feb. 26, 1773	Bedford	English County of Westmoreland
12. Washington	March 28, 1781	Westmoreland	George Washington (President)
13. Fayette	Sept. 26, 1783	Westmoreland	Marquis de la Fayette
14. Franklin	Sept. 9, 1784	Cumberland	Benjamin Franklin (Governor)
15. Montgomery	Sept. 10, 1784	Philadelphia	General Richard Montgomery
16. Dauphin	March 4, 1785	Lancaster	The Dauphin of France
17. Luzerne	Sept. 25, 1786	Northumberland	The Chevalier de la Luzerne
18. Huntingdon	Sept. 20, 1787	Bedford	The Countess of Huntingdon
19. Allegheny	Sept. 24, 1788	Westmoreland, Washington	Allegheny Mts. (Indian name)
20. Mifflin	Sept. 19, 1789	Cumberland, Northumberland	Thomas Mifflin (Governor)
21. Delaware	Sept. 26, 1789	Chester	The Delaware River
22. Lycoming	April 13, 1795	Northumberland	Lycoming Creek (Indian name)
23. Somerset	April 17, 1795	Bedford	English County of Somerset

County	When Formed	Taken From	Source of Name
24. Greene	Feb. 9, 1796	Washington	General Nathaniel Greene
25. Wayne	March 21, 1798	Northampton	General Anthony Wayne
26. Adams	Jan. 22, 1800	York	John Adams (President)
27. Centre	Feb. 13, 1800	Mifflin, Northumberland, Lycoming, Huntingdon	Geographical position
28. Armstrong	March 12, 1800	Allegheny, Westmoreland, Lycoming	General John Armstrong
29. Beaver	March 12, 1800	Allegheny, Washington	The Beaver River
30. Butler	March 12, 1800	Allegheny	General Richard Butler
31. Crawford	March 12, 1800	Allegheny	Colonel William Crawford
32. Erie	March 12, 1800	Allegheny	Lake Erie (Indian name)
33. Mercer	March 12, 1800	Allegheny	General Hugh Mercer
34. Venango	March 12, 1800	Allegheny, Lycoming	Venango River (Indian name)
35. Warren	March 12, 1800	Allegheny, Lycoming	General Joseph Warren
36. Indiana	March 30, 1803	Westmoreland, Lycoming	For the Indians
37. Cambria	March 26, 1804	Huntingdon, Somerset, Bedford	Ancient name of Wales
38. Clearfield	March 26, 1804	Lycoming, Huntingdon	The Clearfield Creek
39. Jefferson	March 26, 1804	Lycoming	Thomas Jefferson (President)
40. McKean	March 26, 1804	Lycoming	Thomas McKean (Governor)
41. Potter	March 26, 1804	Lycoming	General James Potter
42. Tioga	March 26, 1804	Lycoming	The Tioga River (Indian name)
43. Bradford	Feb. 21, 1810	Luzerne, Lycoming	Wm. Bradford (Attorney Gen'l)
44. Susquehanna	Feb. 21, 1810	Luzerne	Susquehanna River (Ind. name)
45. Schuylkill	March 1, 1811	Berks, Northampton	The Schuylkill River (''Hidden stream'')
46. Lehigh	March 6, 1812	Northampton	The Lehigh River (Indian name)

THE FORMATION AND THE NAMING OF COUNTIES—*Continued*

County	When Formed	Taken From	Source of Name
47. Lebanon	Feb. 16, 1813	Dauphin, Lancaster	For Lebanon in Palestine
48. Columbia	March 22, 1813	Northumberland	Poetic name for America
49. Union	March 22, 1813	Northumberland	For patriotic idea of national union
50. Pike	March 26, 1814	Wayne	Gen. Zebulon Montgomery Pike
51. Perry	March 22, 1820	Cumberland	Commodore Oliver Hazard Perry
52. Juniata	March 2, 1831	Mifflin	The Juniata River (Indian name)
53. Monroe	April 1, 1836	Northampton, Pike	James Monroe (President)
54. Clarion	March 11, 1839	Venango, Armstrong	The Clarion River
55. Clinton	June 21, 1839	Lycoming, Centre	DeWitt Clinton (Statesman)
56. Wyoming	April 4, 1842	Luzerne	Indian word
57. Carbon	March 13, 1843	Northampton, Monroe	For Anthracite coal deposits
58. Elk	April 18, 1843	Jefferson, McKean, Clearfield	For Elk Creek, on presence of elks
59. Blair	Feb. 26, 1846	Huntingdon, Bedford	John Blair (Local celebrity)
60. Sullivan	March 15, 1847	Lycoming	General John Sullivan
61. Forest	April 11, 1848	Jefferson, Venango	For its native forests
62. Lawrence	March 20, 1849	Beaver, Mercer	For Perry's flag-ship
63. Fulton	April 19, 1850	Bedford	Robert Fulton (Inventor)
64. Montour	May 3, 1850	Columbia	Madame Catherine Montour
65. Snyder	March 2, 1855	Union	Simon Snyder (Governor)
66. Cameron	March 29, 1860	Clinton, Elk, McKean, Potter	Simon Cameron (Statesman)
67. Lackawanna	Aug. 13, 1878	Luzerne	Lackawanna River (Ind. name)

APPENDIX C

COUNTIES AND COUNTY-SEATS

The counties of Pennsylvania have an average area of 669 square miles. Lycoming County is the largest, with 1,220 square miles; and the adjoining county of Montour, with only 130 square miles, is the smallest. Ten counties have each an area of one thousand square miles or more. Only six counties—Delaware, Lehigh, Montour, Philadelphia, Snyder, and Union—contain less than 350 square miles each.

The counties have an average population of 130,149. Twenty-three counties have each a population of 100,000 or more. Sixteen have between 50,000 and 100,000 each. The remaining twenty-eight fall below 50,000 each; five of these—Cameron, Forest, Fulton, Pike, and Sullivan— have each less than 10,000 inhabitants, Cameron being the smallest in respect to population, with 6,297 people.

Fully half of the county-seats are situated at or reasonably near the geographical centre of the county. Of the remaining thirty-three counties, nineteen have their county towns situated at one end of the county or close to its boundary.

All the county-seats are incorporated either as cities or boroughs. Twenty-one of them have city charters. Taken together, the county towns represent an average population of 53,525 each, and a total population of 3,586,197. Two of them, Philadelphia and Pittsburgh, have 2,412,122 inhabitants. Seven others—Allentown, Erie, Harrisburg, Lancaster, Reading, Scranton, and Wilkes-Barre—have each a population of over 50,000. Ten others—Butler, Easton, Lebanon, New Castle, Nor-

ristown, Pottsville, Washington, Williamsport, and York
—have a population ranging between 20,000 and 50,000.
Eight county-seats—Carlisle, Chambersburg, Greensburg, Meadville, Sunbury, Uniontown, Warren, and West
Chester—have each between 10,000 and 20,000 inhabitants. Eleven others have a population ranging between 5,000 and 10,000. A total of thirty-eight county-
seats contain above 5,000 each. The population of
sixteen others is above the 2,500 mark. Thus only thirteen county towns have a population under 2,500. Seven
of these fall below 1,000, with an average population of
673.

The following table gives the area of each county, the
population of the counties and their county-seats, and
the year in which each county town was laid out.

County	Area in Square Miles	Population (1920)	County-Seat	Population (1920)	County-Seat Laid Out
Adams	528	34,583	Gettysburg	4,439	1790
Allegheny	725	1,185,808	Pittsburgh	588,343	1761
Armstrong	653	75,568	Kittanning	7,153	1803
Beaver	429	111,621	Beaver	4,135	1792
Bedford	1,026	38,277	Bedford	2,330	1766
Berks	865	200,854	Reading	107,784	1748
Blair	534	128,334	Hollidaysburg	4,071	1790
Bradford	1,145	53,166	Towanda	4,269	1812
Bucks	608	82,476	Doylestown	3,837	1778
Butler	790	77,270	Butler	23,778	1803
Cambria	717	197,839	Ebensburg	2,179	1805
Cameron	392	6,297	Emporium	3,036	1861
Carbon	406	62,565	Mauch Chunk	3,666	1820
Centre	1,146	44,304	Bellefonte	3,996	1795
Chester	777	115,120	West Chester	11,717	1786
Clarion	601	36,170	Clarion	2,793	1839
Clearfield	1,142	103,326	Clearfield	8,529	1805
Clinton	878	33,555	Lock Haven	8,557	1834
Columbia	479	48,349	Bloomsburg	7,819	1802
Crawford	1,038	60,667	Meadville	14,568	1795
Cumberland	528	58,578	Carlisle	10,916	1751

County	Area in Square Miles	Population (1920)	County-Seat	Population (1920)	County-Seat Laid Out
Dauphin	521	153,116	Harrisburg	75,917	1785
Delaware	185	173,084	Media	4,109	1849
Elk	806	34,981	Ridgway	6,037	1833
Erie	781	153,536	Erie	93,372	1795
Fayette	795	188,104	Uniontown	15,692	1776
Forest	423	7,477	Tionesta	642	1850
Franklin	751	62,275	Chambersburg	13,171	1764
Fulton	402	9,617	McConnellsburg	689	1786
Greene	574	30,804	Waynesburg	3,332	1796
Huntingdon	918	39,848	Huntingdon	7,051	1767
Indiana	829	80,910	Indiana	7,043	1805
Jefferson	666	62,104	Brookville	3,272	1830
Juniata	392	14,464	Mifflintown	1,083	1791
Lackawanna	451	286,311	Scranton	137,783	1840
Lancaster	941	173,797	Lancaster	53,150	1730
Lawrence	360	85,545	New Castle	44,938	1802
Lebanon	360	63,152	Lebanon	24,643	1750
Lehigh	344	148,101	Allentown	73,502	1751
Luzerne	892	390,991	Wilkes-Barre	73,833	1770
Lycoming	1,220	83,100	Williamsport	36,198	1795
McKean	987	48,934	Smethport	1,568	1807
Mercer	700	93,788	Mercer	1,932	1803
Mifflin	398	31,439	Lewistown	9,849	1791
Monroe	623	24,295	Stroudsburg	5,278	1806
Montgomery	484	199,310	Norristown	32,319	1784
Montour	130	14,080	Danville	6,952	1792
Northampton	372	153,506	Easton	33,813	1750
Northumberland	454	122,079	Sunbury	15,721	1772
Perry	564	22,875	New Bloomfield	778	1823
Philadelphia	133	1,823,779	Philadelphia	1,823,779	1682
Pike	544	6,818	Milford	768	1796
Potter	1,071	21,089	Coudersport	2,836	1807
Schuylkill	777	217,754	Pottsville	21,876	1816
Snyder	311	17,129	Middleburg	984	1800
Somerset	1,034	82,112	Somerset	3,121	1795
Sullivan	458	9,520	Laporte	175	1850
Susquehanna	824	34,763	Montrose	1,661	1812
Tioga	1,142	37,118	Wellsboro	3,452	1806
Union	305	15,850	Lewisburg	3,204	1785
Venango	661	59,184	Franklin	9,970	1795
Warren	902	40,024	Warren	14,272	1795
Washington	862	188,992	Washington	21,480	1781
Wayne	739	27,435	Honesdale	2,756	1827
Westmoreland	1,039	273,568	Greensburg	15,033	1784
Wyoming	397	14,101	Tunkhannock	1,736	1790
York	903	144,521	York	47,512	1741

INDEX TO PLACE NAMES DISCUSSED

NOTE.—This index does not list all the place names that occur in the text, but only the 1,218 names of counties, cities, towns, villages, townships, and streams which have received specific explanation or comment. Some county names that have either been abandoned or have failed to receive final acceptance, and a few important place names that are no longer current, have been included; and these have been printed in italics in order that they may be differentiated from place names now in use.

GENERAL INDEX

English shires, 41, 168; for
French noblemen, 61, 168; from
miscellaneous sources, 159; for
natural features, 119, 138, 168; for
Pennsylvania governors, 78, 168;
for Presidents, 71, 168; for
prominent Pennsylvanians, 152,
168; for women, 114; naming
of, 346-348; owing their existence to ambition of towns to become county-seats, 169; population of, 349-351; summary information about, 346-351; when
organized, 169, 246-248
County names in other states, 40,
44, 54, 56, 62, 74, 75, 77, 79, 88,
99, 103, 106, 107, 109, 111, 121,
130, 136, 140, 150, 164, 167, 326,
327
County names, rejected, 170; unique,
168
County-seats having borrowed names,
172; having Indian names, 172;
having same names as counties,
171; having unique names, 172;
named for geographical features,
172; for local celebrities, 171;
for noted men, 172; population
of, 349-351; summary informa-
tion about, 168-172, 349-351; when
founded, 350, 351
Covington, Leonard, 261
Covode, John 261
Craft, Charles C., 213
Craig, William, 48
Crane, George, 283
Crawford, William, 72, 97-99, 211;
burning of, 99
Cresson, Elliott, 261
Cresson, John C., 262
Croghan, George, 114
Culloden, battle of, 44, 101
Cumberland, Duke of, 44
Cunningham James C., 237
Cunningham, John and Samuel, 97
Curtin, Andrew Gregg, 142, 262
Curtin, Martha, 312
Curwen, John, 274
Custer, George Armstrong, 262

Dallas, Alexander J., 262
Dallas, George M., 262
Danner, Michael, 182
Dauphin of France, 63, 64
Dauphiny, 63, 64

Dawson, George, 274
Dawson, John, 311
Day, Sherman, cited, 149; quoted,
62, 119, 128, 144, 197, 301
Decatur, Stephen, 325
Declaration of Independence, 63, 75;
signers of, 43, 79, 81, 160, 260,
267, 268, 325, 326
Delaware, Forks of the, 47, 48, 333
Delaware, Lord, 139
Delaware and Hudson Company, 94,
197, 206, 213, 226, 277
Delaware, Lackawanna and Western
Railroad, 138, 206, 234
Denny, William, 122
Derr, Lewis, 164
Dickinson, John, 45, 104, 325
Dickinson College, 45
Dickson, Thomas, 213, 226
Dixon, Jeremiah, 312
Doerr, Ludwig: see Lewis Derr
Donehoo, George P., cited, 128, 192
Donner, William H., 214
Donop, A., 187
Dorrance, George, 274
Downing, Thomas, 274
Doyle, William, 38
"Dream counties," 170
Drinker, Henry, 93, 215
DuBois, John, 214, 215
Dunbar, Thomas, 274
Duncan, Samuel, 274
Dunkard Brethren, 242, 308
Dunmore, Lord, of Virginia, 225
Dupetit-Thouars, Aristide Aubert,
308
Duquesne de Menneville, Marquis,
120, 121, 216, 247
Duquesne Steel Company, 216
Durkee, Andrew, 68
Durkee, Barré, 68
Durkee, John, 67, 68
Durkee, Wilkes, 68
Duryea, Abram, 216
Duss, Susie C., 293
Dyberry, Forks of the, 94

East Pittsburgh Improvement Com-
pany, 217, 237
Edmiston, Samuel, 81
Edwards, Daniel, 217
Egle, William H., quoted, 25, 81
Elder, John, quoted, 64
Eldred, C. D., quoted, 125
Ellicott, Andrew, 103, 127, 247

"Westsylvania," 52
Whiskey Insurrection, 53, 58, 72
White, Josiah, 147, 280
Whitefield, George, 115, 251, 303
Wilkes, John, 68, 69
Wilkins, William, 181, 236
Williamstadt, Manor of, 88, 89
Wilmington and Reading Railroad, 313
Wilmot, David, 94, 325
Wilmot Proviso, 94
Wilson, "Aunt Betsy," 318
Wind Gap, the, 322
Winton, William W., 238
Witmer, Abraham, 144, 145, 316
Wolfe, General, 229
Worth, William J., 327

Wray, John, Indian trader, 57
Wright, John, 42
Wright, John A., 176
Wright, Samuel, 210
Wright's Ferry, 42, 210
Wynne, Thomas, 270
Wyoming Massacre, 70, 109, 137, 274

York, Duke of (James II), 40, 56
Youngman, Elias, 80
Young Pretender, the, 44, 101

Zeisberger, David, 314; cited, 284, 287; quoted, 137
Zinzendorf, Count von, 178, 247

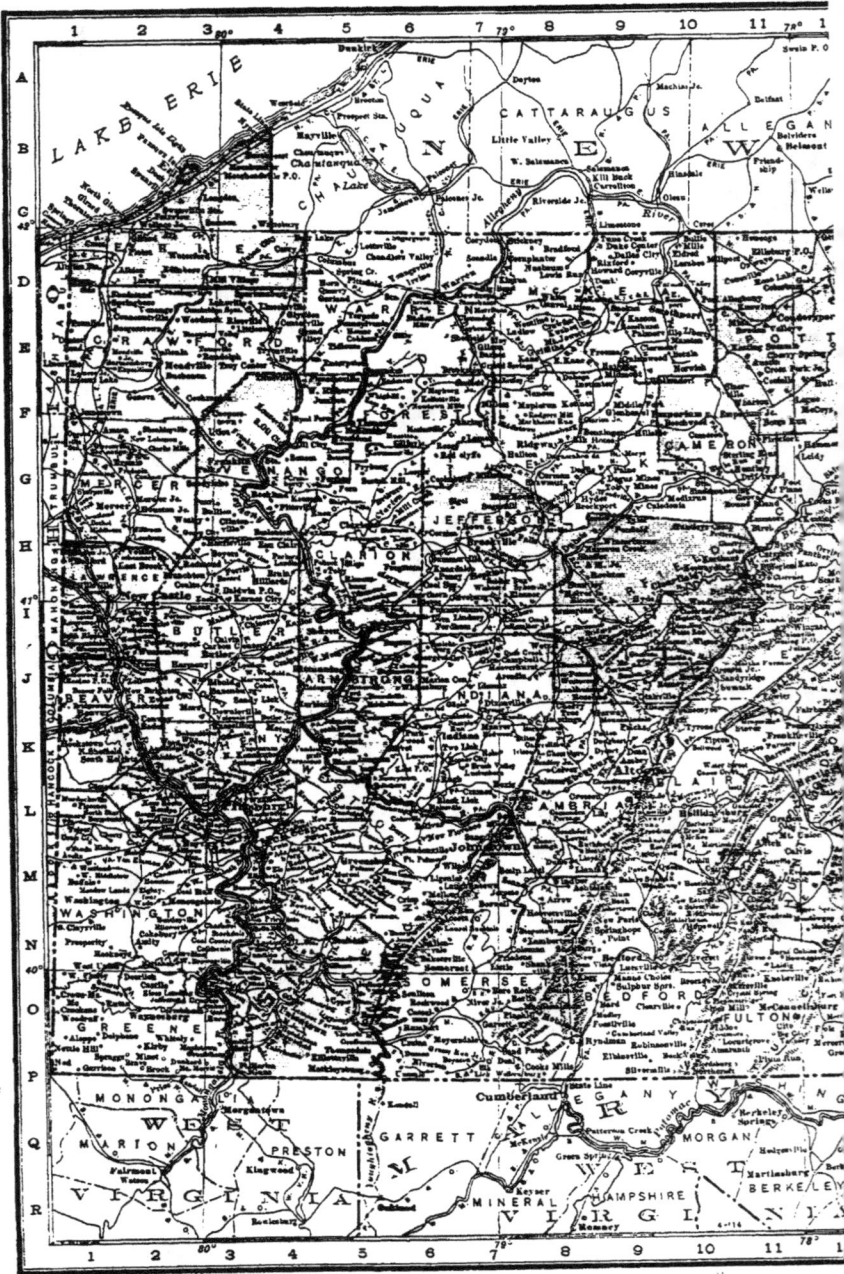

378

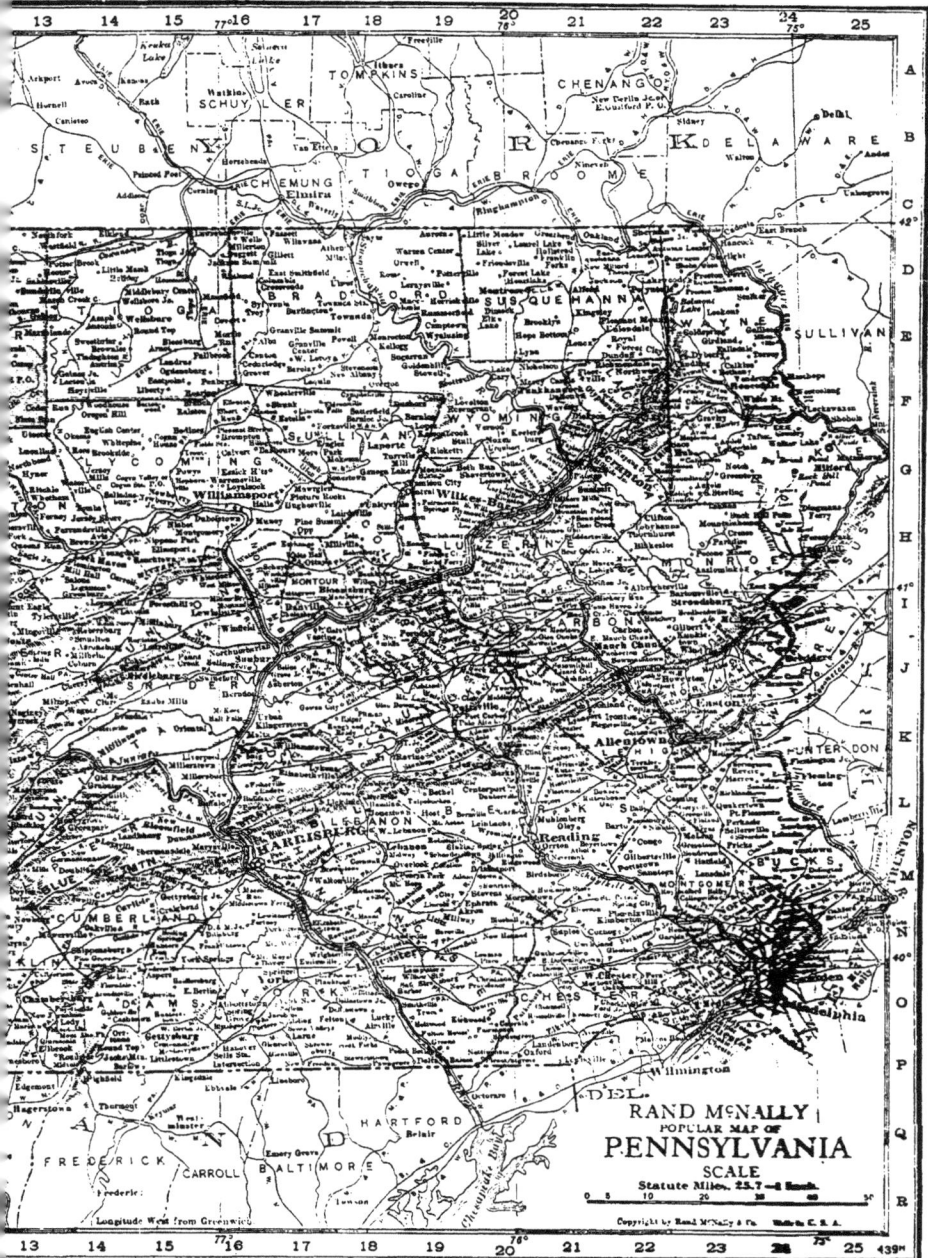

RAND McNALLY
POPULAR MAP OF
PENNSYLVANIA
SCALE
Statute Miles, 25.7 = 1 Inch.

Copyright by Rand McNally & Co.

Longitude West from Greenwich

PENNSYLVANIA

STEUBEN

SCHUYLER

TOMPKINS

CHENANGO

DELAWARE

BROOME

TIOGA

CHEMUNG

Elmira

SUSQUEHANNA

WAYNE

SULLIVAN

BRADFORD

WYOMING

PIKE

MONROE

LUZERNE

Williamsport

CARBON

LEHIGH

HUNTERDON

Allentown

Reading

HARRISBURG

BUCKS

LEBANON

BLUE

CUMBERLAND

MONTGOMERY

CHESTER

YORK

ADAMS

Gettysburg

Wilmington

DEL.

HARTFORD

FREDERICK

CARROLL

BALTIMORE

Hagerstown

379